The Printed Image and the Transformation of Popular Culture

1790-1860

The Printed Image and the Transformation of Popular Culture

1790–1860

PATRICIA ANDERSON

CLARENDON PRESS · OXFORD
1991

Oxford University Press, Walton Street, Oxford OX2 6DP
Oxford New York Toronto
Delhi Bombay Calcutta Madras Karachi
Petaling Jaya Singapore Hong Kong Tokyo
Nairobi Dar es Salaam Cape Town
Melbourne Auckland
and associated companies in
Berlin Ibadan

Oxford is a trade mark of Oxford University Press

Published in the United States
by Oxford University Press, New York

British Library Cataloguing in Publication Data
Data available

Library of Congress Cataloguing in Publication Data

Anderson, Patricia (Patricia J.)
The printed image and the transformation of popular culture, 1790–1860/Patricia Anderson.
Includes bibliographical references and index.
1. Working class—Great Britain—Books and reading—History—19th century. 2. Popular literature—Publishing—Great Britain—History—19th century. 3. Illustrated books—Publishing—Great Britain—History—19th century. 4. Pictures—Great Britain—Printing—History—19th century. 5. Great Britain—Popular culture—History—19th century. 6. Illustration of books—19th century—Great Britain. 7. Popular literature—Great Britain—Illustrations. I. Title.
Z1039.L3A53 1991 302.23'2—dc20 91–2828
ISBN 0–19–811236–X

Phototypeset by Wyvern Typesetting Ltd, Bristol
Printed and bound in Great Britain
by Biddles Ltd, Guildford and King's Lynn

Contents

Illustrations

(Unless otherwise stated, the originals of the illustrations listed below are wood-engravings printed in black and white. Unless otherwise stated, plates are reproduced from the author's own originals.)

Acknowledgements

I have previously published some of the material presented here: 'Pictures for the People: Knight's *Penny Magazine*, an Early Venture into Popular Art Education', *Studies in Art Education*, 28 (Spring 1987), is an abbreviated version of Chapter 2, sections II and III; '"A Revolution in Popular Art": Pictorial Magazines and the Making of a Mass Culture in England, 1832–1860', *Journal of Newspaper and Periodical History*, 6 (Spring 1990), is a synopsis of this book's central arguments; and 'Civilizing the Viewer: Images of Social Virtue in English Popular Magazines, 1830–1860', *Visual Resources* 8, no. 2 (1991), is a theoretical discussion using examples from Chapters 2 and 4. A variation of Chapter 5 is forthcoming in *Victorian Periodicals Review* under the title '"Factory Girl, Apprentice and Clerk"—The Readership of Mass-Market Magazines'.

Introduction

The Printed Image and Cultural Change: English Popular Culture and Illustration

1790–1860

IN 1859 a contributor to the *British Quarterly Review* extravagantly praised such 'marvels' of the time as gas lighting, steamships, and the electric telegraph. Still 'more astonishing' was another contemporary wonder:

> that flood of cheap literature which, like the modern Babylon itself, no living man has ever been able to traverse, which has sprung up, and continues to spring up, with the mysterious fecundity of certain fungi, and which cannot be accounted for in its volume, variety, and universality by any ordinary laws of production.[1]

There is in fact less mystery surrounding the mid-nineteenth-century 'flood of cheap literature' than this passage would suggest. But, literary licence aside, our commentator had rightly remarked that a momentous change had occurred in the dissemination of information and entertainment. Advances in printing technology, reductions in the newspaper tax and paper duty, the widening demand for reading-matter, and publishers' increasing efforts to supply this demand had together promoted the rapid growth of the popular publishing industry in England. Between 1830 and 1860, this growing industry played a fundamental part in the first phase of a broad transformation: the unprecedented expansion of the cultural experience of working people. From the centre of this new and enlarged popular culture, there developed concurrently the beginnings of a modern mass culture. As we will see, in the three decades following 1830 both the

[1] 'Cheap Literature,' *British Quarterly Review*, 29 (Apr. 1859), 316. This journal is not listed in the *Wellesley Index to Victorian Periodicals*, and the article's author is unknown.

printed word and its associated imagery increasingly reached an audience that was not only larger than ever before, but whose number included more than one social class. The interaction of this new mass-market publishing industry and the cultural experience of the English worker is the general subject of this book.

I

The hallmark of a transformed and expanded popular culture was its increasingly pictorial character. This was especially true at the centre of that culture where mass-circulation books and magazines predominated. The introduction into England of mechanized paper-making (1803), the steam-powered press (1814), and multiple-cylinder stereotype printing (1827) permitted the low-cost, high-speed dissemination of the printed word.[2] The same technological advances also made possible the profitable, high-quality mass reproduction of diverse imagery. As a result, illustrations of art, nature, technical processes, famous people, foreign lands, and many other subjects for the first time became widely available and affordable.

From the early 1830s to 1860 pictorial magazines were a major means of diffusing the printed image. For most of these magazines, illustration, rivalled only by sensational fiction, was the main selling-point, and several weekly journals achieved impressive regular sales ranging from 80,000 to more than 400,000 copies per issue.[3] This is not to suggest that a print-centred mass culture would not have emerged without the added impetus of illustration; but it would have done so less rapidly and dramatically. Notwithstanding the attraction of the printed word alone, it is clear that illustrated publications had the draw of greater novelty, and they accordingly found a readier market

[2] Stereotype printing used curved metal plates which could be rapidly cast from original reliefs using papier mâché, clay, or plaster. Multiple cylinders further increased the speed with which impressions could be produced. For further discussion of 19th-cent. printing technology, see e.g. Philip B. Meggs, *A History of Graphic Design* (New York, 1983), 163–4; Michael Twyman, *Printing, 1770–1970* (London, 1970), 51–2; and Geoffrey Wakeman, *Victorian Book Illustration* (Newton Abbot, 1973), 20–2; and see also the *Penny Magazine*, 2 (1833), 379–84, 423–4, 470–2, and 507–11.

[3] For lists of the most representative mid-19th-cent. periodicals and their respective circulations, see Richard D. Altick, *The English Common Reader* (Chicago, 1957) 393–5; and A. Ellegard, *The Readership of the Periodical Press in Mid-Victorian England* (Göteborg, 1957), 35.

among a public whose taste was increasingly for new and varied sources of knowledge and amusement.

But novelty and attendant commercial appeal were by no means the most significant distinction between the printed image and the word. The more crucial difference lay in the image's greater ability to communicate in a time when literacy was not universal. To make both a profit and a cultural impact a non-pictorial publication had to reach an audience who could read, even if many only did so with difficulty. This was not necessarily true of an illustrated magazine whose pictures had the capacity to entertain and inform everyone. In the early and mid-nineteenth century the printed image more than the word represented a cultural break with the past, for it demanded neither formal education nor even basic literacy. The new inexpensive printed image thus became the first medium of regular, ongoing, mass communication. For this reason, the meanings, dissemination, and reception of popular periodical illustration deserve careful study and interpretation.

This is potentially a daunting agenda; for from the 1830s on pictorial magazines so proliferated that those who study them are apt to sympathize with our commentator on 'cheap literature', who found his subject 'too vast to be dealt with as a whole . . . within the compass of a single article'—or even, it might be added, a single book. The focus here then will be on four illustrated weekly magazines: the *Penny Magazine* (1832–45), the *London Journal* (1845–1906), *Reynolds's Miscellany* (1846–69), and *Cassell's Illustrated Family Paper* (1853–1932). These were the first illustrated serial publications to attract and maintain a readership of 1 million or more each, and they provide the basis for a collective case-study of the initial development of a modern mass culture.[4] As these magazines reflect, it was from the outset a culture distinguished by the increasing variety of information and entertainment that it offered, in words—and in pictures.

[4] The circulation of these publications ranged from the *Penny Magazine*'s 200,000 in the early 1830s to the *London Journal*'s 450,000 in 1855. The ratio of 1:5 is widely accepted as a conservative estimate of the relationship between circulation and actual readership—hence the text's reference to a million or more readers for each of the magazines in question.

II

Around the four magazines, their illustrations, and related evidence—other popular periodicals, broadsides, penny story-books, and serials—pivots the following chapters' broad argument: the onset of a mass culture by no means signalled the passive acculturation of the people. Rather, the appeal of the new pictorial magazines derived as much from the readers' long-held social, moral, and aesthetic values as it did from the efforts and ideologies of publishers, editors, writers, and artists. Moreover, other kinds of popular imagery, expressing radical consciousness or alternative taste, survived or developed concurrently. From the early 1830s to 1860 the everyday experience of the people increasingly took in a diversity of cultural levels ranging from traditional to radical, aesthetic to lurid. Thus the emergence of a formative mass culture—at least in its visual forms—was not a process of wholesale repression or replacement.[5]

Even so, this emergence should not be equated with the democratization of culture—with, that is, the eradication of the political, social, economic, and aesthetic distinctions that set high culture apart from the everyday experience of working people. Although it enriched people's lives in many ways, a developing mass culture was in some respects limited in its content. To acknowledge this paradox, we will in later chapters divide our attention between the variety of imagery that became increasingly available in the nineteenth century and the restricted entry into the mass domain of one kind of image: the work of art—or, more precisely, its reproduction.

In recognizing that art was on the whole a marginal part of common experience we distance ourselves from the point of view which celebrates the unprecedented breadth of commercialized mass culture, disregards its aesthetic deficiencies, and fails to consider the economic, social, and political power relations that can be, and were, enacted and reinforced through cultural forms.[6] But to turn from this

[5] For the opposing point of view, see Raymond Williams, 'Radical and/or Respectable', in R. Boston (ed.), *The Press We Deserve* (London, 1970), 18 and 21–3.

[6] The critique here is of what is usually designated as 'liberal pluralism'. For a historical study from this perspective, see J. M. Golby and A. W. Purdue, *The Civilization of the Crowd: Popular Culture in England, 1750–1900* (London, 1984). For further discussion and criticism of pluralist approaches, see Tony Bennett, 'Theories of the Media, Theories of Society', in Michael Gurevitch, T. Bennett, J.

optimistic view of progress through industrialization is not necessarily to adopt wholeheartedly the opposing perspective of radical pessimism. For mass culture cannot be adequately explained merely as an instrument of capitalist domination, robbed of all aesthetic and critical substance, and imposed upon an apathetic working class.[7] If we are to appreciate the historical complexity of early mass culture, then not only must we avoid theories of 'natural' social integration, but also simplistic explanations of cultural forms as the means by which one class imposes its will on another.

This nuanced approach to the relationship of class and culture raises doubts about the usefulness of the concept of social control. We will find that the earliest mass-circulation magazines were consistent in disseminating a particular set of moral and cultural values promoting the 'civilized' behaviour conducive to social cohesion and stability; thus we might be encouraged to assume that these magazines were concerted attempts at social control, and that this was their primary object. There is in fact little or no historical evidence for such a view. Rather, the *Penny Magazine* and its three successors were among the many contemporary cultural forms and processes through which the economically and politically powerful members of society informally and not necessarily deliberately exercised their social, moral, and intellectual leadership.

This idea of leadership derives from the thought of Antonio Gramsci; and from such a theoretical perspective leadership is never merely a euphemism for control pure and simple.[8] As Gramsci realized, in the mid-nineteenth century the effectiveness of authority

Curran, and Janet Woollacott (eds.), *Culture, Society and the Media*, (London, 1982), 39–41; John Clarke and Chas Critcher, *The Devil Makes Work* (London, 1985), 40 ff.; Alan Swingewood, *The Myth of Mass Culture* (London, 1977; reprint edn., 1979), 18–23.

[7] More specifically, I am arguing against the pessimistic position of many Frankfurt School thinkers; for further discussion, see Bennett, 'Theories of the Media', 41–7; and Swingewood, *Mass Culture*, 11–18.

[8] I use the term 'leadership' in the sense of Gramsci's concept of hegemony: see Gramsci, *Selections from the Prison Notebooks*, ed. and trans. Quintin Hoare and Geoffrey Nowell Smith (London, 1971; reprint edn., 1986), esp. 12–13, 242–3, and 264–5. I have also benefited greatly from the following: Peter Bailey, Introduction to the paperback edn. of *Leisure and Class in Victorian England* (London, 1987), 8–18; Tony Bennett, 'Popular Culture and the Turn to Gramsci', in T. Bennett, C. Mercer, and J. Woollacott (eds.), *Popular Culture and Social Relations* (Milton Keynes, 1986), pp. xi-xix; Stuart Hall, 'Cultural Studies', in S. Hall (ed.), *Culture, Media, Language* (London, 1980), 35–6; Ernesto Laclau and Chantal Mouffe, *Hegemony and Socialist Strategy* (London, 1985), esp. 1–42 and 142–5; Chantal

depended upon some form of active consensus (however unequal, uneasy, and temporary that might have been) between two fundamental class groups.[9] On the one hand there was the 'power-bloc'—that is, the gentry, merchants, industrialists, and others who had acquired 'a properly rational social demeanour as defined by their superiors'.[10] On the other hand there was the working class—and here the term 'class' is used somewhat loosely. In considering the period 1830 to 1860, we find little evidence of a fully formed, unified working class. It seems more realistic to think in terms of a less definitive, more fluid social formation composed of such diverse groups of workers as artisans and small tradesmen, street hawkers and entertainers, farm-labourers, servants, and factory operatives. It is in this second sense that 'working class' is to be understood here.[11]

Our recognition of the consensual interaction between the two fundamental class groups takes us well beyond simplistic notions of social control. We avoid too the profound condescension of those who would reduce working people to an undifferentiated, unresisting body lacking both individuality and the capacity for self-determination. To return to the particular subject of this study, workers actively chose to buy pictorial magazines and, in doing so, consented to the values embodied in these publications; their consent was also a matter of choice and accorded with their individual and collective needs as an emergent class.

As we persist in our effort to develop a nuanced understanding of the relationship of class and culture, we find that notions of domination and control are not the only ones to prove unsatisfactory. The

Mouffe, *Gramsci and Marxist Theory* (London, 1979), esp. 1–18, 168–204 and 190–200; ead., 'Hegemony and Ideology in Gramsci', in T. Bennett, G. Martin, C. Mercer and J. Woollacott (eds.), *Culture, Ideology and Social Process* (London, 1981), 219–34; and Swingewood, *Mass Culture*, 76–8 and 82–6; Gareth Stedman Jones argues that there is little to differentiate between social control and the informal exercise of authority (hegemony): see 'Class Expression versus Social Control', in Jones, *Languages of Class* (Cambridge, 1983), 86.

[9] I refer here to Gramsci's idea of negotiated consent: see *Prison Notebooks*, 12, 182, 242.

[10] Robert Gray, 'Bourgeois Hegemony in Victorian Britain', in Bennett *et al.*, *Culture, Ideology and Social Process*, 239.

[11] On the diversity of 19th-cent. English workers, see David Vincent, *Bread, Knowledge and Freedom: A Study of Nineteenth-Century Working Class Autobiography* (London, 1981; reprint edn., 1982), 7; and on the need for a comprehensive definition of 'working class', see John Burnett, David Mayall, and D. Vincent, *The Autobiography of the Working Class* (Brighton, 1984), i. p. xxxi.

kind of reductionism that would align class and culture in direct and static correspondence is also unconvincing. Indications are that in the mid-nineteenth century there was no specific, dominant, and cohesive middle-class culture.[12] Neither, it seems, was there a pure oppositional working-class culture of the sort that E. P. Thompson and others have postulated.[13] Available evidence suggests a wider, more varied phenomenon. By the late eighteenth century there had long been a multi-faceted culture of the people. From the early 1830s, as it changed and expanded, it increasingly but in no a priori way embodied aesthetic, social, and moral diversity: for instance, high and low taste in reading, pictures, and theatrical entertainments; oppositional and conformist social and political values; religious faith, respectability, and rowdy tendencies. This is not to say that there was no form of worker-consciousness or cultural expression, but rather that we need to locate these in an appropriately broad and dynamic cultural context.

III

Such an endeavour will entail some rethinking of our usual understanding and periodization of popular culture, and it would now be useful to clarify certain key terms and concepts. In particular 'popular', 'mass', and their cultural opposite, 'high', call for definition. To take the most straightforward first, 'high' as used here in connection with culture refers to the objects of fine art (especially, for this book's purposes, painting, sculpture, and expensive limited-run

[12] Chap. 2 develops this part of the argument further; and, for a comparable view, see Raymond Williams, 'Minority and Popular Culture', in Michael Smith, Stanley Parker, and Cyril Smith (eds.), *Leisure and Society in Britain* (London, 1973), 22 ff.

[13] E. P. Thompson, *The Making of the English Working Class* (1963; reprint edn., Harmondsworth, 1978); Patricia Hollis, *The Pauper Press* (London, 1970); G. S. Jones, 'Working-Class Culture and Working-Class Politics in London, 1870–1900', *Journal of Social History*, 7 (Summer 1974), 498 and *passim*; Martha Vicinus, *The Industrial Muse* (London, 1974); and see also Eileen Yeo, 'Culture and Constraint in Working-Class Movements, 1830–55', in E. and S. Yeo (eds.), *Popular Culture and Class Conflict, 1590–1914* (Brighton, 1981), 155, 172–3, and *passim*. Among those who have expressed a view similar to the one adopted here, see Stuart Hall, 'Notes on Deconstructing the "Popular"', in R. Samuel (ed.), *People's History and Socialist Theory* (London, 1981), 238; and Swingewood, *Mass Culture*, 39 and *passim*. Of related interest is G. S. Jones, 'Rethinking Chartism', in Jones, *Languages of Class*, 90–178; Jones argues that neither Chartism nor early radicalism were expressions of a class-specific ideology—they were instances of struggle between the 'people' and a power-bloc.

prints), the aesthetic theories, canons of taste, traditions, general knowledge, and formal education that signalled and accrued to social and economic privilege.

The definition of 'popular' is more complicated, for the term has several possible meanings.[14] There is, for example, a common tendency to add a class dimension to its general dictionary sense of prevalent among and approved by the people. Adherents to E. P. Thompson's approach are particularly apt to equate 'popular' with 'working-class'.[15] This interchange is not only conceptually confusing but also inimical to a nuanced approach to the relationship of class and culture. When we consider people's everyday experience between 1790 and 1832, the period just before the appearance of the pictorial magazines, a broadly descriptive definition is most appropriate. 'Popular' in this context may thus be defined as the concept and word designating the entire culture and associated artefacts of, and available to, working people.[16] It need hardly be added that this culture and its specific forms were distinct from the precious objects and exclusivist high culture of the more advantaged and powerful strata of society.

This distinction between two fundamental cultural levels should not be hardened into a purely class-based concept of popular culture. The latter was only in part expressive of worker radicalism and cannot on that ground be interpreted as an emergent class culture built wholly and exclusively on oppositional consciousness. In other words, in the period in question popular culture was a varied and variable experience. This is not, however, to espouse a form of celebratory populism and overlook that popular culture in the broad sense used here must also be understood as part of a larger social configuration. For such a culture was one site where the dynamic, uneven relationship between the people and the power-bloc was enacted.[17] Like the transformed culture that followed, popular

[14] Hall, 'Deconstructing the "Popular"', 231.

[15] See n. 13 above, first part, and also, among others, Charles Elkins, 'The Voice of the Poor: The Broadside as a Medium of Popular Culture and Dissent in Victorian England', *Journal of Popular Culture* 14 (1980): 262–74; and R. D. Storch, 'Persistence and Change in Nineteenth-Century Popular Culture', in R. D. Storch (ed.), *Popular Culture and Custom in Nineteenth-Century England* (London, 1982), 1–19.

[16] This definition derives from the comparable ones given in Peter Burke, *Popular Culture in Early Modern Europe* (London, 1978), p. xi; and Hugh Cunningham, *Leisure in the Industrial Revolution* (London, 1980), 37–8.

[17] Hall, 'Deconstructing the "Popular"', 235ff.

culture between 1790 and 1832 was a means for the dissemination and reception of certain restrictive social values variously expressed in both written and pictorial form.

Applied to the cultural history of the later period, the 1830s to 1860, 'popular' has continuing usefulness as a common-sense description of any generally accessible, widely shared interest or activity, or of the taste of a majority of ordinary people, or of the commercial success of particular cultural artefacts—most notably, the four previously named, high-circulation pictorial magazines. But when we try to characterize the new culture that grew up around these magazines, the term 'popular' lacks sufficient conceptual and historical specificity. From 1832, with the publication and unprecedented sales of the *Penny Magazine*, common cultural experience changed quickly and decisively. In describing that change and its impact on people's lives and perceptions, the most pertinent term and concept is not 'popular' but 'mass'.

Here again definition is no simple matter. It is thus understandable that historians in general have not addressed the problem directly, and that much of the literature on periodicals, leisure, and entertainment tends to lack rigour in employing the term 'mass'.[18] Indeed there is little doubt that the concept ultimately eludes the niceties of any fixed quantitative or qualitative definition. What we might productively bear in mind, though, is a historically specific set of considerations that later references to 'mass' or 'the mass' will take in.

Certainly, a central aspect of any mass phenomenon is the great many people involved. From the 1830s the number of those able to participate in the cultural experience afforded by print grew substantially. Among the chief factors in this development were changes in the taxation policies affecting the press. Decreases in the newspaper tax (1836) and the paper duty (1837) lessened publishers' costs and enabled them to increase or at least maintain their output of low-priced publications, especially periodicals. The repeal of the former tax in 1855 further facilitated the large-scale publication and distribution of 'cheap literature'. As the *British Quarterly Review*'s expert on the subject expressed it,

[18] See, among others, Burke, *Popular Culture*, 72; Elkins, 'Voice of the Poor', 263–4; R. Johnson, 'Really Useful Knowledge', in J. Clarke, C. Critcher and R. Johnson (eds.), *Working-Class Culture* (London, 1979), 235; L. Lowenthal, 'Historical Preface to the Popular Culture Debate', in N. Jacobs (ed.), *Culture for the Millions?*, intro. P. Lazarsfeld (Boston, 1964), 28–42; and Vicinus, *Industrial Muse*, 238–49.

> the abolition of the Stamp Duty on Newspapers and the consequent reduction of prices, enlargement of size, and wider diffusion of the daily and weekly press mark an era in our progress from the old region of enormous expenditure and fiscal restraint to an age when journalism may be said to be as universal as air or light.[19]

In considering the size of the market to which this expanding industry catered, there is little point in trying to designate some minimum number that would necessarily constitute a mass, for any such number would always be relative to time and place. For example, in mid-nineteenth-century England, with its population of 12–13 million, a mass audience might arguably comprise significantly fewer people than would its present-day counterpart in a now heavily populated nation. What identifies the *Penny Magazine* and its successors as artefacts of a formative mass culture is not just the size of the readership, but the fact that there was a contemporary awareness that these publications were indeed notable for and previously unequalled in their circulation figures.[20] What was also new about these figures was the fact that they were achieved regularly and sustained over a period of years. Certain earlier broadsides had reached sales of up to half a million each, but these were isolated occurrences which were not duplicated with sufficient frequency or regularity to be described collectively as mass culture.

As suggested earlier, certain crucial technological advances were integral to the development of such a culture. The introduction of steam-powered printing and related processes provided the level of mechanization necessary for the large-scale production of print and imagery. Bound in with this advancement was the growing sophistication of publishers who increasingly realized that culture was a

[19] 'Cheap Literature', 316. The paper duty, a particularly contentious tax, stayed in effect until 1861; on this and related fiscal policies, see H. R. Fox Bourne, *English Newspapers*, 2 vols. (London, 1887), ii. 232 ff.; C. D. Collet, *History of the Taxes on Knowledge*, 2 vols. (London, 1899); Charles Knight, *The Case of the Authors as Regards the Paper Duty* (London, 1851); id., *The Struggles of a Book against Excessive Taxation*, 2nd edn. (London, 1850); Alan J. Lee, *The Origins of the Popular Press in England* (London, 1976), 45–9, 95–7; Joel H. Wiener, *The War of the Unstamped* (Ithaca, NY, and London, 1969); and Francis Williams, *Dangerous Estate: The Anatomy of Newspapers* (London, 1957), 123 and *passim*.

[20] See, e.g. James G. Bertram, *Some Memories of Books, Authors and Events* (London 1893), 140; 'Cheap Literature', 320 ff.; Edward Cowper, Evidence given before the Select Committee on Arts and Manufactures, 17 June 1836, *Report*, vol. 9.1, pp. 50–1; Charles Knight, *The Old Printer and the Modern Press* (London, 1854), 254 ff.

marketable commodity and that technology could be used specifically for its widespread and profitable sale. For all such awareness on the part of its producers, the emergent mass culture was not fully commercialized in the sense that the publishing industry was unequivocally profit-motivated or predominantly organized into limited companies. Between 1830 and 1860 most publishing houses operated as sole proprietorships or partnerships that had established their initial capital with personal funds, family money, or informal backing. In addition, many publishers not only saw themselves as businessmen, but also as humanitarians or reformers; they often involved themselves deeply in the editorial as opposed to the strictly managerial end of the business in order to be all the more active in furthering their particular interest or cause. But if the mass-market publishing industry at mid-century was not as commercialized as it would later become, those who controlled it were none the less astute enough to employ new profit-enhancing technology and to use marketing strategies effective in achieving the unprecedented distribution which we have already noted.

Of even greater interest here than the supply side of the formative culture is its obverse: people's widespread desire and, as the nineteenth century wore on, enhanced ability to consume cultural products.[21] It is in fact at the level of consumption rather than production that we find the most significant aspect of the new mass culture: its social diversity. Such a culture was never exclusively the experience of any one group or class, and for this reason 'mass' must be understood to designate multiple social layers. Finally, also significantly, the concept of 'mass' carries with it a historical perception of unprecedentedness. Later chapters will indicate that there was among both the producers and consumers of the emerging culture a shared consciousness that they were participating in a fundamental and far-reaching change in the structure of knowledge and communication. And, as one group of contemporary observers remarked, this was a change that involved 'the great *mass* of the population'.[22]

It is hardly to be expected that these definitions will find a consensus

[21] This was an outgrowth of the generalized consumer revolution which had begun in England in the 18th cent.; see Neil McKendrick, John Brewer, and J. H. Plumb, *The Birth of a Consumer Society* (London, 1982).

[22] General Literature Committee, Society for Promoting Christian Knowledge, 21 May 1832, report transcribed in the Committee Minutes, vol. for 1832–4, SPCK Archive, London. The italics are mine.

of agreement among scholars. Primarily they are working definitions appropriate to the particular focus of this study. Nevertheless the intention has been to propose meanings sufficiently precise, yet also broad enough to have potential usefulness for other similar analyses of early and mid-nineteenth-century society and culture.[23] The distinction made here between 'popular' and 'mass' bears directly on the periodization of the cultural history of the people. That is, before 1832 there was a non-élitist popular culture of the working population; after 1832 this gave way to a greatly enlarged cultural experience, some of which continued to be mainly of and for working people. The central and greater part of this transformed and expanded culture, however, was not just the domain of the working populace, but of an unprecedentedly numerous and socially diverse public—in other words, the mass. But both before and after this transition there was another level of cultural terrain. Reminding us that neither the old popular nor the new mass culture were manifestations of aesthetic or social democracy, there remained at mid-century, and remains today, the heartland of exclusivist privilege and power—high culture.

IV

In taking inexpensive printed imagery as both the subject-matter and evidence for much of its argument, this study fills something of a gap in the literature on nineteenth-century popular culture. With comparatively few exceptions, what has been written about popular illustration fails to situate it in any wider social or cultural context.[24]

[23] In formulating definitions, I have been helped by the following: Asa Briggs, 'The Language of "Mass" and "Masses" in Nineteenth-Century England', in D. E. Martin and D. Rubinstein (eds.), *Ideology and the Labour Movement* (London, 1979), 62–83; H. J. Gans, *Popular Culture and High Culture* (New York, 1974); Jon P. Klancher, *The Making of English Reading Audiences, 1790–1832* (London and Madison, Wis., 1987), 76–97; Leo Lowenthal, 'Historical Perspectives of Popular Culture', in B. Rosenberg and D. M. White (eds.), *Mass Culture* (New York, 1957), 46–58; Dwight MacDonald, 'A Theory of Mass Culture', ibid. 59–73; J. A. Maravall, *Culture of the Baroque* (Manchester, 1986), 79–103; Swingewood, *Mass Culture*, 106–7 and 109–10; John A. Walker, *Art in the Age of Mass Media* (London, 1983), 18; and R. Williams, *Keywords: A Vocabulary of Culture and Society* (New York, 1976), 158–63 and 198–9.

[24] Among the important exceptions are Peter Bailey, 'Ally Sloper's Half-Holiday: Comic Art in the 1880s,' *History Workshop* 11 (1983), 4–31; Allan Ellenius, 'Reproducing Art as a Paradigm of Communication: The Case of the Nineteenth-Century Periodicals', *Figura*, NS 21 (1984), 69–92; Celina Fox, 'The Development of Social Reportage in English Periodical Illustration during the 1840s and Early 1850s', *Past*

It is the context of imagery that is of particular interest here for, as we will see, when, where, and by what means an image is reproduced together affect its meaning. We will find that illustration—most notably art reproduction—often had implicit contemporary social meanings which are sometimes still accessible.[25]

This book also relies upon archival material, parliamentary reports, newspapers, and the like. In addition, workers' autobiographies offer clues to the role of the working class in the creation of a formative mass culture. But, as others have recognized, these autobiographies pose problems as well. First, by the very fact of having written a book, the autobiographers were not typical working people, and we must be cautious about generalizing from their experiences.[26] More troublesome still is the matter of autobiographical reticence in a number of areas. Literary conventions and the dictates of editors and publishers together determined what was 'appropriate' to an autobiography and undoubtedly limited the scope of reminiscences.[27] It

and Present, 74 (1977), 90–111; ead., *Graphic Journalism in England during the 1830s and 40s* (Ph.D. diss. (Oxford, 1974); published, London and New York, 1988); ead. 'Political Caricature and Freedom of the Press in Early Nineteenth-Century England', in G. Boyce, J. Curran and P. Wingate (eds.), *Newspaper History* (London, 1978), 227–46; ead. and M. Wolff, 'Pictures from Magazines', in H. J. Dyos and M. Wolff (eds.), *The Victorian City*, 2 vols. (London, 1973), ii. 559–82; M. D. George, *Hogarth to Cruikshank* (London, 1967); W. M. Ivins, *Prints and Visual Communications* (London, 1953; reprint edn., New York, 1969); and, on music-hall song sheet illustration, Jane Traies, 'Jones and the Working Girl: Class Marginality in Music-Hall Song, 1860–1900', in J. S. Bratton (ed.), *Music Hall: Performance and Style* (Milton Keynes, 1986), 23–48. The work of Celina Fox, cited above, is of particular interest in relation to this study; written from a different theoretical stance than mine, her thorough analyses of popular imagery have none the less anticipated certain points which I develop in my discussion of the *Penny Magazine*: see chap. 2, sections II and III, and Chap. 2, nn. 25 and 26.

[25] For the theoretical basis of the pictorial analyses in later chapters, see Roland Barthes, 'Rhetoric of the Image', in *Image–Music–Text*, trans. Stephen Heath (New York, 1977), 32–51; and 'The Photographic Message', ibid. 15–31; Walter Benjamin, 'The Work of Art in the Age of Mechanical Reproduction', in *Illuminations* (Frankfurt, 1955: *Illumination–*; trans. H. Zohn, New York, 1969; reprint edn., New York, 1978), 217–51; John Berger, *Ways of Seeing* (Harmondsworth, 1972; reprint edn., 1976), see esp. 7–33. Of related interest for its attention to cultural context is the analytical method described in Umberto Eco, 'Rhetoric and Ideology in Sue's *Les Mystères de Paris*', *International Social Science Journal* 19 (1967), 552–4.

[26] See John Burnett (ed.), *Useful Toil: Autobiographies of Working People from the 1820s to the 1920s* (Harmondsworth, 1984), 11; id., *Destiny Obscure: Autobiographies of Childhood, Education and Family* (1982; reprint edn., Harmondsworth, 1984), 12; and Vincent, *Bread, Knowledge and Freedom*, 9.

[27] Burnett, *Useful Toil*, 12–13; id., *Destiny Obscure*, 11–12; and Vincent, *Bread, Knowledge and Freedom*, 10–11.

appears that among those subjects generally deemed inappropriate was the place of imagery in working-class life. Even so, a few autobiographers commented directly, if briefly, on this theme, and one even went so far as to admit that he 'hated all books but those of pictures'.[28] On the whole, though, out of a sampling of some fifty autobiographers, most did not express their response to imagery, their pictorial taste, or the uses to which they put printed illustration. Occasionally such reticence functions as negative evidence and allows some inference to be drawn. More often than not the autobiographies are not amenable even to speculation. It seems clear nevertheless that culture emanates from both producers and consumers; and if we are to recognize adequately the role of the latter, then we must use available evidence, however fragmentary. The alternative is our own silence.

Finally, a word or two about the geographical scope and chronology of this book. As is no doubt already apparent, what follows concentrates wholly on England. It is possible, however, that much of what will be said could have wider bearing, since all four of the pivotal magazines also circulated in Scotland, Wales and Ireland. As for chronology, there is here, as with most periodization, a degree of inexactitude. Often what will be said about the years between 1790 and 1832 might well be applicable to the 1780s or even the decade or so before. Much the same holds true for the period 1832 to 1860, and at least some of the cultural conditions that characterized these decades continued to prevail for perhaps another twenty years.

The year 1860 does not then represent any kind of watershed between one kind of culture and its later replacement. The first phase of a new mass culture was well under way by this date and continued on into the 1880s.[29] But 1860 does present a convenient stopping-point: the sources up to then are relatively manageable in quantity, and the time-span takes in the kinds of change that most concern us here. By 1855 the *London Journal*, *Reynolds's Miscellany*, and *Cassell's Paper* had achieved peak circulations of 450,000, 250,000, and 200,000 respectively and, five years later, were still maintaining a similarly high level of regular sales. This five-year period has proved

[28] William Hutton, *The Life of William Hutton* (London and Birmingham, 1817), 79.

[29] For discussion of the phase following, see Hall, 'Deconstructing the "Popular"', 229–31.

to be sufficient as an indicator of commercial success and long enough for related cultural effects to be apparent.

At the other end of the chronology, the year 1790 closely coincides with the earliest memory of the majority of autobiographers. It also preceded the onset of mass culture by some four decades, a length of time adequate to reveal the fundamental character of an older popular culture just before its transformation and expansion. This older culture found expression through the printed imagery that stood at the centre of popular pictorial experience. What follows next is an attempt to reconstruct some of that experience—and revive that imagery.

1

The Printed Image in Transition: Popular Pictorial Experience

1790–1832

AMONG the contemporary scenes illustrated in an 1808 survey of London life and monuments was the annual Royal Academy exhibition of oil paintings. Beneath the high ceilings and large windows of the exhibition room, historical and mythological subjects, animal and genre paintings, landscape and portraiture congested the walls. The stylish crowd of viewers posed, preened, strolled, and conversed. Few gave more than passing attention to the art. They had little need to do so, for such imagery was a commonplace in their lives.

The same London survey also illustrated a different kind of contemporary visual experience. Just a few streets away from the exhibition, in a room of less generous proportion and lighting, another group was assembled. Variously absorbed in needlework, slopwork, winding candlewicks, and picking horsehair, the room's occupants, like the crowd at the exhibition, took scant notice of their surroundings. And they too had little need to do so. In the workhouse of the parish of St James the walls were completely bare.[1]

Between these extremes of aesthetic abundance and visual deprivation lay the experience of the majority of English working people. Those who managed to subsist outside the confines of the prison, asylum, and workhouse were not entirely without the stimulus of imagery. Nature, architecture, public monuments, and commercial signs were all sources of colour, line, and form.[2] So too were the

[1] R. Ackermann, *The Microcosm of London*, 3 vols. (London, 1808), illus. facing i. 10, and between iii. 240 and 241. When this work was published, the Royal Academy was quartered in Somerset House; it moved to a wing of the National Gallery, Trafalgar Square, in 1839, and then to Burlington House in 1869.

[2] For illustrations or commentaries indicative of working people's experience of the natural and man-made environment, see, among many other sources, Thomas

ornamented stages of travelling puppet shows, the painted posters of fairs and circuses, and the scenes of murder and execution that drew crowds to itinerant peep-shows.[3]

But the imagery that was part of the environment, or an aspect of entertainment, was not specifically intended to provide working people with either instruction or aesthetic experience. Fairs and shows, moreover, were only occasional, often fortuitous events; and the more constant sights of daily surroundings must, with familiarity, have lost much of their power to stimulate the eye and arouse the intellect. Thus, if most workers of the late eighteenth and early nineteenth centuries managed to escape the bleakness of the institution, theirs was still by no means the consistently rich and varied experience of imagery that was taken for granted by patrons of the Academy and others equally privileged. At that time it was the rare worker, if any at all, who had seen an original work of fine art in a gallery or museum.

Between 1790 and 1832, then, it was not the establishments of high culture, nor the physical environment, nor even popular entertainment that provided English workers with their most sustained source of aesthetic experience, visual information, and pictorial amusement. Rather, such stimulus came mainly from the imagery dispensed through the medium of print. In the late eighteenth century Thomas Bewick's popularization of the process of wood-engraving, together with early nineteenth-century advances in mechanized printing,

Carter, *Memoirs of a Working Man* (London, 1845), 30 and 125; Thomas Cooper, *Life of Thomas Cooper* (London, 1872), 61; James Elmes and Thomas Shepherd, *London and its Environs in the Nineteenth Century* (London, 1829), *passim*; John H. Harris, *John Harris, the Cornish Poet: The Story of his Life* (London, 1884), 19–20; George Holyoake, *Sixty Years of an Agitator's Life* (London, 1892; reprint edn., London, 1906), 17; and David Love, *The Life, Adventures and Experience of D. Love* (Nottingham, 1823), 147–9.

[3] For representative illustrations of circuses, fairs, puppet shows, and their imagery, see E. B. Chancellor, *The XVIIIth Century in London* (London, 1920), fig. 3; Samuel McKechnie, *Popular Entertainments through the Ages* (New York and London, 1931; reprint edn., London 1969), figs. facing 32, 80, 89, 96, and 97; H. Morley, *Memoirs of Bartholomew Fair* (London, 1857), figs. on 355, 363, and 364; and W. H. Pyne, *Costume of Great Britain* (London, 1808), n.p., see under 'A Country Fair' and illustration facing; and see also R. D. Altick, *The Shows of London* (Cambridge and London, 1978). For a comment on peep shows, see Asa Briggs, *Mass Entertainment* (Adelaide, 1960), 14; and for a representation of the viewers, see Thomas Rowlandson, *Sketches of the Lower Orders* (London, 1820), 'Raree-Show', n.p.

made illustration increasingly available to a widening public.[4] And without doubt that public included working people.

Until 1832, though, it was the middle strata of society that primarily benefited from the burgeoning of pictorial publishing.[5] Economic limitations excluded the majority of workers from all but participation on the fringes of the growing trade in illustration. In a time when a working man's weekly income might be as low as 6 shillings, to own a picture-book or single print was an uncommon luxury that no worker so advantaged took for granted.[6] As the Lancashire weaver and Peterloo activist Samuel Bamford remembered, more prosperous workers might after assiduous hoarding take 'every farthing [they] could scrape together' and purchase the occasional broadside or chapbook—which for 1 or 2 pennies might include a single small woodcut at its head.[7]

Those whose income or frugality were insufficient for such purchases gained access to the printed image from a variety of alternative sources. Coffee-houses contained printed matter, some of it pictorial; many charity and Sunday schools supplied picture books and other illustrated material for use in the classroom, or to be awarded as prizes for diligence; and it was not unknown for sympathetic booksellers to grant borrowing privileges to the trustworthy.[8] From time to time workers in the larger towns and cities must have paused to gaze at the many fine engravings and other pictorial material arrayed in print and bookshop windows. Certainly they had greater oppor-

[4] On Bewick and the history of British wood-engraving in general, see W. A. Chatto, 'The History and Practice of Wood-Engraving', *Illustrated London News*, 11 May 1844, 309–10; Austin Dobson, *Thomas Bewick and his Pupils* (London, 1884); Albert Garrett, *A History of British Wood Engraving* (Atlantic Highlands, NJ, 1978); Thomas Gretton, *Murders and Moralities* (London, 1980), 8–9; Kenneth Lindley, *The Woodblock Engravers* (Newton Abbot, 1970); and Philip Meggs, *A History of Graphic Design* (New York, 1983), 150–1; on early 19th-cent. printing technology, see Introduction, n. 2, above. On print and its dissemination before the period considered here, see Roger Chartier, *The Culture of Print: Power and the Uses of Print in Early Modern Europe*, trans. L. G. Cochrane (Cambridge, 1989); and Margaret Spufford, *Small Books and Pleasant Histories: Popular Fiction and its Readership in Seventeenth-Century England* (Cambridge, 1981).

[5] Richard D. Altick, *The English Common Reader* (Chicago, 1957), 38–41, 51 ff., and 85 ff.

[6] On workers' wages, 1790 to the 1830s, see J. F. C. Harrison, *Early Victorian Britain* ([London], 1979), 53ff.; and E. H. Hunt, 'Wages', in J. Langton and R. J. Morris (eds.), *Atlas of Industrializing Britain, 1780–1914* (London, 1986), 65.

[7] Samuel Bamford, *Early Days* (1848–9; reprint edn., New York, 1967), 90.

[8] Carter, *Memoirs*, 20–1 and 186–7; T. W. Laqueur, *Religion and Respectability* (New Haven, Conn., 1976), 7 and 203.

tunity to do so than their rural counterparts. Thus, although the generality of workers had extremely limited experience of original works of painting and sculpture, at least the urban dwellers among them could on occasion study the art reproductions and other striking prints on display in many a shop-window. No matter where a worker lived, however, at an average cost of 2*s*. 6*d*. each, the quality print-seller's wares were beyond the means of even the relatively well-off artisan.[9]

I

The comparatively restricted access to pictorial material in rural areas and, regardless of locale, its often prohibitive cost could not repress people's widespread interest in the printed image. Rather, workers of all types and from diverse environments sought to incorporate it into their daily lives. The imagery that most typically came their way—through saving and purchase, charity, or chance—was thus closely bound in with other aspects of their cultural experience. One historian has convincingly described this experience as three cultures. There was first of all a predominant popular culture of entertainment characterized by a 'live-and-let-live hedonism'. In opposition to this culture were two others: a religious culture centred around Methodism, but taking in Anglican Evangelicalism; and a culture of secular radicalism which combined the politics of protest with the creed of self-improvement.[10]

With certain qualifications to be discussed later, the printed imagery most common in the everyday life of the people conforms to this descriptive model. But one reservation must be expressed immediately: the model does not distinguish between the experience of urban and rural workers; and, as we have just seen, in the case of the printed image and opportunities for viewing it, the distinction

[9] On the print trade and the cost of prints, see M. D. George, *Hogarth to Cruikshank* (London, 1967), 17; David Kunzle, *The Early Comic Strip* (Berkeley, 1973), 426; and Henry Vizetelly, *Glances Back through Seventy Years*, 2 vols. (London, 1893), i. 88; for an illustration showing people's fascination with a print-shop window display, see Robert Dighton's 1790 *A Windy Day: Scene outside the Shop of Bowles, the Printseller*, reproduced in Thomas Burke, *The Streets of London* (London, 1940), frontispiece; of related interest is S. Taubert, *Bibliopola: Picture and Texts about the Book Trade*, 2 vols. (London, 1966).

[10] Hugh Cunningham, *Leisure in the Industrial Revolution* (London, 1980), 37–41.

needs to be made.[11] Even so, the idea of the geographical uniformity of people's overall cultural experience still has application here. We have already noted, for instance, that most workers—on farms, in villages, towns, or in cities—could not afford the price required to own any illustrative material other than the odd penny print or picture-book. It will also become apparent as we progress with our survey that, whether they occurred often or rarely, many of the circumstances in which working people might potentially encounter or acquire imagery were not geographically differentiated. So it seems that while we must acknowledge the local divergency of some kinds of pictorial experience, we must equally remember that this did not negate a more general cultural coherence manifested through the printed image.

In both country and city, then, but with varying frequency, working people saw printed imagery, usually woodcuts, providing diverse kinds and levels of entertainment. The walls and windows of inns, shops, and other premises were a source of information and at least occasional pictorial diversion. As print replaced the bellmen, advertising bills and cards became an increasingly common sight in village, town, and city. Before the mid- to late 1830s the majority of printed wall advertisements were not illustrated, or included only the odd asterisk or pointing finger for emphasis. None the less the pictorial bill was not entirely unknown, and many working people would have been familiar with such stock images as the horses and riders commonly used to illustrate race bills. One typical example, an 1829 advertisement for the Yarmouth races, presented viewers with a tiny cut of two jockeys and their mounts in a neck-and-neck race; the well-detailed composition also incorporated a flagman and two cheering spectators. Another fairly common sight must have been the stock-cuts of acrobats and tightrope walkers, frequently reproduced on announcements of coming circuses, fairs, and theatrical events like '*Monsieur Longuemare* . . . on the TIGHT ROPE' at Davis's Amphitheatre near Westminster Bridge, 28 April 1823.[12] Trade cards, usually displayed in shop-windows, were illustrated more

[11] Cunningham, nevertheless, is persuasive when he questions the usefulness of such a distinction for understanding other forms of leisure: *Leisure in the Industrial Revolution*, 10.

[12] For an illustration of the race bill mentioned in the text, see John Lewis, *Printed Ephemera* (Ipswich, 1962), 118. For examples of circus and theatrical bills, see London Playbills, 171, British Library, London; and see also Morley, *Bartholomew Fair*, 355. For commentary on posted bills, racing and theatrical advertisements,

often than posted bills and encompassed a range of subject-matter. Among the many images that passers-by might view were Chinese merchants drinking tea, Turks imbibing coffee, and Englishmen enjoying pipe tobacco; elsewhere, meanwhile, cupids, goddesses, flowers, scrolls, and acanthus helped to promote such products as Fashionable Linen Drapery and Cheap Hats; or such enterprises as Richard Warren, Perfumer; Graham, Printer at Alnwick; and J. Garnett, Chemist, Druggist, etc.[13]

The interior walls of many public houses were also a source of printed imagery. To some patrons, perhaps, these woodcuts and engravings were bland entertainment when compared to the pleasures of the main attraction of such establishments. But at least one working man, a London ribbon-weaver, was sufficiently impressed to recall the 'framed engravings of naval battles hung round the walls' of a 'respectable' Clerkenwell public house in 1824. More than their subject-matter, however, it was the general character of these prints that struck him. For they, like the rest of the interior, were 'neat and sober' and thus harmonized with the clientele whose number included 'carpenters, bricklayers and labourers'.[14]

But these and other offerings of walls and windows provided imagery of secondary importance in the lives of most workers. More central to their experience of printed pictorial entertainment were the woodcut illustrations of the broadside and chapbook.[15] Sold by printers, booksellers, chapmen at fairs, and street vendors, both kinds of publication had wide distribution. A broadside—that is, a single

and the early use of imagery in advertising, see J. D. Burn, *Commercial Enterprise and Social Progress* (London, 1858); id., *The Language of the Walls* (Manchester and London, 1855); James Cleaver, *A History of Graphic Art* (London, 1963), 174–6; Patricia Hollis, *The Pauper Press* (London, 1970), 114–15; N. McKendrick, J. Brewer, and J. H. Plumb, *The Birth of a Consumer Society* (London, 1982), 273 ff.; and Frank Presbrey, *The History and Development of Advertising* (New York, 1929; reprint edn., New York, 1968), 84–5 and 110–11.

[13] The text's description of trade cards is based on examples from Window Bills and Advertisements, John Johnson Collection, Bodleian Library, Oxford; and Blanche Cirker, (ed.), *1800 Woodcuts by Thomas Bewick and His School* (New York, 1962), plates 183–6.

[14] 'A Working Man', *Scenes from My Life*, ed. R. Maguire (London, 1858), 21–2.

[15] Among the many compilations, studies, and discussions of broadsides and chapbooks are J. Ashton, *Chap Books of the Eighteenth Century* (London, 1882; reprint edn., New York, 1966); Robert Collinson, *The Story of Street Literature* (London, 1973); Gretton, *Murders and Moralities*; Charles Hindley, *Curiosities of Street Literature* (London, 1871; reprint edn., New York, 1970); id., *History of the Catnach Press* (London, 1887; reprint edn., Detroit, 1969); Louis James, *Print and*

sheet with a poem, song, story, and perhaps one woodcut—cost a penny or halfpenny, while a chapbook—a miniature, usually soft-cover story-book of a dozen or so pages—sold for slightly more at 1*d*. to 3*d*. Those unable to afford such prices might patronize one of the coffee-houses or pubs where the latest broadsides were pasted on the walls or passed from hand to hand. It was also not uncommon for workers to pool resources and share a penny ballad or book between two families.[16] And, at no cost whatever, the shop-window of town and city was a constant means of viewing at least some of this material and taking in the pictorial entertainment it afforded. Bamford recalled a Manchester bookshop 'kept by one Swindells, a printer' and described what must have been a fairly typical display of illustrated wares: 'In the spacious windows of this shop . . . were exhibited numerous songs, ballads, tales and other publications with horrid and awful-looking woodcuts at the head; which publications, with their cuts, had a strong command on my attention.'[17]

The subject matter of the displays that so attracted Bamford and others revolved around a few constant main themes: real or fictitious scandals, often humorously treated; love, sex, and marriage; illness, misfortune, and death; crime and punishment. The broadsides in particular repeated endless variations on these themes in both ballad and prose forms. A nineteenth-century collector and compiler of street literature, Charles Hindley, pointed out that the stock-in-trade of such publishers of popular entertainment as James Catnach and John Pitts was 'doubtful scandals, "cooked" assassinations, sudden deaths of eminent individuals, apocryphal elopements, real or catch-penny accounts of murders, impossible robberies, delusive suicides, dark deeds and public executions.'[18]

the People (London, 1976), 38–40 and *passim*; Victor E. Neuburg, 'The Literature of the Street', in H. J. Dyos and M. Wolff (eds.), *The Victorian City*, 2 vols. (London, 1973), i. 191–209; id., *The Penny Histories* (London, 1968); id., *Popular Literature* (Harmondsworth, 1977); Edwin Pearson, *Banbury Chap Books* (London, 1890; reprint edn., New York, 1972); Leslie Shepard, *The History of Street Literature* (Newton Abbot, 1973); and Martha Vicinus, *The Industrial Muse* (London, 1974). Unpublished primary material can be found in various collections: e.g., the John Johnson Collection, Bodleian Library; the S. Baring-Gould and Thomas Crampton collections of ballads, and several similar unnamed collections, all in the British Library.

[16] L. Shepard, *John Pitts, Ballad Printer of Seven Dials* (London, 1969), 83.

[17] Bamford, *Early Days*, 83.

[18] Hindley, *Curiosities*, 75. On Catnach and Pitts, see id., *The Life and Times of James Catnach* (London, 1878; reprint edn., Detroit, 1968); and Shepard, *John Pitts*.

These subjects and themes were commonly, though not invariably, illustrated and, as much as the publishers' stock of cuts allowed, the imagery corresponded to the texts. Where they existed, such correspondences tended to be rather loose and generalized, while the use of fairly standardized stock imagery meant that the chosen illustrations were often only pallid reflections of the textual accounts. This was most true in the case of broadsides dealing with sex and love. Extravagant and often highly suggestive passages on illicit passion, heart-rending longings, and cold-blooded betrayal frequently had as their visual accompaniment such innocuous images as prim-looking, not overly attractive young women or, alternatively, sedate and heavily garbed couples strolling chastely through the countryside.[19] Sometimes the choices were not so much bland as surprising. In one such instance a ballad entitled 'The Constant Lovers' was illustrated with the image of a well-nourished duck, captured in print at some point before the ballad's conclusion determined his and the happier fate of the protagonists: 'So the constant lovers got married, and had an excellent fat duck for dinner.'[20]

In contrast, illustrations of crime and punishment were both to the point and not without emotive force. In the starkness of their style and the finality of their content, stock images of the gallows (figure 1) must have aroused at least a small *frisson* of pleasurable dread in many viewers.[21] Similarly, broadside depictions of violent crime were surely graphic enough to satisfy all but the most blood thirsty of pictorial tastes. A case in point is the image of a manic-looking young man relentlessly tightening a rope around the neck of his prone and weakly struggling female victim (figure 2). Probably the majority of viewers cared little that the text described a knifing while the picture showed murder by strangulation—the level of violence portrayed was after all true to the spirit of its description.

The working people who wrote about their lives and tastes remained remarkably silent on the subject of broadsides, feeling perhaps that reminiscences of such entertainment would not have been in keeping with the self-consciously literary and hortatory tone that characterized many of their autobiographies. However, the

[19] For examples, see Hindley, *Curiosities*, 14, 17, 23, and 34; and Shepard, *Street Literature*, 195.

[20] For a reproduction of this broadside, see Shepard, *Street Literature*, 176.

[21] On the iconography of punishment and the viewers' role in the 'spectacle of the scaffold', see Michel Foucault, *Discipline and Punish*, trans. Alan Sheridan (New York, 1979), 32–72, 94–5, and *passim*.

The Trial and Execution of

Thomas Hubbard, for House Breaking, and

William Cattermole, for setting fire to a stack of Hay,

Who suffered at Ipswich, on Saturday, April 25, 1829, pursuant to their sentence at Bury Lent Assizes.

WILLIAM CATTERMOLE was indicted for having in the afternoon of the 12th of November last, maliciously set fire to a stack of clover hay, in the parish of Letheringham, the joint property of Jas. Glandfield and others.

Wm. Plant, a labourer, worked last Nov. on the farm at Letheringham, occupied by Mr. Glandfield and others; on the 12th of Nov. last, saw the prisoner about 8 or 9 o' clock in the morning, going towards the Lawn Field; saw him come home about a quarter after 4, in the afternoon. There was a little stack of clover, of about 2 jags, which came off 6 acres, in Mr. Glandfield's yard; I passed the stack a ¼ past 4, about five minutes before I saw the prisoner; there was no appearance of any fire; I went through the barn, which is a few yards from the stack; I was on the front side of the barn when I saw the prisoner; who was pulling some beans from the stack close to the barn-door; he saw me come into the barn, and I talked to him at the barn

James Glandfield—Prisoner was employed on my land; I had no particular dispute. About a fortnight or three weeks before the fire happened the prisoner was dissatisfied with his pay, but I dont recollect what the prisoner said.

The Jury retired for some time. On their return they pronounced a verdict of Guilty. The verdict was received with surprise by the Judge and the whole Court.

The Learned Judge proceeded in the most impressive and feeling manner, to pass the awful sentence of Death, which the prisoner heard with apparent indifference.

LAMENTATION.

William Cattermole is my name,
I've sham'd my friends in the town,
And now that I am doom'd to die,
I hope the youth that see me die,

I'm brought to grief and shame,
In my bloom I am cut down.
In tender years with scorn,
May be warn'd by my downfall.

THOMAS HUBBARD was placed at the bar, charged with breaking into the dwelling house of George Rant, of Mendham, Gent. and stealing

1. Execution broadside, 1829

HORRID MURDER,

Committed by a young Man on a young Woman.

George Caddell became acquainted with Miss Price and a degree of intimacy subsisted between them, and Miss Price, degraded as she was by the unfortunate step she had taken, still thought herself an equal match for one of Mr. Caddell's rank their intended marriage. Miss Price met him at the time appointed, on the road leading to Burton, at a house known by the name of "The Nag's Head." Having accompanied her supposed lover into the fields, and walked about till towards evening, they

2. Early nineteenth-century murder broadside

commercial success of broadsides in general and the wide circulation of certain specific examples are together a strong indication that the publishers of such material reached their targeted audience. The large print-runs and frequent reissuing of certain categories of broadsides further suggest that among the most profitable and popular were those treating love and courtship. Rivalling these were the almanac sheets with their small traditional images of the labours of the months and their 'Wonderful Predictions and Remarkable Prophecies' for the coming year.[22]

But above all it was the murder and execution broadsides that had the most notably large following. Catnach's 1823 account of the execution of the murderer John Thurtell sold 500,000 copies, while two later Catnach broadsides—the 'last Dying Speech and Confession of William Corder, Murderer of Maria Marten' (1828) and 'John Holloway, the Brighton Wife Murderer' (1831)—had respective sales of 1,166,000 and 500,000 copies.[23] On these and other similar broadsides bold headlines and such typical catchwords and phrases as '*Dreadful*, HORRIBLE, Cruel and Inhuman, SHOCKING RAPE AND MURDER, and *HORRID MURDER!*' not only promoted sales: they also on occasion enhanced a purported 'Likeness of the Murderer' whose benign-looking stock countenance might otherwise have been mistaken for an ordinarily mild and law-abiding individual (figure 3).

It is possible that workers saved these images of murder and its punishment and used them to relieve the bareness of their walls. Illustrator John Leech would later suggest this pictorially in an engraving showing the interior of a working family's home. On the wall over the mantle he depicted a broadside image of the murderer Greenacre and, above it, a stock gallows scene.[24] His intent was to satirize popular taste of the 1840s, but he perhaps also identified an aspect of household embellishment which was not uncommon a few years earlier. If so, then it would not have been as grisly a mode of

[22] For an illustration of an almanac broadside published by Catnach in 1825, see James, *Print*, 55; see also his commentary, 53–9. My conclusions about the relative popularity of subject-matter are based on the following samplings: the Baring-Gould Collection of Ballads printed in London, vols. 1, 2, and 3, British Library; id., Collection printed in Newcastle, vols. 1.1 and 1.2, British Library; the Crampton Collection, vols. 1, 2, and 3, British Library; and the Catnach catalogue of ballads for 1832, reproduced in Shepard, *Street Literature*, 216–23.

[23] Altick, *Common Reader*, 288; J. Holloway, 'Broadside Verse Traditions', *Listener*, 21 May 1970, 684. Neuburg, *Popular Literature*, 138, has a reproduction of the Corder broadside.

[24] The engraving is from *Punch* 17 (1849), 117.

3. Broadside image of the murderer
John Thurtell, 1823

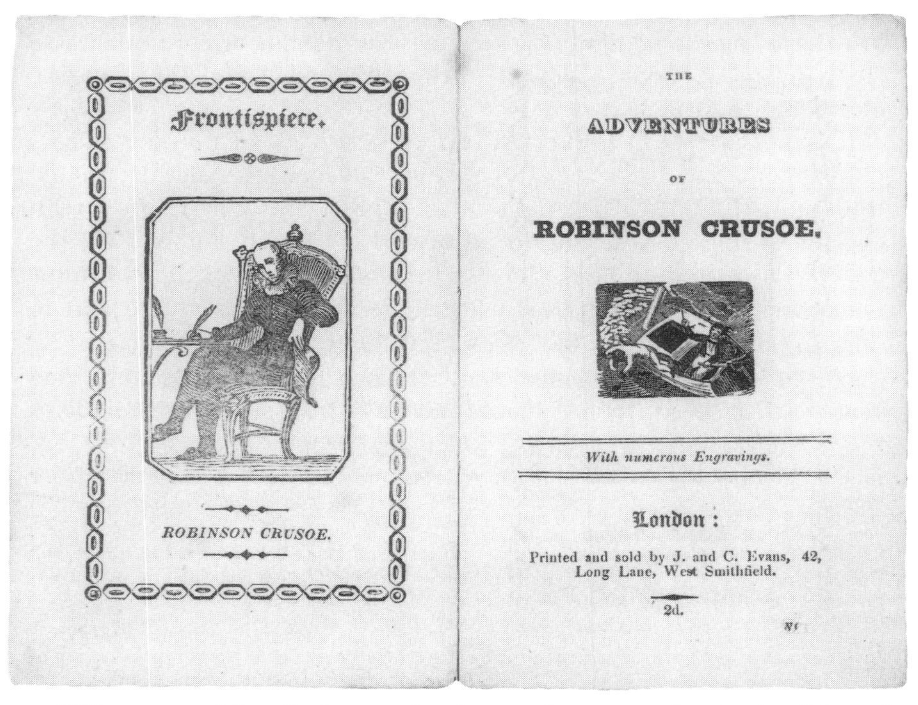

4. Title-page and frontispiece, early nineteenth-century chapbook edition of *Robinson Crusoe*

interior decoration as it might today seem. For the eighteenth- and nineteenth-century lore relating to dream interpretation and fortune-telling deemed the image of the gallows to be 'a most fortunate omen', the indicator of coming riches and 'great honours'. In a similarly happy vein, murder was paradoxically 'a sign of long life', while 'to imagine you see a murderer' meant 'good news' on the way.[25] Perhaps, though, in a world where pictures were often expensive and difficult to come by, it was simply the appeal of any wall decoration, rather than a specific image, that most mattered.

By the turn of the nineteenth century, at least some workers must have been able to exercise a greater amount of choice in imagery for their homes. In the cities, street vendors who pinned their wares to open umbrellas offered penny prints of varying quality, usually purchased from waste-paper dealers. Additionally, as both the collector Hindley and the publisher Charles Knight recalled, there were broadside-style prints, sometimes red- or blue-tinted, which workers could buy cheaply from itinerant pedlars at markets and fairs.[26] According to Hindley, the subjects of these prints were standard genre scenes such as 'The Curate Going Out on Duty', 'The Countryman in London', and 'Troubled with Gout'. Other scenes—'Love in a Village' and 'Out of Place and Unpensioned'—touched more closely on the workers' lived experience and perhaps for that reason may have been more popular. But there is no direct evidence one way or another: on this point too the autobiographers remained mute.

They were somewhat more forthcoming about their preferences in chapbook tales and images. This is fortunate, because beyond the fact that many chapbooks circulated in the thousands in the eighteenth century, no figures have emerged to show comparative sales and relative popularity. From readers' and others' accounts, it seems that the most widely circulated chapbooks included *Nixon's Prophecies*, *Mother Shipton's Legacy*, and other guides to the future; traditional romances such as *Guy of Warwick*; and the stories and pictures of fairies, giants, and fabulous exploits found in works like *Mother Bunche's Fairy Tales*.[27] Once again Bamford is the most

[25] From a dictionary list of typical items in dream and fortune-telling booklets, reproduced in Collinson, *Story of Street Literature*, 129–43.

[26] Hindley, *Life of Catnach*, 23; Knight, 'Address to Readers', *Penny Magazine*, 5 (1836), 516; for commentary on and illustration of the umbrella print-sellers, see Peter Jackson, *George Scharfe's London* (London, 1987), 48.

[27] Altick, *Common Reader*, 38; Neuburg, *Penny Histories*, 9–20. For representative

articulate source. Among the chapbook stories and images that drew him to Swindell's shop window were *Jack the Giant Killer*, *Saint George and the Dragon*, *Jack and the Beanstalk*, *The Seven Champions of Christendom*, *Fair Rosamund*, *The Witches of the Woodlands*, and 'such like romances'. A one-time Yarrow serving-girl, Janet Bathgate, indicated a similar taste, echoing Bamford's mention of *Jack and the Beanstalk* and adding *Robinson Crusoe* to his selection.[28]

Among younger readers at least, the latter title was perhaps the best loved of all. One worker reminiscence after another makes approving reference to this story of high adventure, faith, and self-reliance. Chartist shoemaker Thomas Cooper, for example, remembered it as one of his favourite works, placing it near the top of a list in which he included such other prized classics as the *Arabian Nights*, Shakespeare's plays, *Paradise Lost*, and Byron's *Childe Harold*.[29] Illustrations undoubtedly added to the story's appeal, and many inexpensive editions had at least one or two; figure 4 shows a typical example dating to about 1820. The following incident, recounted by the son of the Cornish miner and poet John Harris, is a touching indication of the value attached to even a modest, single-image version of Defoe's tale: 'His father to show appreciation of his progress, presented John with a penny abridgment of "Robinson Crusoe" with a pictorial frontispiece. Except the school primer, this was the first book which he could call his own and it was carried to his bedroom every night.'[30]

Like the broadside publishers, those who printed and sold chapbooks—some, such as Catnach, handling both kinds of publication—kept a stock of images to be used and reused. As a nineteenth-century compilation of Banbury chapbooks illustrates, there were groups of stories—for instance, *Jack and the Giants*, *Tom Thumb*, and *Tom, Tom the Piper's Son*—each with episodes similar enough to allow publishers to interchange the same set of engraved blocks among two or more illustrated chapbooks.[31] Reused or otherwise,

illustrations, see ibid., 81ff.; and Pearson, *Banbury Chap Books*, 33, 36, and *passim*.

[28] Bamford, *Early Days*, 90; Janet Bathgate, *Aunt Janet's Legacy to Her Nieces* (Selkirk, 1894).

[29] Cooper, *Life*, 33.

[30] Harris, *John Harris . . . Life*, 17.

[31] Pearson, *Banbury Chap Books*, 15. On the publishers of chapbooks, see Neuburg, *Penny Histories*, 34–44 and 66–71.

much of the imagery of late eighteenth- and early nineteenth-century chapbooks differed from that of the broadsides in its generally higher level of stylistic sophistication. This distinction was due to the more frequent use in chapbooks of wood-engravings rather than woodcuts, the former technique enabling the engraver to introduce finer lines and greater detail. Publishers like Catnach and Thomas Saint of Newcastle augmented their stock of cuts with engravings commissioned from the young Bewick and, later, some of his pupils.[32] The charm of the Bewick images is apparent; but even those cuts which seem crude by comparison often show a certain vitality, and on occasion they too must have enhanced the popular appeal of the chapbook literature.

II

The illustrated chapbook was also integral to the second kind of popular experience that many working lives embraced: the culture of religion. *The Pilgrims: An Allegory*, *The History of Joseph and his Brethren*, *Daniel in the Den of Lions*, *General Resurrection*, *The History of Joseph of Arimathea*, and the much-loved *Foxe's Martyrs* are just a few of the many works that were sold and distributed in the 1790s and early 1800s under the auspices of organizations such as the Church of England's Society for Promoting Christian Knowledge (SPCK), the Evangelical Religious Tract Society, and Hannah More's Cheap Repository of Moral and Religious Tracts.[33] The Repository in particular was adept at conveying its messages in entertaining form, using to advantage the brisk narrative, lively images, and intriguing titles that typified chapbooks designed more

[32] For representative examples, see Cirker, *1800 Woodcuts by Thomas Bewick*. On the difference in appearance and process between woodcuts and engravings, see Gretton, *Murders and Moralities*, 9; Meggs, *History of Graphic Design*, 150; and Michael Twyman, *Printing, 1770–1970* (London, 1970), 21.

[33] On the history and activities of these societies, see W. O. B. Allen and E. McClure, *Two Hundred Years: The History of the SPCK* (London, 1898); Altick, *Common Reader*, 100 ff.; W. K. L. Clarke, *History of the SPCK* (London, 1959); S. G. Green, *Story of the Religious Tract Society* (London, 1899); M. G. Jones, *Hannah More* (Cambridge, 1952); Susan Pedersen, 'Hannah More Meets Simple Simon: Tracts, Chapbooks and Popular Culture in Late Eighteenth-Century England', *Journal of British Studies*, 25 (Jan. 1986), 84–113; and R. K. Webb, *The British Working Class Reader, 1790–1848* (London, 1955), 25–8. For reproductions of illustrations from some of the works named in the text, see Ashton, *Chap-Books*, 3–24, 25, and *passim*.

purely for amusement. More and her associates marshalled—among others—*The Lancashire Collier Girl*; *Tom White, the Postilion*; *Two Soldiers*; *Betty Brown, the Orange Girl*; *Sorrowful Sam*; and *Sinful Sally* in a concerted attack on the perceived vulgarity, licentiousness, profanity, and indecency of the secular broadsides and chapbooks.[34]

Among the Repository's front-line literary and pictorial arsenal was the story of the *Two Shoemakers*.[35] Representative of many other similar works, the *Shoemakers* sold in penny-parts, each with a dozen or so pages and an illustration at the head. The image shown in figure 5 introduced the first part and encapsulated the plot as a whole, a variation on a common contemporary theme: the behaviours, rewards, and punishments associated with industry and idleness. At the left of the picture sits James Stock, hard at work on an item of footwear. The product of a thrifty, church-going family, he presented the viewer with a clear instance of 'upbringing tells'. No less was true of his fellow apprentice, 'idle Jack Brown'. The text unequivocally intended the reader to make a causal connection between Jack's irreligious family background and his uncompromisingly supine and unoccupied image at the bottom right of the illustration. The eventual fates of the two young men are also consistent with their contrasting pictorial representation. The ever-diligent James worked and saved, halfpence by halfpence, 'without spending a single farthing on his own diversions', and 'became a Creditable Tradesman'. Jack, on the other hand, proceeded inevitably from idleness into profligacy and crime, and ended his career in prison.

In recounting their literary preferences the autobiographers remark little, if at all, upon Repository publications or the comparable efforts of other religious organizations. This lends credence to the opinion of some scholars that the middle classes were the principal consumers of religious tracts.[36] Weighing against this view is the impressively wide circulation of tract literature: SPCK publications numbered 1,500,000 in 1827; the Religious Tract Society printed 314,000 tracts in 1804; and by March of 1796 the Cheap Repository had achieved a total sales and distribution of 2 million.[37] Frequently given out at no

[34] On the style and content of these and other Repository chapbooks, see Pederson, 'Hannah More', 88–97.

[35] Although the edition cited and illustrated here was published in Dublin, numerous similar editions and reprints circulated throughout England and the rest of Great Britain.

[36] For example, Webb, *Working Class Reader*, 28.

[37] Altick, *Common Reader*, 101; Pedersen, 'Hannah More', 112.

charge, religious reading material presumably reached a significant number of workers' households. And while texts might often have remained unread, their less demanding illustrations must have attracted at least passing attention and thus have become part of popular experience of the printed image.

There is less uncertainty about the appeal of one central publication of the Religious Tract Society. Sold in penny-parts, charitably distributed, or awarded as Sunday school prizes, inexpensive abridged versions of *The Pilgrim's Progress* almost invariably figured among even the most meagre of household libraries. Among others, Janet Bathgate and a Kent shoemaker, William Burch, recalled copies in their family homes.[38] Neither mentioned imagery; but most of the chapbook versions had at least one woodcut or engraving, and Bathgate's and Burch's copies were probably not unlike the Tract Society's edition of about 1815, whose pictorial title page is reproduced in figure 6. As we have rather come to expect, on the subject of popular reading and illustration it is again Bamford whose memory was most vivid. Recollecting his early impressions of Bunyan's allegory, he wrote:

> The first book which attracted my particular notice was 'The Pilgrim's Progress' with rude woodcuts; it excited my curiosity in an extraordinary degree. There was 'Christian knocking at the strait gate', his 'fight with Apollyon', his 'passing near the lions', his 'escape from Giant Despair', his 'perils at Vanity Fair', his arrival in the 'land of Beulah', and his final passage to 'Eternal Rest'; all these were matters for the exercise of my feeling and my imagination.[39]

In the 1790s and first thirty years of the nineteenth century the chapbook-style tract appears to have been the religious organizations' main vehicle for disseminating imagery. But during this time several societies and individuals began to expand their efforts to include the publication of periodical literature, some of which was illustrated.[40] The Tract Society, for example, entered the field in 1824 and, with characteristic munificence, produced 339,000 copies of *The Child's Companion; or, Sunday Scholar's Reward* and 206,000 numbers of an adult version, *The Tract Magazine; or, Christian Miscellany*.[41]

[38] Bathgate, *Aunt Janet's Legacy*, 48; William Burch, *Life, Sermons and Letters*, ed. T. Russell (n.p., 1866), 25. On Sunday school prize-books, see Laqueur, *Religion and Respectability*, 118 and 206.

[39] Bamford, *Early Days*, 40.

[40] For a general discussion, see Laqueur, *Religion and Respectability*, 206–8.

[41] Green, *Religious Tract Society*, 30–3.

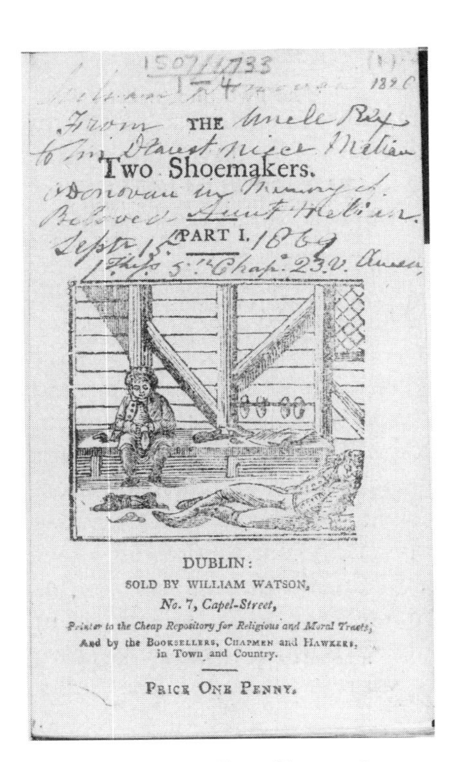

THE

Two Shoemakers.

PART I.

DUBLIN:

SOLD BY WILLIAM WATSON,

No. 7, Capel-Street,

Printer to the Cheap Repository for Religious and Moral Tracts;

And by the BOOKSELLERS, CHAPMEN and HAWKERS, in Town and Country.

PRICE ONE PENNY.

5. Title-page, *Two Shoemakers*, 1810

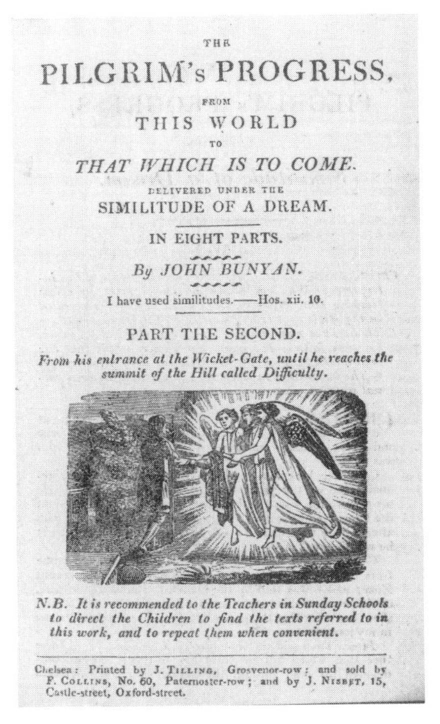

THE

PILGRIM's PROGRESS,

FROM

THIS WORLD

TO

THAT WHICH IS TO COME.

DELIVERED UNDER THE

SIMILITUDE OF A DREAM.

IN EIGHT PARTS.

By JOHN BUNYAN.

I have used similitudes.——Hos. xii. 10.

PART THE SECOND.

From his entrance at the Wicket-Gate, until he reaches the summit of the Hill called Difficulty.

N.B. It is recommended to the Teachers in Sunday Schools to direct the Children to find the texts referred to in this work, and to repeat them when convenient.

Chelsea: Printed by J. TILLING, Grosvenor-row; and sold by F. COLLINS, No. 60, Paternoster-row; and by J. NISBET, 15, Castle-street, Oxford-street.

6. Title-page, *Pilgrim's Progress*, 1815

7. The Bell-Ringer, 1820

The pictures and texts of these magazines were consistent with the Society's wish to counteract the 'mass of evil literature' of a secular nature. In the first issue of the *Child's Companion* (January 1824), the illustration and its accompanying text portrayed two earnest and —considering the intended audience—inappropriately well-dressed boys on their way to Sunday school, to celebrate in exemplary fashion 'THE FIRST SABBATH OF THE YEAR'. The initial and concurrent number of the *Tract Magazine* illustrated a 'poor man's' family engaged in home Bible study—a central activity, presumably, in the text's programme for 'a new year of redemption'.

There was a measure of realism in the *Tract Magazine*'s introductory image. As many of the autobiographers indicated, few households lacked a bible.[42] But if bibles were a commonplace, illustrated versions were not. In the period considered here only a very few inexpensive editions contained cuts or engravings.[43] Moreover, the great majority of autobiographers who referred to a family bible made no mention of pictures. From the only two to do so—Cooper and the Colchester tailor Thomas Carter—we can infer that ownership of, or even access to, an illustrated bible was rare enough to merit retrospective notice. Carter recalled with some fondness the generosity of a shopkeeper who allowed him to browse through a bible 'crowded with engravings, which were called embellishments'. For Cooper and his family it was an apparent source of great pride that his father had managed to purchase an engraved bible. He remembered how 'on rainy Sundays' his mother would unwrap this 'treasure' from 'its careful cover'; and then the young Carter, feeling 'privileged', would 'gaze and admire while she slowly turned over that superb store of pictures'.[44] These fragments of evidence are only suggestive. But, in combination with what is known of publishing history in general, it seems that working people had little experience of pictorial bibles until the late 1830s, when publishers like Charles Knight made them affordable to a wider public.

The role of Methodism in the dissemination and popularization of religious imagery of all kinds should not be overlooked. As part of its

[42] Bamford, *Early Days*, 89; Bathgate, *Aunt Janet's Legacy*, 48; Burch, *Life*, 28 and *passim*; Cooper, *Life*, 8; Joseph Livesey, *The Life and Teachings of Joseph Livesey* (London, 1886), 5; see also David Vincent, *Bread, Knowledge and Freedom* (London, 1981), 110–11.

[43] For an example of Bible illustration from *c.*1803, see Pearson, *Banbury Chap Books*, 90.

[44] Carter, *Memoirs*, 20; Cooper, *Life*, 8.

general philosophy of encouraging learning, the sect not only produced its own pamphlet and periodical literature—some of it illustrated—but also distributed at small cost several publications of other organizations: for example, the kind of chapbook-style tracts discussed above.[45] Methodism, moreover, was a major impetus behind the rapid growth of Sunday schools in the early nineteenth century—and these in turn were one of the most important and constant sources of popular religious imagery.[46]

At the core of the Sunday schools' curricula, whether Methodist, Dissenting, or Church of England, was the illustrated Scripture lesson. The SPCK, for example, had been distributing pictorial lesson books to schools since 1705. More popular among the Chapel-affiliated schools were the two series of Old and New Testament prints which the energetic Evangelical Mrs Sarah Trimmer had 'Designed to Illustrate Scripture Lessons'. The two series together contained 130 or so engravings, whose number included representations of Adam and Eve in the garden, Noah's Ark, David and Goliath, the birth of Christ, the raising of Lazarus, and many more scenes.[47]

On occasion, pictorial chapbook editions of *Pilgrim's Progress* may also have assisted in the teaching and learning of Scriptures. To prompt teachers, the title page of the Tract Society's abridgment incorporated the following pedagogical suggestion: 'N.B. It is recommended to the Teachers in Sunday Schools to direct the Children to find the texts referred to in this work, and to repeat them when convenient' (see figure 6). The libraries of the various Sunday schools might also have included Cheap Repository stories and magazines like the *Child's Companion*. Nearly always, among their store of literature were the little books, many of them illustrated, which rewarded the conscientious and, perhaps, inspired many others. Among the more frequently awarded prizes were *Foxe's Book of*

[45] Altick, *Common Reader*, 35–8; H. F. Mathews, *Methodism and the Education of the People, 1791–1851* (London, 1949), especially 71ff.; and see also R. F. Wearmouth, *Methodism and the Working-Class Movements in England, 1800–1850* (London, 1937). For examples of illustration—portraits of 'Preachers of the Gospel', see the *Methodist Magazine* 21, 30, 44 (1798, 1807, 1821).

[46] Mathews, *Methodism*, 39 ff. The most useful study of Sunday schools in general is Laqueur, *Religion and Respectability*: see esp. 113–19 and 204–6.

[47] For an illustration of 'Samson Destroying the Feasting Place of the Philistines' from an SPCK lesson book, see Allen and McClure, *Two Hundred Years*, 185. Trimmer's *Series of Prints* . . . appeared in numerous editions dating back to the 1780s and still being reissued in 1840; biographical information is contained in *Some Account of the Life and Writings of Mrs. Trimmer* (London, 1825).

Martyrs, Milton's *Paradise Lost* and Bunyan's unfailingly popular *Pilgrim's Progress*.

The Sunday schools and religious organizations were the major, but not exclusive, disseminators of popular religious imagery. In addition to their other output, publishers such as Catnach and Pitts produced chapbook editions of saleable works like *Foxe's Martyrs* and *Pilgrim's Progress*. They also printed religious broadsides; and, as one early nineteenth-century example illustrating the Nativity suggests, trade was particularly brisk at Christmastime.[48] The iconography of Christmas was not, however, the only subject-matter of the religious broadside. Illustrations of Old Testament stories, martyrdoms, the Crucifixion, Christ in Majesty, and the Day of Judgement were all common.[49] From time to time such uplifting images were also part of the scenery of the street and blazoned the messages of self-appointed itinerant preachers like Joseph Hill, the 'Bell-Ringer' (figure 7)—a religious enthusiast whose vigorous peals matched the evangelical fervour with which he expounded a text.[50] The general popularity and influence of the kind of broadside that inspired Hill and, presumably, other less eccentric believers, cannot be determined. The autobiographies have yielded no pertinent references, and circulation figures, if they were ever recorded, no longer exist.

III

A similar lack of evidence dogs the analysis of pictorial artefacts of the third significant type of contemporary popular experience, the culture of radicalism. Surviving examples are not only scarce, but they also do not figure in the recollections of our sampling of autobiographers. As a result, the printed imagery of radicalism is now for the most part detached from whatever lived experience it once represented.

In the 1790s and early 1800s the political concerns of radicalism

[48] For a reproduction of this example, see Gretton, *Murders and Moralities*, 119, fig. 86.

[49] For examples, see ibid., figs. 85, 88, 89, and *passim*. Others can be found in the Baring-Gould Newcastle Collection (1.1, fo. 3, and 1.2, fo. 159), British Library, and several unnamed British Library collections of broadsides; for general commentary, see Collinson, *Story of Street Literature*, chap. 9.

[50] T. L. Busby, *Costume of the Lower Orders* (London, 1820), commentary on the 'Bell-Ringer', n.p.

found printed expression in broadsides, posted bills, pamphlets, the widely circulated writings of Thomas Paine, and newspapers like the *Black Dwarf* and Cobbett's *Political Register*; meanwhile, the culture's central preoccupation with self-help and improvement similarly manifested itself in the diverse educational literature, posters, pamphlets and circulars of working-men's libraries, mechanics' institutes and other such organizations.[51] Of this material only a small proportion of what remains is illustrated. And, because of its cost, much of this was inaccessible to working people except through shop-windows or circulation in pubs, coffee-houses, and, perhaps, mechanics' institutes and similar establishments. This was the case with satirical cartoons by artists such as Gillray and Cruikshank.[52]

It was probably also true of the most widely circulated of all illustrated political literature: the pamphlets published by William Hone between 1819 and 1820—for example, *The Man in the Moon*, *The Political 'A, Apple Pie' . . . for the Instruction and Amusement of the Rising Generation*, *The Real or Constitutional House that Jack Built*, and *The Political House that Jack Built* (figure 8).[53] Of these the last publication, a protest against the 'gagging' effect of the 1819 Newspaper Stamp Act, had the highest cumulative circulation: 100,000 by 1822. Bamford and Cooper recalled having read Hone's publications but do not refer specifically to *Political House*.[54] This is not particularly surprising since, like other Hone pamphlets, a standard edition cost 1*s*., while a deluxe edition with coloured illustrations sold for 3*s*. – both prices well out of reach for all but the most prosperous of artisans. Other working people who might have managed to acquire a copy of a Hone pamphlet presumably did

[51] For discussions of this material, see Charles Elkins, 'The Voice of the Poor', *Journal of Popular Culture* 14 (1980), 262–74; Hollis, *Pauper Press*; James, *Print*, 62–81; Neuburg, *Popular Literature*, 107 and 122; E. P. Thompson, *The Making of the English Working Class* (1963; reprint edn., Harmondsworth, 1978), 788–94 and *passim*; Vicinus, *Industrial Muse*, chap. 2; and Raymond Williams, *The Long Revolution* (London, 1961), 186–9. Many primary source items, such as circulars, which pertain to the reading-matter and activities of mechanics' institutes and libraries are interspersed amongst the correspondence of the Society for the Diffusion of Useful Knowledge (SDUK), University College London Library.

[52] James, *Print*, 71.

[53] For illustrations and discussion, see Neuburg, *Popular Literature*, 148–9; E. Rickword (ed.), *Radical Squibs and Loyal Ripostes* (Bath, 1971), 23 ff., 59 ff., 135 ff., and 311 ff.; and Brian Simon, *Studies in the History of Education, 1780–1870* (London, 1960), between 176 and 177.

[54] Samuel Bamford, *Passages in the Life of a Radical* (1848–9); reprint ed; W. H. Chaloner (New York, 1967), 280–1; Cooper, *Life*, 36.

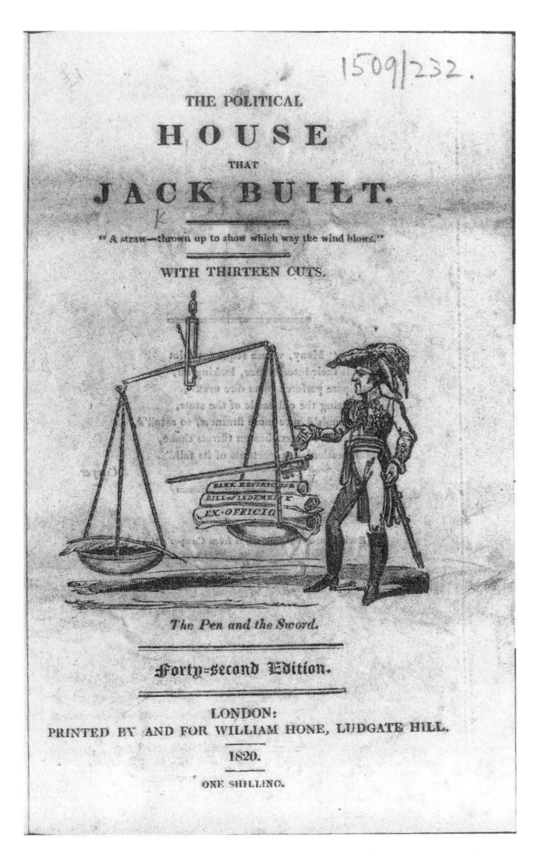

THE POLITICAL

HOUSE

THAT

JACK BUILT.

"A straw—thrown up to show which way the wind blows."

WITH THIRTEEN CUTS.

The Pen and the Sword.

Forty-second Edition.

LONDON:
PRINTED BY AND FOR WILLIAM HONE, LUDGATE HILL.

1820.

ONE SHILLING.

8. Title-page, Hone's *Political House that Jack Built*, 1820

The last Dying Speech and Confession of

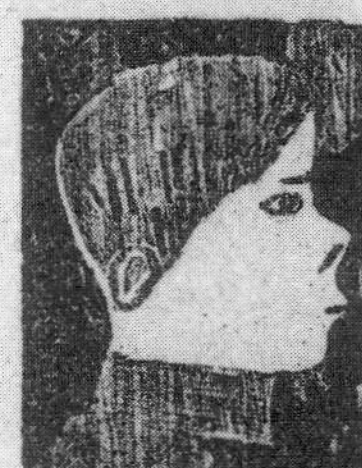

JOSHUA SLADE,

Who received Sentence of Death at Huntingdon Assizes on Tuesday the 31st of July, 1827, for the Murder of the Rev. J. Waterhouse, at Little Stukeley, 3rd of July preceding, and executed on the 1st of September. With the Transportation for Life of William Heddings, one of his Associates, for Burglary.

9. Execution broadside, 1829

so through the philanthropy of well-off reformers who distributed political literature purchased in batches at a reduced price. For most, however, the pubs and other establishments mentioned above must have provided their only glimpses of Hone's images of political protest.

A few pamphlets, less lavishly produced with perhaps only a single illustration on the cover or title-page, might have been within the means of a slightly larger group. Threepence, for example, could buy Richard Carlile's *Life and History of Swing, the Kent Rick-Burner*, 'Written by Himself' in 1830. This price included a cover graphically illustrated with the image of a grossly bloated landowner, looming on horseback above a ragged labourer, his dying wife, and their five weeping children.[55]

For the majority, the broadsheet, rather than the pamphlet, remained the most affordable source of political illustration. Typical of surviving examples from this period are those that celebrated the reform of the rotten borough system, commemorated the Cato Street conspiracy and 'the blood stained crew at Peterloo', or commented pictorially on social and constitutional inequities. In an 1829 broadside of the latter type from the Catnach press, fifteen small cuts, arranged somewhat like a modern comic strip, depict several political figures in the guise of stagecoach drivers; they variously simper, scowl, leer, or posture arrogantly; several clutch whips or riding crops. A final cut shows 'John Bull, broke down'—bent over with the weight of a sackful of taxation and other burdens, he remarks: 'These fellows drive me hard. I must carry less baggage.'[56] Although Catnach's trade in broadsides of this sort was an ongoing aspect of his business, such material was only a small part of his total publications. It is suggestive that out of the 735 titles in his 1832 catalogue of ballad sheets, only seventeen are even remotely indicative of radical content. Of these less than half imply any clear element of protest.[57]

Catnach's comparatively modest output of specifically political

[55] Illustrated in James, *Print*, 97.

[56] For an illustration, see Gretton, *Murders and Moralities*, 75, fig. 41; for reproductions and commentary on other examples mentioned in the text, see ibid., 81, fig. 48; Hindley, *Curiosities*, 45–6 and 98; James, *Print*, 77.

[57] The catalogue is reproduced in full in Shepard, *Street Literature*, 216–23; titles suggestive of protest or dissatisfaction include 'Poor Mechanic's Boy', 'Poor Little Sweep', 'Poverty's No Sin', and 'Time to Remember the Poor'. Other titles are more ambiguous as indicators of content: e.g. 'Carpet Weaver', 'Dustman', and 'Roving Journeyman'.

ballads was a businesslike response to what seems to have been the proportionate lack of market demand for such material. The cumulative evidence of the autobiographies is that work and the pursuit of general knowledge took precedence over oppositional political activity and interests. However, in the period considered here, the overwhelming concern for improved working conditions and educational opportunity was not well reflected in the pictorial material then available. Some early union certificates and trade society membership cards were engraved with coats of arms or similar emblematic representations. But there are very few known examples dating before 1840 and the autobiographies say nothing about such imagery.[58] Illustration associated with self-instruction seems to have been particularly scant at this time. Among the autobiographers only Cooper recollected encountering printed imagery of a broadly educational sort. In the small library of his hometown, Gainsborough, he studied 'Stanley's "History of Philosophers", and its large full-length portraits, [and] Ogilvy's "Embassies to Japan and China", with their large curious engravings.'[59] Cooper's experience does indeed seem to have been unusual, for as late as the 1840s many working men's institutes and libraries keenly felt the lack of both illustrated books and pictorial decoration for their walls.[60] Before 1832 this need would have been even more acute, and those who practised the creed of self-help must have done so largely without the benefit of pictures.

Children from working homes fared slightly better than their elders. By the early 1800s most workers managed to send their children to charity or Sunday schools for a year or two of primary education. In most of these schools the classroom walls had at least some form of rudimentary decoration such as printed pictorial maps, an engraved portrait or two, or a set of alphabet pictures. In his fictionalized autobiography of 'an intelligent artisan' Thomas Wright (the 'Journeyman Engineer') included the description of an infant-

[58] An undated, perhaps early 19th-cent., example of a local society of tin-plate workers membership card is illustrated in R. A. Leeson, *Travelling Brothers* (London, 1979), between 240 and 241; for discussions of later union imagery, see id., *United We Stand* (Bath, 1971); and John Gorman *Images of Labour* (London, 1985).

[59] Cooper, *Life*, 51.

[60] The SDUK's correspondence contains numerous requests from working men's organizations for donations of, or reduced prices for, illustrated books and prints suitable for use on walls; among other examples is the Wakefield Mechanics' Institution letter to secretary Thomas Coates, 26 Aug. 1842. See also the discussion of mechanics' institutes in C. P. Darcy, *The Encouragement of the Fine Arts in Lancashire, 1760–1860* (Manchester, 1976), 104–12.

school classroom that presumably bore some resemblance to the actual appearance of many such premises: 'the school-roomly appearance of the apartment was completed, and the business of its walls relieved by a number of alphabetical and other cards, and cheap coloured prints of Scriptural subjects being hung round the room'. The autobiography of a Southwark working man also contains a description of a classroom. James Bonwick remembered that on the walls of the Borough Road schoolroom in the 1820s there hung Scripture maps for learning Biblical geography and, in a prominent position, 'the portrait of George III, with the motto "The Patron of Education and Friend of the Poor"'.[61]

While classroom decor might vary from school to school, most were consistent in supplying a few illustrated primers for the use of their pupils. Among the well-favoured examples were the *Salisbury Reader* and Catnach's *Child's Easy Primer*. Apart from the Bible, these primers were the first, often the only, books to which a poor child might normally have access. With their woodcut embellishments, these books held considerable appeal for at least some of their young users. Joseph Gutteridge, a ribbon-weaver, remembered that school picture books were 'full of wonders to my youthful imagination'; and a Gloucester shoemaker and sometime poet, Henry Herbert, was inspired to reminisce in verse about his first school texts:

> Neat little books with pictures in
> Were placed within my hand,
> And could not fail my heart to win,
> Which felt this magic wand.[62]

IV

The pictorial experiences of early schooling lay at the periphery of the culture of radicalism. At its core there was no significant body of widely affordable illustrated material designed specifically to promote

[61] Wright, *Johnny Robinson*, 2 vols. (London, 1868), i. 84; Bonwick, excerpts from his autobiography in John Burnett, *Destiny Obscure* (1982; reprint edn., Harmondsworth, 1984), 171 and 174; see also Twyman, *Printing*, 94–6, on early pictorial maps.

[62] Gutteridge, *Autobiography*, 85; Herbert, *Autobiography of . . . a Gloucestershire Shoemaker . . .* (Gloucester, 1866; reprint edn., 1876), 6; and see also Harris, *John Harris*, 17. For illustrations and description of school primers and alphabet books, see Laqueur, *Religion and Respectability*, 114–15; Mathews, *Methodism*, 50 ff.; Pearson, *Banbury Chap Books*, 30 and 87; and Shepard, *Street Literature*, 153.

social change and intellectual improvement. This scarcity of radical imagery and the fact that the majority of autobiographers do not mention political literature, illustrated or otherwise, is consistent with the idea that radicalism in all its guises was a minority culture—at least when compared to popular entertainment.[63] We might therefore wish to reassess the view of some historians that before 1830 radicalism was a widespread expression of formative working-class consciousness.[64] From the evidence relating to printed imagery, it seems that in popular consciousness a radical vision of change had neither the vividness of broadside scenes of love and death, nor the compelling appeal of little woodcut images of Robinson Crusoe and Jack the Giant Killer. Shortly, though, this would begin to change: as we will later note, from 1832, as discontents mounted, the imagery of protest became more prevalent.

The influence of the culture of religion is somewhat more problematic. Was it a minority culture, or did it in its own way have as great an appeal as popular entertainment? The abundance of religious literature produced from the late eighteenth century on, its favourable recollection by some of the autobiographers, and its wide distribution at little or no cost, suggest a need for further research into the impact of this material. It may be that the concept of a minority culture does not accord sufficient importance to the role of religion in people's lives.

There is also other evidence that the three-part model of popular experience may require a further qualification. Is it entirely correct to say that radicalism and religion opposed the wider culture of pure entertainment? It is undoubtedly true that the radical proponents of social and personal improvement, committed Methodists, Evangelicals, and others directed their efforts and rhetoric against the hedonism of many popular enthusiasms. But at another level of cultural expression—the point where social and moral values become embedded in texts—there was a measure of commonalty among the three cultures. Not only is there much that entertained in the written and pictorial expressions of religion and radicalism, but there are also, more significantly, signs in some of the broadsides and chapbooks examined here that printed entertainment had by the 1790s

[63] Cunningham, *Leisure in the Industrial Revolution*, 38.

[64] Thompson, *Making of the English Working Class*; and see also e.g. Hollis, *Pauper Press* and G. S. Jones, 'Working-Class Culture and Working-Class Politics in London, 1870–1900', *Journal of Social History*, 7 (1974), 498 and *passim*.

assimilated many of the values of the other two cultures. The broadside collections are replete with romantic ballads, accounts of sexual and other adventures, almanac sheets, and New Year's verses, all of which combine social moralizing, religion, and patriotism with humour, hedonism, and sensation. And what was that popular hero Robinson Crusoe, if not a model of hard work, self-restraint, and time well used?[65] Similarly the 'last dying speeches' of the murder and execution sheets were more than just conventions. They were also expressions of a widespread system of civilized values relating to religious belief and the virtues of work and self-discipline. Such 'speeches' and 'confessions' are so numerous and similar that one key representative example should be adequate to illustrate the point. In his 'Last Dying Speech and Confession' (1828), Catnach's 'best-selling' murderer, William Corder, described in graphic detail his scuffle with the victim, her shooting and burial, and, of course, the 'vast quantity of blood [that] issued from the wound'. Then, as convention dictated, the murderer expressed guilt and repentance. But it was not the blood on his hands that caused him remorse. Rather, it was the lapses in social virtue that he regretted: 'I have been guilty of great idleness and at times led a dissolute life, but I hope by the mercy of God to be forgiven.'[66]

The values embedded in the literature of entertainment were not usually as overtly moralistic in their presentation as those in, say, a religious tract. Nor did they represent any explicit or concerted vision of social change on the part of those who produced broadsides and chapbooks. They are, however, an instance of the extent to which social and moral authority could exert itself in even the most popular and frivolous of cultural forms. Moreover, the fact that entertainment, religion, and radicalism thus shared certain values is a significant indicator that these cultures were not monolithic and, on one level at least, had the capacity to intermingle.

[65] Among the many representative examples showing the values content of broadsides are those contained in the Baring-Gould Collection of Ballads, 2 vols., Newcastle, vol. 1.1, fo. 3; Ballads and Other Broadside Sheets Published by J. Pitts *et al.* fo. 62; and Miscellaneous Broadsides . . ., ff. 60 and 61—all in the British Library; on the complex structure of values in *Robinson Crusoe*, see Christopher Hill, 'Robinson Crusoe', *History Workshop*, 8, (1980), 7–24.

[66] For a facsimile of the Corder confession, see Hindley, *Life of Catnach*, 187; see also Neuburg, *Popular Literature*, 138; for other examples, see id., *Catnach Press*, 67; Baring-Gould Newcastle Collection, vol. 1.2, fo. 121; Miscellaneous Broadsides, fos. 3 and 27; and, also in the British Library, Broadsheets Relating to . . . Traitors, Murderers and Malefactors, nos. 1, 8, and *passim*.

V

On another level—the iconographic—each of the three kinds of popular experience was loosely linked to the visual forms of high culture. For example, political broadsides often depicted an English oak with branches bearing taxation and other such oppressive fruits—an image whose ultimate derivation was the trees of virtue and vice in medieval illuminated manuscripts. Trade society imagery similarly had iconographic connections with both heraldry and the emblematic imagery of baroque painting. The imagery of popular religion—representations of the Nativity or Crucifixion, for example—drew even more directly upon the standard iconography of sixteenth- and seventeenth-century religious art. Even purported 'likenesses of murderers', execution scenes, and other stock images of broadsides and chapbooks were for the most part simplified versions of the pictorial conventions of portraiture, history painting, and so on.[67]

But these kinds of iconographic linkages by no means signalled the existence of any sort of emergent democracy of imagery. The popular printed image was in form and content far removed from original art, quality prints, and expensive book illustration. The style of the mostly anonymous artists whose work became the stock of popular publishers was, at best, unsophisticated, at worst, crude (figure 9). More often than not, pictures were ill-matched to texts to such an extent that there was nothing unusual in the sight of the face of an elderly bearded gentleman at the head of a ballad entitled 'The Primrose Girl'. That same face also adorned a jingoistic song about the French navy and appeared again at the top of a religious poem. The stock image of a sailing ship illustrated everything from tales of shipwreck, sailors, and military victories (not necessarily naval) to love ballads, murderers' confessions, and stories of religious conversion.[68]

And what of the workers who were the main audience for this kind of inexpensively produced imagery? Were they satisfied with its quality and content? Of the autobiographers only Carter explicitly

[67] For discussion and illustration of some of these points, see Gretton, *Murders and Moralities*, 18, 60, 99, 110, 114–15, 119, and 124–7; and Leeson, *United We Stand*, 8 ff.; James, *Print*, 79, reproduces an example of the Tree of Taxation.

[68] These and many other examples abound in the collections cited in nn. 65 and 66 above.

expressed any dissatisfaction. Recalling the 'embellished' bible of his youthful experience, he remarked that its engravings were 'sorry affairs with regard to both design and execution'. In support of this criticism he gave two examples of images that were in his view more than just 'a little ludicrous'. In the first a figure that should have been portrayed with a beam of light obscuring his vision had instead 'a fair-sized beam [of wood]' protruding from his eye. To Carter's even greater disgust, in a scene from the life of Paul—the restoration of his sight—it was not scales but rather 'a set of balances' that fell from the saint's eyes.[69]

It may be that most people were not as visually fastidious as Carter. Many after all chose to buy or look at broadsides and chap-books and perhaps found little to fault in their illustrations. Bamford for one, we are reminded, was considerably charmed by the woodcuts in a printer's window. But whatever people might have felt about the quality of the images they saw, they were not necessarily happy about their available quantity. The occasional fragment of commentary suggests that working people wanted printed imagery in their lives and at times felt its lack. The son of an impoverished tradesman, for instance, remembered that in the early 1800s most poor households were 'almost bookless' and 'ill-provided' with any sort of illustrated material.[70]

There is some additional evidence which may also, indirectly, indicate people's wish for increased access to the printed image. This evidence bears on other kinds of pictorial material, but from it we can perhaps infer a level of need that took in the general desire for more *printed* illustration. In one case the want of pictorial stimulus among a group of country people was such that even a comparative commonplace like an inn-sign aroused great interest. Adam Rushton, a Kent farm-labourer and later factory-worker, recollected that he and others in his village were very curious and indulged in 'much cogitation' about the possible meaning of the figures on the new sign at the George and Dragon inn. Rushton proposed an interpretation that apparently satisfied most of the onlookers. The 'fearful dragon', he explained, was 'Alcohol . . . seeking whom it might devour'. St George, on the other hand, was not unlike 'the great temperance cause . . . enthusiastically pursuing' and soon to 'destroy the great

[69] Carter, *Memoirs*, 21.

[70] 'An Irreconcileable' [W. B. Rands], 'The Penny Magazine', *St. Pauls Magazine*, 12 (1873), 543–4.

dragon of strong drink, and so to deliver mankind'. George Holyoake also remembered the wonder he felt as a young man when he first saw the newly painted sign at the Fox tavern in Birmingham: 'a very wonderful fox it seemed to me. The sharp-nosed, bushy-tailed animal was rushing to cover—on the sign. I had never seen a fox or a cover, except on that sign. I had only seen a workshop.'[71]

Perhaps the most compelling indication that people wanted more and different imagery in their lives is the effort that many gave to creating their own pictures. For example, drawing and other sorts of artistic activity were a major preoccupation of Cooper's youth: 'I fell upon the project of drawing with slate and pencil but became still more attached to cutting out shapes in paper. With a pair of scissors, I used often to work for hours, making figures of men, horses, cows, dogs, and birds.'[72] He was not alone in this enthusiasm—his closest boyhood friend also drew pictures and cut shapes from paper and, like Cooper, favoured animals as subject-matter. Still other autobiographers similarly recalled making their own imagery: a Yorkshire stencil painter, Christopher Thomson, did so with 'colours and drawings to copy' borrowed from a sympathetic shop-owner; another young worker sketched with bits of chalk on the floor of the boiler-room where he was employed; and others drew with chalk or charcoal on their household hearths.[73] The only female among the sampling of autobiographers also felt a need to create her own imagery. As a young serving-girl, Janet Bathgate was given some 'green cloth and yellow thread' which she used to sew a stitchery map of the lake and surroundings near her place of work.[74]

The kind of artistic endeavour just described, people's general interest in, and frequent lack of, pictorial material, the stylistic shortcomings and repetitiveness of much affordable printed imagery, and the possibility that some viewers found such imagery wanting, are together indicative that working people represented a potential market for more and better imagery than what was currently available to them. As noted previously, in the early nineteenth century the technology of engraving and printing was well enough developed to

[71] Adam Rushton, *My Life as a Farmer's Boy, Factory Lad, Teacher and Preacher* (Manchester, 1909), 16–17; Holyoake, *Sixty Years*, 17.

[72] Cooper, *Life*, 7–8 and 17.

[73] Christopher Thomson, *Autobiography of an Artisan* (London, 1847), 74; Leeson, *United We Stand*, 21; Samuel Bamford, *Walks in South Lancashire* (Blackley, 1844; reprint edn., Brighton, 1972), 212.

[74] Bathgate, *Aunt Janet's Legacy*, 104–5.

supply such a market. But few publishers of the time realized the value of the new processes for the production of good-quality, inexpensive, and commercially profitable illustration; and fewer still envisioned the enormous market for printed imagery that would soon emerge.

VI

By the 1820s, however, this situation was beginning to change. The publisher John Limbird, for example, began producing a weekly pictorial miscellany in 1823. At twopence an issue, his *Mirror of Literature, Amusement and Instruction* was within the reach of artisans and probably many other workers.[75] But the autobiographers do not mention this publication, and later nineteenth-century opinion was that the *Mirror*'s audience of 80,000 or so came mainly from 'the upper and middle classes'.[76]

Another kind of pictorial publication was initially more successful in attracting a readership comprising a significant number of working people. This was the *Library of Useful Knowledge*, issued in monthly parts by the utilitarian Society for the Diffusion of Useful Knowledge (SDUK), whose purpose was to counteract what they feared might be the disruptive influence of the radical press through the publication of cheap, informative, morally improving, and politically innocuous literary and pictorial works. Among the earliest of such publications, the *Useful Knowledge* series had in its first year (1828–9) sales ranging from 22,000 to 33,000 per month. But by 1832 the appeal of long articles and accompanying illustrations treating the natural sciences and other such weighty subjects had waned, and sales had declined to a disappointing 6,000 to 10,000. With the possible exception of maps and almanacs, other SDUK publications of this period followed a similar pattern; thus the illustrated *Library of Entertaining Knowledge* may have been a little less ponderous than its 'useful' counterpart, but it was still only marginally profitable, if at all.[77]

Before 1832 the most successful venture into low-cost pictorial

[75] Henry Brougham, *Practical Observations on the Education of the People* (1825; reprint edn., Boston, 1826), 7.

[76] *Bookseller*, 30 Nov. 1859, 1326–7.

[77] On the SDUK, its membership, aims and publications, see Brougham, 'Society for the Diffusion of Useful Knowledge', *Edinburgh Review* 46 (1827): 235–44; Brougham correspondence, T. Coates to Brougham, 1836–54, and C. Knight to Brougham, 1832–58, University College London Library; Monica Grobel, 'The

publishing for working people was the *Mechanic's Magazine*, which first appeared in 1823. As the title suggests, its editor, J. C. Robertson, a one-time civil engineer and patent agent, aimed the magazine specifically at a readership of literate working men, promising them 'sixteen closely printed pages' and numerous illustrations every Saturday.[78] Indeed, for threepence an issue, readers could browse through the guaranteed number of pages and study diagrams and discussions of 'new Discoveries, Inventions and Improvements', 'Secret Processes', 'Economical Receipts', 'Practical Applications of Mineralogy and Chemistry', and more.

The magazine augmented its primarily technical content with 'Essays on Men and Manners, Tales, Adventures, Anecdotes, Poetry', and 'occasionally Portraits of eminent Mechanics'. The image of one such mechanic, that 'great Improver of the Steam Engine', James Watt, introduced the magazine's first number (figure 10). In the biographical notices that accompanied this and other such portraits, Robertson invariably emphasized the subject's personal and vocational virtues. It was thus no mere likeness of Watt that the viewer saw: it was also an exemplar of wisdom and kindness, skill and inventiveness, perseverance and exertion, improvement and success. The magazine achieved its own measure of success with its mixture of technical information, literary entertainment, and biographical homilies. By 1824 it had a regular circulation of 16,000; and, as its editorial correspondence makes clear, the readership largely comprised Robertson's intended audience of 'Mechanics and Artisans'.[79]

This is not, however, to suggest that the *Mechanic's Magazine* replaced other forms of popular imagery. It had not in fact the power

Society for the Diffusion of Useful Knowledge, 1826–1848', 4 vols., Ph.D. diss. (London, 1932); C. Knight, *Passages of a Working Life*, 3 vols. (London, 1864), ii. 113–35 and *passim*; Harold Smith, *The Society for the Diffusion of Useful Knowledge, 1826–1846*, Dalhousie Library Occasional Paper, 8. (Halifax, Nova Scotia, 1974); and Webb, *Working Class Reader*, 68–72. The major source on the SDUK is its archive at University College London Library. Specific sections are cited in notes to subsequent chapters.

[78] Opening editorial statement, Sat., 30 Aug., *Mechanic's Magazine*, 1 (1823), 16; on Robertson and the magazine, see Altick, *Common Reader*, 393; Brougham, *Practical Observations*, 7; *Dictionary of National Biography*, under 'Robertson, Joseph Clinton'; *Gentleman's Magazine*, NS 38/2 (1852), 548; Robertson to Robert Peel, 22 Apr. 1825, and id., to Charles Babbage, 30 Apr. 1833, Add. MSS 40377, 71 and 37187, 515, British Library.

[79] See also Robertson, evidence before the Select Committee on Arts and Manufactures, 2 Sept. 1835, *Report*, vol. 5, 119, items 1586–8.

Mechanic's Magazine.

——— Industry! rough power!
Whom labour still attends, and sweat, and pain;
Yet, the kind source of every gentle art,
And all the soft civility of life.

Thomson.

No. 1.] SATURDAY, AUGUST 30, 1823. [Price 3*d.*

JAMES WATT.

MEMOIR OF JAMES WATT,

THE GREAT IMPROVER OF THE STEAM-ENGINE.

Many great and distinguished men, the ornaments of the last and present centuries, have been more known and much more talked of than James Watt; but, perhaps, no one of them was the fortunate author of so much real good to mankind or has equal claims on their gratitude. Now, indeed, it is generally known, that he was one of the most successful and skilful inventors of machinery of the age. His good fortune may encourage, and his perseverance instruct the present and all future generations of mechanics; and, therefore, his biography has been selected, as it seems particularly well adapted, for the first number of a work which is to be entirely devoted to their amusement and improvement. Mr. Watt was also a kind good-hearted man—giving lustre to his art, not only by the prodigious power he created, but by the life he led. He acquired wealth and honour by his own exertions, and was praised for his wisdom as well as for his skill. Though we do not pretend to assert that there is any thing in mechanical pursuits which peculi-

B

10. James Watt, *Mechanic's Magazine*, 1823

to do so. In the 1820s, and throughout the period discussed here, working people were not the passive recipients of whatever imagery publishers directed their way. They were instead active consumers and viewers.[80] From what was affordable and accessible, they made their choices and incorporated these into their wider cultural life. It was not the producers, but the consumers, who made the *Mechanic's Magazine*, *Pilgrim's Progress*, *Robinson Crusoe*, and the Corder execution part of the culture that most workers shared.

But pictorial choices were by no means unlimited in possibility. Missing from the everyday experience of many working people—especially those in rural areas—was a wide array of imagery: informative scenes of travel and adventure, naturalistic landscapes, accurate depictions of historical events, believable representations of plant and animal life, recognizable landmarks, realistic portraiture, and quality reproductions of painting and sculpture. In the cities and towns, as much as the villages and farms, the vast majority had no hope of owning the kind of books, prints, and magazines that transmitted such images. Early in 1832, though, this situation would quickly and dramatically change. A new illustrated publication, the *Penny Magazine*, would enter the market and offer people the choice of an unprecedented variety of printed imagery. Until such time, however, there remained a vast difference between the pictorial world of the English worker and the crowded walls of an Academy exhibition.

[80] On the dynamic role of the consumer in cultural production, see Janet Wolff, *The Social Production of Art* (London, 1981), 95–7.

2

The New Printed Image: The *Penny Magazine* and the Mass Circulation of Illustration

1832-1845

EARLY in March of 1832 Member of Parliament Matthew D. Hill and his neighbour, author, editor, and publisher Charles Knight (figure 11), walked to town from their homes in Hampstead. On this occasion, Knight later recalled, their talk was of the current lack of wholesome and affordable literature for the masses. As a possible solution to this problem, Hill suggested an inexpensive magazine: '"Let us," he exclaimed, "see what something cheap and good can accomplish! Let us have a Penny Magazine!" "And what shall be its title?" said I. "THE PENNY MAGAZINE."'[1]

Knight acted 'at once' upon this conversation. He approached the Society for the Diffusion of Useful Knowledge, for which he was already the official publisher, secured that organization's nominal sponsorship of the proposed venture, and took on himself the dual role of editor and publisher. He then proceeded with typical energy, and some three weeks later, on 31 March, he brought out the first number of the new illustrated miscellany, the *Penny Magazine*.[2]

[1] Knight, *Passages of a Working Life*, 3 vols., (London, 1864), ii. 180.

[2] On the *Penny Magazine*, see SDUK General Committee Minutes, 2 Sept. and 18 Dec. 1832, and 14 Feb. 1834, Penny Publication Committee Minutes, 24 Feb. to 19 Aug. 1832, and Publication Committee Minutes, 23 Mar. and 25 Oct. 1836, and 3 July 1838, SDUK papers 2, 6, and 10, University College London Library; and see also R. D. Altick, *The English Common Reader*, (Chicago, 1957), 332–9; Scott Bennett, 'The Editorial Character and Readership of the *Penny Magazine*: An Analysis', *Victorian Periodicals Review*, 17 (1984), 126–41; id., 'Revolutions in Thought: Serial Publication and the Mass Market for Reading', in Joanne Shattock and Michael Wolff (eds.), *The Victorian Periodical Press*, (Toronto, 1982), 225–57; Eric de Mare, *The Victorian Woodblock Illustrators*, (London, 1980), 74–5;

THE ILLUSTRATED LONDON NEWS, MARCH 22, 1873.—265

THE LATE CHARLES KNIGHT.

11. Charles Knight, *Illustrated London News*, 22 March 1873

Apart from personal enthusiasm and editorial expertise, there were two reasons why Knight was able so rapidly to turn an informally conceived idea into a viable publishing endeavour. First of all, for some years prior to 1832 his business had had the necessary level of mechanization. His earlier publications for the SDUK, such as the *Library of Entertaining Knowledge*, had been printed through the use of steam power and the process of stereotyping, which together were well suited to the efficient production of a large-run illustrated magazine. Secondly, in his four-year association with the SDUK, Knight had personally established throughout the United Kingdom a large network of wholesalers and retailers through which to market his own and the Society's publications. In 1832, to reinforce and expand these connections, he sent out a traveller to further promote the *Penny Magazine*. Thus in June of that year he was able to report to the SDUK that 'the machinery for circulating the *Penny Magazine* extends to the most opulent bookseller and to the keeper of a stall—to the publisher of the country Newspaper and the hawker of worn-out Reprints.'[3]

Knight's 'machinery' did its job well. By December of 1832 the *Penny Magazine*'s circulation had climbed to an unprecedented 200,000—a figure which, Knight 'fairly calculated', indicated an actual readership of 1 million.[4] The magazine maintained this high circulation throughout the first three years of its publication life and thus brought information and imagery to a large number of working

A. Ellenius, 'Reproducing Art as a Paradigm of Communication', *Figura*, NS 21 (1984), 71–8: Celina Fox, 'The Development of Social Reportage in English Periodical Illustration', *Past and Present* 74 (1977): 103–4; ead., *Graphic Journalism in England in the 1830s and 40s* (Ph.D. diss. (Oxford, 1974); published, London and New York, 1988), 7–9, 18–19, 23, 138–57, and *passim*; ead., 'Political Caricature and the Freedom of the Press in Early Nineteenth-Century England', in G. Boyce, J. Curran and P. Wingate (eds.), *Newspaper History*, (London, 1978), 239 and 245; J. F. C. Harrison, *Learning and Living, 1790–1960* (Toronto, 1961), 28–30; Patricia Hollis, *The Pauper Press* (London, 1970), 20–1, 106, 137–8 f., 296, and *passim*; Mason Jackson, *The Pictorial Press* (London, 1885), 276 f.; Louis James, *Fiction for the Working Man* (Oxford, 1963), 15–16; Knight, *Passages*, ii. 179–94, 321–2, and *passim*; and R. K. Webb, *The British Working Class Reader, 1790–1848* (London, 1955), 77–80. For additional biographical information on Knight, see A. C. Cherry, 'A Life of Charles Knight', M.A. thesis, University of London, 1943; and Alice A. Clowes, *Charles Knight* (London, 1892).

[3] Knight, Proposal for the *Penny Cyclopedia*, 21 June 1832, SDUK papers 53, quoted in Bennett, 'Revolutions in Thought', 244; on the marketing of the *Penny Magazine*, and other SDUK publications, see ibid. 230–1 and 242–6.

[4] Knight, *Passages*, ii. 184.

people. As one of Knight's contemporaries observed, this was imagery 'which they never could behold before . . . and literally at the price they used to give for a song'.[5]

For Knight the *Penny Magazine* was more than just a successful commercial venture. It was also, more importantly, a mission into the field of popular education. Like most members of the SDUK and many other reformers of the time, he was worried about worker unrest and the potential threat to social stability of the radical press. Even more, he deplored the generally poor quality of literature and imagery then available to working people; and he sympathized as well with their demands for access to such preserves of art, high culture, and instructive amusement as galleries, the British Museum, the Tower, and Kew Gardens.[6] Thus at its outset he regarded the *Penny Magazine* partly as an antidote to the forces of social disruption and, above all, as a new medium for the dissemination of much-needed general knowledge and diverse imagery.

I

In the introduction to the first issue, Knight addressed his intended readership—'the many persons whose time and whose means are equally limited'. He explained that his 'little Miscellany' would on the one hand 'enlarge the range of observation [and] add to the store of facts', and on the other, 'awaken the reason and lead the imagination into innocent and agreeable trains of thought'.[7] Implicit in these

[5] Edward Cowper, witness before the Select Committee on Arts and Manufactures, 1836, quoted ibid. 223.

[6] For Knight's views on working-class educational needs, popular literature and related matters, see Knight, 'Diffusion of Useful Knowledge', *Plain Englishman* 3 (1823): n.p.; id., 'Education of the People', *London Magazine*, 3rd ser., 1 (1828), 2–3 and 12; id., *Knowledge is Power* (London, 1859), 3; and id., *Passages*, ii. 26–7, 80, and *passim*. On the condition-of-England question, the radical press, and attempts by the government and various reformers to address social problems, see W. L. Burn, *The Age of Equipoise* (New York, 1965), chap. 5; Harrison, *Learning*, 27–37; Hollis, *Pauper Press*, *passim*; Harold Perkin, *The Origins of Modern English Society, 1780–1880* (London, 1969), 290–338; R. D. Storch, 'The Problem of Working-Class Leisure: Some Roots of Middle-Class Moral Reform in the Industrial North: 1825–1850', in A. P. Donadjgrodzki (ed.), *Social Control in Nineteenth Century England* (London, 1977), 138–42 and 147–9; David Vincent, *Bread, Knowledge and Freedom* (London, 1981), 133–9 and *passim*; and Webb, *Working Class Reader*, chaps. 2 and 3. On the SDUK, see Chap. 1, n. 77, above.

[7] 'Reading for All', *Penny Magazine* (hereafter *PM*) 1 (1832), 1.

remarks was a concept of education that would form the basis of the magazine's editorial policy during the first five years of its operation. In Knight's view, education in its fullest sense was a twofold enterprise entailing both factual instruction in a range of general subjects and the inculcation of a particular set of social virtues.[8]

Accordingly the magazine united two kinds of content. First, and predominantly, it provided its readers with relatively objective factual information on such subjects as science, geography, history, and art. Its distinguishing feature and major selling-point—high-quality wood-engraved illustration—complemented and clarified most of this textual instruction. Thus the magazine included abundant pictorial material, much of which was new to a working-class audience: elaborate diagrams of scientific and mechanical devices; artistically rendered pictures of foreign lands, plants, and animals (figure 12); accurate representations of religious monuments and noteworthy ruins; detailed scenes of contemporary life and architecture (figure 13); individualized portraits of famous people (figure 14); and well-executed illustrations of works of art (figures 15 to 19).[9]

Sometimes, in keeping with the second aspect of Knight's concept of education, pictures and texts incorporated one or more interwoven social and moral themes. For example, the interested reader of articles on natural history and geography was, on occasion, regaled with anecdotes about the 'docility' of the Newfoundland dog, the 'economical' habits of Icelandic mice, the parental 'solicitude' of storks, the 'frugality' of Swedish peasants, and the 'temperance' of Lombardy labourers. Similarly, medical and scientific articles statistically demonstrated that moral restraint prolonged life, hard work cured fatigue, and self-discipline would decrease the birth rate. Additionally, from essays on new inventions and modern life, the reader learned that English civilization was technologically and culturally superior to all others, that its continued existence required an ordered and harmonious society, and that both civilization and order depended upon the moral improvement of the English worker. In this way, the *Penny Magazine* encouraged the cultivation of such 'civilized' and English virtues as temperance and other forms of

[8] Knight, 'Education of the People', 10–12; id., *Rights of Industry* (London, 1831), 169–70; and *Passages*, ii. 243–4.

[9] For examples not illustrated here, see among many others *PM* 3 (1834), 40, 73, 76, 117, and 429; and see also Bennett, 'Editorial Character . . . of the *Penny Magazine*'.

THE PENNY MAGAZINE

OF THE

Society for the Diffusion of Useful Knowledge.

141.] PUBLISHED EVERY SATURDAY. [June 14, 1834.

THE FLAMINGO

[Flamingoes.]

The flamingo, although one of the most remarkable of the aquatic tribe for its size and appearance, is by no means well known as regards its habits and manners. This bird, with a smaller body than the stork, has the neck and legs much longer, and indeed there is no other bird in which they are so disproportionately long.

12. Flamingoes, *Penny Magazine*, 1834

13. East India House, London, *Penny Magazine*, 1834

14. Benjamin Franklin, *Penny Magazine*, 1834

continence, self-help, industriousness, frugality, and a sense of duty to one's family and employers.[10]

Although discussions of any number of subjects might include this kind of thematic material, its pictorial expression appears to have been confined mainly to two groups of imagery. The first consists of portraits created specifically to illustrate short biographies of exemplary individuals. Almost invariably, the authors of such pieces integrated biographical and historical detail with laudatory descriptions of their subjects' personal qualities. These descriptions recalled the magazine's themes, and the writers' apparent intention was to improve the reader by offering for emulation appropriate examples from real life. The accompanying portraits reflected this intention, and in each case the artist not only depicted the physical image of the subject, but also gave visible form to his abstract virtues. In one such portrait John Wesley's intense frown and strongly drawn chin helped to evince the truth of textual assertions that he was a model of diligence and 'persevering regard to method'. Similarly, the artist who portrayed John Locke gave him the lofty forehead and smooth untroubled face appropriate to one who was a 'noble example . . . of the union of high intellect and equally high virtue'. And, finally, Benjamin Franklin's unlined face, bland gaze, and calm smile visually confirmed that here indeed was a man with a 'perfection of common sense', 'singular powers of . . . self-control', and 'cool tenacity of temper and purpose' (figure 14).[11]

In its ability to provide exemplars of social and personal virtue portraiture was secondary to another larger group of illustrations: representations of paintings and sculpture. Pictures of this sort are distinguishable from the portraits by the greater complexity of their interaction with their associated commentaries. Through such interaction and the shifts in meaning that resulted, the imagery and discourse of art reinforced the magazine's themes—and, as we are about to see, provided Knight with his most effective vehicle for popularizing high culture and, simultaneously, civilizing the reader.

II

Certain analysts of culture have suggested that the medium for transmitting an image—book, newspaper, magazine—can also be the

[10] This description of the magazine's themes is based on a sampling of issues from 1832–1834.

[11] *PM*, 1 (1832), 110 and 205; and 3 (1834), 24.

agency by which that image's meaning is altered.[12] Its position on the page, the caption, text, and name of the publication together provide a context for the picture, a context which directs the reader-viewer's attention toward a specific message which may, or may not, be literally depicted. Something of this sort appears to have happened when Charles Knight decided to use art reproductions in his magazine. When introduced into that context, the works represented lost some of their original significance and took on new social and cultural connotations.

In one notable example an illustration of a third-century BC statue, *The Dying Gladiator*, was placed under the magazine's title, identified as 'a man of toil, who has lived a laborious life', and described, in both prose and poetry, as the stoical victim of a highly 'uncivilized' society (figure 15).[13] The textual theme of forbearance, and the statue's new visual association with the names of the magazine and its sponsor, together modified the meaning of the image. No longer just a figure of antiquity, it had become as well a role-model for the contemporary reader-viewer. For here was one who was also a worker, who therefore suffered, but who endured his suffering in a 'manly' way. Visually this is evidenced by the figure's third-century BC version of the 'stiff upper-lip'—a departure from the original statue's agonized scowl.[14] The gladiator's *Penny Magazine*-generated stoicism was the more remarkable because, as the author of the text repeatedly pointed out, this worker of antiquity, unlike the fortunate reader, lived in an unstable, uncivilized, and thoroughly un-English world.

In other words, it could be argued that the *Penny Magazine*'s *Gladiator* embodied three messages. The first was literal and consisted simply of the actual appearance of the image (linear representation of prone figure); the second was linguistic and found expression in the caption and accompanying commentary. Finally, most significantly, there was the third message, which arose from the interaction of the first two *and* their socially and culturally symbolic context—the

[12] Roland Barthes, 'The Photographic Message', in *Image-Music-Text* (New York, 1977), 15–16; Walter Benjamin, 'The Work of Art in the Age of Mechanical Reproduction', in *Illuminations* (1955; reprint edn., New York, 1978), 219–22; John Berger, *Ways of Seeing* (Harmondsworth, 1976), 24–33.

[13] *PM* 2 (1833), 9. The statue was misnamed in the 19th cent. It has been reidentified as *The Dying Gaul*.

[14] For a comparative photograph, see Helen Gardner, *Art through the Ages*, 7th edn. (New York, 1980), 145.

THE PENNY MAGAZINE

OF THE

Society for the Diffusion of Useful Knowledge.

50.] PUBLISHED EVERY SATURDAY. [JANUARY 12, 1833.

THE DYING GLADIATOR.

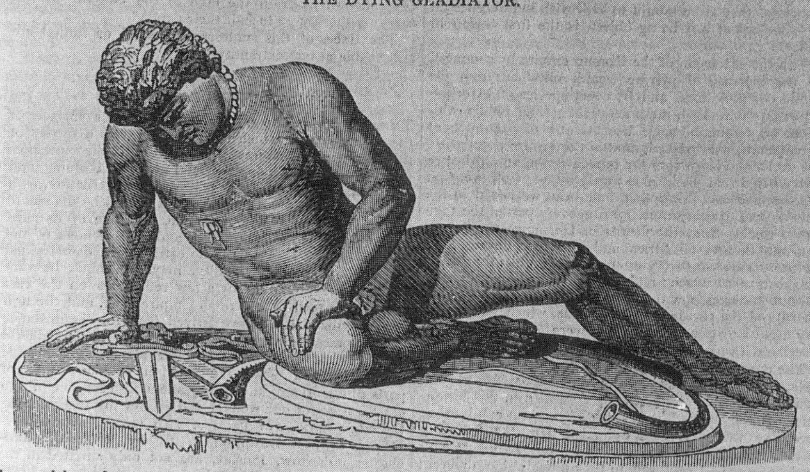

THIS celebrated statue, which is now at Rome, has given rise to much discussion, and it is at least doubtful whether it bears its right name. It is thus described by Winkelmann (vol. ii. p. 241, French ed.):—"It represents a man of toil, who has lived a laborious life, as we may see from the countenance, from one of the hands, which is genuine, and from the soles of the feet. He has a cord round his neck, which is knotted under the chin; he is lying on an oval buckler, on which we see a kind of broken horn*." The rest of Winkelmann's remarks are little to the purpose.

Pliny, in a long chapter of his thirty fourth book, wherein he enumerates the most famous statuaries who worked in metal, mentions one called Ctesilaus, who appears to have lived near, or shortly after, the time of Phidias. "He made," says Pliny, "a wounded man expiring (or fainting), and he succeeded in expressing exactly how much vitality still remained." It is possible that this bronze or metal figure may be the original of the marble figure now in Rome, to which we give the name of the Dying Gladiator. As far as we can judge from the attitude, the armour, the general character of the figure, and the deep expression of pain and intense agony, the whole composition may very possibly be intended to represent the death of one of those wretched beings, who were compelled to slaughter each other for the amusement of the Roman capital. The broken horn is, however, considered by some critics as an objection to this statue being a representation of a gladiator; the signal for the combat, they say, might be given with a horn, but what had the fighter to do with one? This seems to us a small objection. The presence of the horn does not necessarily imply that it belonged to the gladiator; it is a symbol, a kind of short-hand, which brings to recollection the crowded amphitheatre, the eager populace, the devoted victims, the signal for attack; and the sad contrast to all this is exhibited in the figure of the dying man. As to any difficulty that may be raised about the kind of armour, or the cord round the neck, this may be removed by considering that the Romans had gladiators from all countries, and that these men often fought with their native weapons, and after the fashion of their own country. The savage directors of these spectacles knew full well the feelings of animosity with which uncivilized nations are apt to regard one another, and they found no way so ready for exhibiting to the populace all the bloody circumstances of a real battle, as to match together people of different nations.

Whether this figure be that of a dying gladiator or not, it is pretty certain it will long retain the name, at least in the popular opinion in this country, as it has furnished the subject for some of the noblest lines that one of the first of modern poets ever penned:—

"I see before me the gladiator lie
He leans upon his hand—his manly brow
Consents to death, but conquers agony,
And his droop'd head sinks gradually low—
And through his side the last drops, ebbing slow
From the red gash, fall heavy, one by one,
Like the first of a thunder-shower; and now
The arena swims around him—he is gone,
Ere ceased the inhuman shout which hail'd the wretch who won.

"He heard it, but he heeded not—his eyes
Were with his heart, and that was far away;
He reck'd not of the life he lost, nor prize,
But where his rude hut by the Danube lay,
There were his young barbarians all at play,
There was their Dacian mother—he, their sire,
Butcher'd to make a Roman holiday—
All this rush'd with his blood.—Shall he expire,
And unavenged?—Arise, ye Goths, and glut your ire!"

* This horn, which was broken, has been restored, and that near the right hand is entirely modern.

VOL. II. C

15. *The Dying Gladiator*, *Penny Magazine*, 1833

magazine, that is.[15] In the combined image, text, and context of the *Gladiator* there was thus an undepicted, unwritten exhortation to the reader: work hard, exercise restraint, and value what you have—in short, be civilized.

The third message, then, was a connoted one, and it depended on the existence of some degree of cultural knowledge or experience shared by the reader-viewers, the magazine's editor, and the contributing authors—whose number, incidentally, included both the eminent and the obscure: William Hone, who submitted a short piece on Charing Cross for the first number; art critic Anna Jameson, whose series on early Italian painters enhanced the magazine's sales in the 1840s; naturalist James Rennie, who supplied essays on insects and birds; John Kitto, a deaf former workhouse inmate, who wrote travelogues; and a teenage girl, Emily Shore, who, in the two years before her death at nineteen from tuberculosis, contributed articles on nature.[16] The artists' role in the transmission of the third message was probably purely mechanical. If the magazine's better-known artists—engraver William Harvey, chief engraver John Jackson (a one-time pupil of Bewick), and F. W. Fairholt, draughtsman of many of the art reproductions—were typical, then we can infer that the others, for whom there is little or no biographical information, were also young, or comparatively so, and striving for professional advancement. Moreover, according to Knight, they were well paid.[17] It seems safe then to assume that an ample salary and steady employment would have given most, if not all, of the magazine's artists sufficient motives for doing as they were directed—creating, adapting, or merely copying images to suit both specific texts and overall editorial policy.

[15] For the theoretical basis of my analysis of the *Gladiator* and of various other illustrations in this and subsequent chapters, see Barthes, 'The Rhetoric of the Image', in *Image-Music-Text*, 32–51.

[16] *Dictionary of National Biography* (*DNB*), under 'Rennie, James'; Knight to Hone [Mar. 1832], Hone correspondence, Add. MS, 40120.2, fo. 37, British Library; Knight, *Passages*, ii. 185–9; M. Shore (ed.), *Journal of Emily Shore* (London, 1898), 219–20, 231, 235–6; C. Thomas, *Love and Work Enough: Life of Anna Jameson* (Toronto, 1967), 165–6.

[17] On the *Penny Magazine* artists, see de Mare, *Woodblock Illustrators*, 35–7; *DNB*, under 'Fairholt, Frederick', 'Harvey, William', and 'Jackson, John'; Austin Dobson, *Thomas Bewick and His Pupils* (London, 1884), 216; id., *William Hogarth* (London, 1907), 175; Rodney Engen, *Dictionary of Victorian Wood Engravers* (Cambridge, 1985), under 'Fairholt, F.', 'Harvey, W.', 'Jackson, J.', and 'Sly, Stephen'; and Knight, 'Commercial History of a Penny Magazine,' *PM* 2 (1833), 420.

Like *The Dying Gladiator*, several other reproduced works of art embodied a connoted message and served as exemplars for the nineteenth-century reader-viewer. A statue of Diana, for instance, illustrated chastity and maidenly modesty; Carracci's Mary was the epitome of maternal sensibility; and *The Last Supper* depicted seemly behaviour in trying circumstances. Frequently the artists themselves were held up as models of industriousness and dedication. Leonardo da Vinci earned praise for his 'untiring industry and continued perseverance', while Rubens was deemed noteworthy for 'raising himself' through 'the most remarkable industry as well as fertility'.[18]

Very often works of art were chosen for their ability to civilize by *negative* example. In pictures of this type what was portrayed was not a role-model to be emulated, but rather a situation, vice, or emotion to be avoided. Since it was important that the meaning of such images was not misconstrued, the associated commentary helped to clarify the underlying message. A critical analysis of Murillo's *Young Beggar* (figure 16) thus included the following remarks: 'The roughness of the skin attests the idleness of this unhappy child; his morals are in some measure written upon the squalidness of his limbs.'[19] In company with this text, the image became an implicit warning against the moral debility that led inevitably to physical infirmity. In another instance the discussion of a reproduction of *Niobe* informed the reader of the severe penalties incurred by those who have a 'pride of heart' and 'insolence' beyond what is appropriate to their allotted position in an ordered world.[20] Even the nineteenth century's most admired specimen of Hellenism, the *Laocoön* (figure 17), became a *Penny Magazine* negative exemplar. Presented from the social and moral perspective of a disapproving commentator, the statue admonished against a lack of emotional restraint that mere adversity could not excuse: 'the agony is that of despair; there is nothing like the resistance of true courage; nor does there appear to us, in the position of the serpent which is attacking the father, any sufficient cause for the total despair with which he is overwhelmed.'[21]

The art works most frequently reproduced in the *Penny Magazine* were the engravings of William Hogarth. In 1834 and 1835 the magazine used a total of twenty-four such prints.[22] The reasons for

[18] *PM* 1 (1832), 118; 3 (1834), 92–3; and 4 (1835), 4 and 73.
[19] *PM* 3 (1834), 114.
[20] *PM* 2 (1833), 41.
[21] *PM* 1 (1832), 314.
[22] *PM* 3 (1834), 122 has a list of these prints.

THE PENNY MAGAZINE

OF THE

Society for the Diffusion of Useful Knowledge.

127.] PUBLISHED EVERY SATURDAY. [March 29, 1834.

MURILLO.

['The Young Beggar,' from Murillo.]

Bartolomeo Esteban Murillo, the most celebrated painter of the Spanish school, was born at or near Seville, in the year 1618. Having exhibited a very early inclination for the art, he was placed under the instruction of his uncle, Juan del Castillo. The favourite subjects of this artist were fairs and markets; and several pieces of this description were executed by Murillo previously to their separation, which took place in consequence of the removal of the uncle to Cadiz. The youth, being thus left to himself, was obliged to earn his subsistence by painting banners and small pictures for exportation to America. This sort of work did not, perhaps, advance him in the points most essential; but, as he had full employment, he acquired facility, and began to distinguish himself as an able colourist.

Vol. III. Q

16. *The Young Beggar*, *Penny Magazine*, 1834

THE PENNY MAGAZINE

OF THE

Society for the Diffusion of Useful Knowledge.

39.] PUBLISHED EVERY SATURDAY. [November 10, 1832.

THE LAOCOON.

[The Group of the Laocoon, at Rome.]

The story of Laocoon is told by Virgil, and will form the best introduction to our notice of the celebrated group known by that name. The terrible fate of the unfortunate man and his children was brought upon them, according to the poet, by the father's disobedience to the will of Minerva: —

"Laocoon, Neptune's priest by lot that year,
With solemn pomp then sacrific'd a steer:
When, dreadful to behold, from sea we spied
Two serpents rank'd abreast the seas divide,
And smoothly sweep along the swelling tide.
Their flaming crests above the waves they show,
Their bellies seem to burn the seas below:
Their speckled tails advance to steer their course,
And on the sounding shore the flying billows force.
And now the strand, and now the plain they held,
Their ardent eyes with bloody streaks were fill'd:
Their nimble tongues they brandish'd as they came,
And lick'd their hissing jaws that sputter'd flame.
We fled amaz'd; their destin'd way they take,
And to Laocoon and his children make:
And first around the tender boys they wind,
Then with their sharpen'd fangs their limbs and bodies grind.

Vol. I. 2 S

17. *Laocoön*, *Penny Magazine*, 1832

Hogarth's appeal are fairly obvious: he was English, his works reproduced easily, and their openly moralistic subjects—*The Rake's Progress*, *Beer Street*, and *Gin Lane*—were 'made to order' for the purpose of civilizing by negative example. The discussion accompanying a scene from the series *Marriage à la Mode* shows the extent to which the *Penny Magazine*'s art criticism typically emphasized the moralistic content of Hogarth's work. A full-page reproduction revealed a young husband and wife, both the worse for wear after a night of heavy drinking and other indulgences—as evinced by the disarray of their home and attire. In this instance the couple's nocturnal extravagances were well matched by the verbal improvidence of the commentator as he warned the reader against 'evil passions and corrupting idleness', 'the vain pursuit of pleasures', 'withering satiety', 'poison in the cup', and 'the ruin which has overwhelmed thousands'.[23] Similarly, in other examples, Hogarth's *Distrest Poet* illustrated a homily on misguided young men with a 'dreamy belief' in genius rather than industriousness; and *The Politician*, whose subject absent-mindedly sets fire to his hat, was the inspiration for an admonitory discussion of political hotheadedness.[24]

Of all his works, Hogarth's *Industry and Idleness* was perhaps best suited to the magazine's concept of improvement through art; the series depicted both good and bad examples of behaviour and showed the attendant consequences of each. Out of the twelve prints in the original series the magazine reproduced eight. The first of these (figure 18) depicted the interior of a weaver's shop and introduced the series' main characters, a pair of apprentices. With the help of the accompanying text, this illustration also demonstrated the contrast between the two young men: the reader-viewer could thus identify the idle apprentice by his 'vulgar countenance' and sleeping posture, while his hard-working counterpart was conversely recognizable by his 'intelligent countenance' and diligence at the loom.[25] In a subsequent illustration (figure 19) the industrious apprentice, now a self-improved London magistrate, could be seen sentencing his one-time fellow worker for thievery and murder—the fruits of idleness. Collectively, this and other illustrations from the same series had instructional value of a particularly high order, for, as figure 19 suggests, just

[23] *PM* 3 (1834), 124 and 125.

[24] Ibid. 329–30; and 481–2.

[25] Ibid. 209 and 211; Fox, *Graphic Journalism*, 145, and 'Social Reportage', 103–4, has also commented on the magazine's use of *Industry and Idleness* to promote virtue and discourage vice.

Monthly Supplement of
THE PENNY MAGAZINE
OF THE
Society for the Diffusion of Useful Knowledge.

139.] April 30, to May 31, 1834.

HOGARTH AND HIS WORKS.—No. II.

" The drunkard shall come to poverty, and drowsiness shall clothe a man with rags."—*Proverbs*, xxiii., 21.
" The hand of the diligent maketh rich."—*Proverbs*, x., 4.

[Apprentices at their Looms.]

About the middle of the last century an old play, called 'Eastward Hoe,' was revived at Drury Lane Theatre; it had been previously published in Dodsley's 'Collection.' To this play it is said that Hogarth was indebted for the suggestion of the contrast between the courses of a faithful and virtuous, and a careless and vicious apprentice, which he has delineated in his series of prints called 'Industry and Idleness.' This is by no means improbable, although the painter's treatment of the subject is essentially different from that in the drama. 'Eastward Hoe,' which was the joint production of Ben Jonson, George Chapman, and John Marston, and was first published in 1605, is founded upon an entirely different state of manners from those which prevailed in the days of Hogarth—contrasting as much as the stuffed hose, the long-waisted doublet, and the high-peaked hat of the time of James I., contrasted with the square-cut coat, the long-flapped waistcoat, the periwig, and the buckles, of the time of George II. Before we proceed to our main object of describing this series of the works of Hogarth, it may not be uninstructive to furnish our readers with an introductory account of that remarkable and once formidable body,—the London apprentices.

To most readers the vivid and amusing description of the manners and habits of the London apprentices in early times, given by the pen of the 'Author of Waverley' in the 'Fortunes of Nigel' must be well known. The characters of Jin Vin and Frank Tunstall may be considered as no less correct than animated representations of the class to which they belonged. But it is not merely in works of fiction that we meet with frequent notices of the apprentices of London. The chronicles and other records of former times offer many particulars of the manners and conduct of a class of society which has long ceased to exist as a separate body. So entirely is this the case, that it may perhaps be to many persons a matter of surprise that they should ever have had that consequence which at one time they certainly possessed. This consequence was owing to several circumstances. It is well known that the custom which still exists of learning handicraft

18. *Industry and Idleness*: apprentices at their looms, *Penny Magazine*, 1834

Several other instances could be mentioned of persons, members of the Corporation at the latter end of the last century, who had raised themselves from an original equally low with those we have named; and this has been often the case with those who attained to the chief magistracy of London. This is easily accounted for; for while experience shows this dignity to be attainable by the lowest, this high place, like others, appears the most splendid to those who are at the greatest distance from it, and who have therefore a stimulus in pressing forward to it, unfelt by those who have always seen it as a near object.

When it is considered how many virtues and how much knowledge go to make up the character of a good tradesman, it must be a matter of proud satisfaction that the highest municipal honours have fallen upon many who have risen to commercial eminence from small beginnings. Such men have invariably been benefactors of their species. To industry they must have united great economy; and judicious economy is the main-spring of all profitable industry,—the source from which all the great private and public works of man are created and upheld. The opulence of individuals, founded upon their industry and frugality, has raised up some of the most valuable institutions of our own and other countries;—the poverty of individuals, produced by their wasteful expenditure, has destroyed many of the most splendid creations of wealth and taste, and has involved in that destruction the prosperity, not only of families, but of whole districts. History is full of such examples. But these considerations extend beyond individual interests. Nations depend for their prosperity, and consequently their strength and happiness, upon the industry of private men. Their aggregate industry makes up a flourishing community. The eloquent divine, whom we have already quoted, truly says, "It is industry whereto the public state of the world, and of each commonweal therein, is indebted for its being, in all conveniences and embellishments belonging to life, advanced above rude and sordid barbarism; yea, whereto mankind doth owe all that good learning,—that morality,—those improvements of soul, which elevate us beyond brutes.

"To industrious study is to be ascribed the invention and perfection of all those arts whereby human life is civilized, and the world cultivated with numberless accommodations, ornaments, and beauties.

"All the comely, the stately, the pleasant, and useful works which we do view with delight, or enjoy with comfort, industry did contrive them, industry did frame them.

"Doth any country flourish in wealth, in grandeur, in prosperity? It must be imputed to industry,—to the industry of its governors settling good order,—to the industry of its people following profitable occupations:—so did Cato, in that notable oration of his in 'Sallust,' tell the Roman senate that it was not by the force of their arms, but by the industry of their ancestors, that the commonwealth did arise to such a pitch of greatness. When sloth creepeth in, then all things corrupt and decay; then the public state doth sink into disorder, penury, and a disgraceful condition."

"Thou shalt do no unrighteousness in judgment."—*Leviticus*, xiv. 15.
"The wicked is snared in the work of his own hands."—*Psalm* xix. 16.

[THE IDLE APPRENTICE COMMITTED FOR TRIAL BY THE INDUSTRIOUS APPRENTICE, WHO HAS BECOME A MAGISTRATE OF LONDON.]

We have little to say in explanation of the above noble picture. The murderer is at the bar of justice—his accomplice is giving evidence against him—his weeping mother is pressing forward in her agony to implore mercy. The magistrate is the former fellow-apprentice of the criminal. The curtain may fall. The tragedy is ripe. The execution and the Lord Mayor's Show are the accessories which can add nothing to its lessons.

*** The Office of the Society for the Diffusion of Useful Knowledge is at 59, Lincoln's Inn Fields.

LONDON:—CHARLES KNIGHT, 22, LUDGATE STREET.

Printed by WILLIAM CLOWES, Duke Street, Lambeth.

19. *Industry and Idleness*: the idle apprentice committed for trial by the industrious apprentice, *Penny Magazine*, 1834

one image could inspire prodigies of moralizing prose, classical references, and biblical quotations. And, in each case, picture, prose, and literary allusions together reiterated the same themes: improve yourself; cultivate industriousness; practise economy—be civilized.

III

In their attempt to fathom the connoted meanings of the *Penny Magazine*'s art reproductions, the above analyses are in some part interpretive. Knight's papers have not survived and we cannot know conclusively that he had the precise editorial intentions just indicated. None the less, we can note that all of the interpretations given here are fully consistent with the magazine's textual themes and with its aim to provide the English worker with 'agreeable and innocent' knowledge.

It is also, however, important to emphasize that in its thematic use of art reproduction the magazine was not merely serving its own idiosyncratic social purposes. Rather, there is clear evidence linking its view of art to an established aesthetic tradition: that body of thought which equated art with intellectual and moral elevation and advanced civilization, and artists with virtue and industriousness.[26] Both explicitly and implicitly, the magazine's selection of art reproductions and the content of associated texts derived directly from the ideas of the most noted past and contemporary art critics

[26] Among the many works comprising this tradition are Archibald Alison, *Essays on the Nature and Principles of Taste*, revised edn., 2 vols. (Edinburgh, 1811), ii. 418, 432–3, 436 and 438–41; Denis Diderot, *Essays in Painting* (1766), excerpted in L. Eitner, *Neoclassicism and Romanticism 1750–1850*, 2 vols., Sources and Documents in the History of Art Series (Englewood Cliffs, NJ, 1970), i. 63; id., *Pensées détachées sur la peinture* (1776–81), in Eitner, i. 64–6; William Hazlitt, 'The Principal Picture Galleries in England', 'Criticisms on Marriage à-la-Mode', and 'Fine Arts', in Hazlitt, *Collected Works*, ed. A. R. Waller and Arnold Glover (London, 1903), ix. 7–8, 77, 80–1 and 390–1; Charles Lamb, 'On the Genius and Character of Hogarth', in *The Life, Letters and Writings of Charles Lamb*, 6 vols., ed. P. Fitzgerald (London, 1876), iv. 287–313; Joshua Reynolds, *Discourses on Art*, ed. R. Wark (San Marino, Calif., 1959), 35, 169–71 and *passim*; Lord Shaftesbury, *Characteristics of Men, Morals, Opinions, Times* (1711), 2 vols., ed. J. M. Robertson (London, 1900), i. 217; id., 'Plastics or the Original Progress of Designatory Art' (1712), in *Second Characters or the Language of Forms*, ed. Benjamin Rand (Cambridge, 1914), 102; see also ibid., pp. xxvii, 60, and 98–101; J. J. Winckelmann, *Reflections on the Painting and Sculpture of the Greeks*, trans. H. Fuseli (London, 1765), 31 and 63–4; and see Eitner, *Neoclassicism*, i. 55; David Irwin (ed.), *Winckelmann: Writings on Art* (London, 1972), intro., 30–42; and Wark, pp. xviii-xxii; see also Fox, *Graphic Journalism*, 8–9, and 'Political Caricature', 239.

and theorists. For example, several contributors cited Sir Joshua Reynolds's *Discourses*, the writings of art historian J. J. Winckelmann, and essayist Charles Lamb's assessment of the 'Genius and Character of Hogarth'.[27] In addition, the magazine's frequent use of reproductions of works by Rubens, da Vinci and Raphael reflected the preferences of the prominent contemporary critic William Hazlitt. Finally, much of the general pictorial content—illustrations of peasants and their rustic dwellings, trees, ruins, bridges, and birds—corresponded closely to ideas on the picturesque expressed by another eminent writer, Archibald Alison, whose essays on taste were well known in the early nineteenth century.[28]

It was not coincidental that aesthetic tradition and current criticism found their way into the *Penny Magazine* and enhanced its themes. The predominance of art reproduction and the magazine's characteristic sensitivity to the practical contemporary application of tradition arguably generated from the efforts and ideas of one person primarily: the editor and publisher, Charles Knight. It seems clear that the other most likely source of editorial and pictorial policy, the SDUK committee that had originally authorized the *Penny Magazine*, had little to do with its use of visual material, art criticism, and related tradition. The Society's records show that the penny publication committee made Knight responsible for the magazine's content. The committee reserved the right to review and revise any issue before publication, but the evidence is that it rarely, if ever, exercised this option.[29] It also seems unlikely that other SDUK members contributed significantly to shaping the magazine's pictorial policy. Although one member, Henry Hallam, had earlier written a treatise on taste, and another, H. B. Ker, had contributed 'Lives' of Wren and Michelangelo to the magazine, neither this nor any other evidence suggests that the Society as a whole, or any individual member, had Knight's well-developed concept of the instructional value and civilizing power of pictures.[30] Even the chairman, Lord Brougham, who had opinions on nearly everything, was com-

[27] *PM* 1 (1832), 67, 314, and 362; 2 (1833), 9, 126, and 498; 3 (1834), 122, 126, 258 and 378–9; and 4 (1835), 5 and 87–8.

[28] Hazlitt, 'Fine Arts', in *Works*, ix. *passim*; and Alison, *Taste*, i. 42–56.

[29] Penny Publication Committee Minutes, 8 Mar. 1832; Publication Committee Minutes, 23 Mar. 1836 and 3 July 1838; and Miscellaneous Sub-Committee Minutes, 8, 20 Dec. 1838.

[30] H. Hallam, 'Enquiry into the Principles of Taste', *Edinburgh Review* (*ER*), 7 (1806), 295–328; *DNB*, under 'Ker, H. B.'

paratively reticent about art. In two articles on the subject he showed, at best, only a nebulous appreciation of its educative potential.[31]

Knight's understanding of art and the didactic possibilities of imagery was considerably more sophisticated. After he had finished his formal schooling, and had entered his father's printing business, he set himself a disciplined programme of reading in history, philosophy, and the arts; and he followed this programme diligently for some twenty years. By the time he had begun publishing the *Penny Magazine*, he knew and admired the work of such 'brilliant' critics as Hazlitt and Lamb and, in all probability, was also familiar with the ideas of Winckelmann, Reynolds, Alison, and Edmund Burke on 'the Sublime and the Beautiful'.[32] But his interest in art and other visual forms had not begun with his reading of the critics. Even as a boy he had admired 'the grandeur of Rafaelle', 'gazed' with appreciation upon Murillo's *Boy and Puppies*, and looked with less approval at Lely's portrayals of 'King Charles' "beauties" . . . profusely displaying their charms'. A few years after, he had been impressed with 'the patriotic enthusiasm' that had inspired a caricature of Napoleon as an ineffectual 'vapouring little man'; and during the same period —'those times of paper-currency and protection'—he had pondered the dubious symbolic appropriateness of a large painted image of 'the classical horn of plenty'.[33]

Knight's youthful interest in imagery continued into later life. He was, for instance, among the first to appreciate the aesthetic and educational potential of 'Talbotype' photography; in addition, several years before the Art Union conceived the idea of selling art reproductions, he had proposed to the SDUK that they should publish inexpensive wood-engravings of 'celebrated paintings . . . so as to diffuse generally a taste for the Fine Arts.'[34] Knight was never able to realize this particular proposal. However, in addition to the *Penny Magazine*, he succeeded in producing such illustrated works as

[31] Brougham, 'False Taste', *ER* 69 (1839), 214–30; and, with C. H. Parry, an article on Fuseli, *ER* 2 (1803), 453–62. For Brougham's thoughts on a range of topics, see Brougham, *Opinions* (London, 1837).

[32] Knight, *Passages*, i. 272; and ii. 109 and 265; Charles Knight (ed.), *Pictorial Gallery of the Arts*, 2 vols. (1845–7; 2nd edn., London, [1858]), ii. 38, 238, 262, and *passim*; *PM* 1 (1832) 383; on his efforts at self-education, see Knight, *Passages*, i. 67–9, 81 and *passim*.

[33] Knight, *Passages*, i. 52–3 and 56–7.

[34] Ibid. ii. 228; Arts Committee Minutes, 25 Jan. 1831.

the *Gallery of Portraits* (1832–4), the *Pictorial Bible* (1835–7), an illustrated edition of Shakespeare (1837), and the *Pictorial History of England* (1837–44). He would later express considerable gratification that through such publications, high-quality wood-engravings had become the 'marked feature' of his business, and he claimed credit for the popularization of both the concept and the word 'pictorial'.[35]

Knight's wide-ranging appreciation and promotion of illustration were aspects of his belief that 'intellectual culture' did not merely 'depend upon books and lectures'. Pictures, he believed, were 'true eye-knowledge' and as such could not only 'add both to the information and enjoyment of the reader', but were also 'sometimes more instructive than words'.[36] Moreover, as the *Penny Magazine*'s content reflects, in its editor's view some kinds of pictures had greater educational merit than others. 'Faithful and spirited copies of the greatest productions of PAINTING and SCULPTURE', he wrote, were among the most 'valuable accessories of knowledge [and] instruments of education'.[37]

But the imagery of art was more to Knight than just a pedagogical tool. He also had a larger concept of what should be the role of the aesthetic in everyday life. In an 1848 address to the Nottingham Mechanics' Institute, he spoke eloquently on this subject. Expressing first his approval of the many pictures hanging in the Institute hall, he then continued:

> I would not have in any mechanics' institution, as I would not have in any school throughout the land, bare naked walls for the eye to rest on undelighted. I do know, and the experience of the wise teaches me to believe, that we cannot be surrounded too much with the beautiful in art; in civic halls, and wherever men congregate together for public business, or meet for social purposes; in our own houses, where prints and casts of rare sculpture are the best and least expensive luxuries; and what is still more to the purpose, in the humblest cottage in the land. I do not think it is possible to make the people too familiar with high models of art, because in so doing a refinement is given to the understanding, and what is spiritual and grand in our nature may be developed by the presence of these beautiful creations, which, without presumption, I venture to think are emanations through the mind of man of the power of the Deity.[38]

[35] Knight, *Passages*, ii. 253 and 262.

[36] Ibid. 262 and 284; and iii. 82.

[37] Charles Knight, *Pictorial Half-Hours: or Miscellanies of Art* . . . (London, 1850–1), quoted in Ellenius, 'Reproducing Art', 77.

[38] Address delivered 3 Mar. 1848, quoted in Knight, *Passages*, iii. 83.

Additional evidence, from the magazine, Knight's memoirs, and other sources, further links his interests with the magazine's textual and pictorial content. For example, quotations from the work of his friend Allan Cunningham, author of *Lives of the Most Eminent Painters* (1830), contributed to the length of a seven-page essay on Hogarth, while the same piece also incorporated a substantial excerpt from Knight's 1831 treatise on the rights of industry. Another article, on working men's libraries, was sprinkled with references to Knight's favourite authors. Elsewhere, similarly, the magazine's only double-spread set of illustrations reproduced scenes from Windsor, his birthplace and home until 1822.[39] But perhaps the most compelling indication that Knight controlled the *Penny Magazine*'s editorial policy is the fact that he also controlled its finances. Throughout most of the magazine's publication life, he was the SDUK's creditor.[40] It therefore seems unlikely that the Society's publication committee significantly influenced his editorial decisions.

IV

The extent to which Knight controlled both the finances and the formal character of the magazine suggests that when we attempt to analyse the motives behind that publication we should look to Knight rather than the SDUK. This approach is a departure from most other assessments of the magazine, which have tended to overstate the relationship of its content to the SDUK's utilitarian ideals and social purposes.[41] This is not to imply that Knight had no concerns in common with his magazine's nominal sponsor. As indicated at the beginning of this chapter, he shared the Society's worries about worker unrest and the influence of the unstamped press. We have also seen that these social fears found their expression in the magazine's studious avoidance of radical political discourse and in its use of art to provide positive and negative exemplars of behaviour.

There is other evidence, however, which indicates that much of Knight's interest in the magazine was purely professional and not

[39] *PM* 2 (1833), 252–3, 373–5; 3 (1834), 377–84; Knight, *Passages*, ii. 185 and 307; for Knight's favourite authors, see his *Half-Hours with the Best Authors* (London, n.d.); and *Passages*, *passim*.

[40] SDUK secretary, T. Coates, to Knight, 22 Aug. 1833, General Committee letter-book, SDUK papers, 19; and Bennett, 'Revolutions in Thought', 231.

[41] See e.g. Fox, *Graphic Journalism*, 23, 156, and *passim*; and Fox, 'Political Caricature', Hollis, and Webb, all cited in n. 2 above.

directly related to his SDUK affiliation. For, unlike others on the publication committee, he was both a businessman and a publisher, and his specialized knowledge led him to believe that an illustrated miscellany could be a profitable endeavour. He had in fact been one of the first publishers to appreciate the potential of stereotyping; and he thus recognized that the speed and low cost of this mode of reproduction would enable him to provide illustrated reading-matter to a large market whose major affordable form of pictorial entertainment had been the often crude and repetitive stock woodcuts of broadsides and chapbooks.

In the late 1820s Knight had approved of the general idea, although not the quality, of the illustrations in John Limbird's *Mirror*; and probably the *Penny Magazine*'s miscellany format owed something to the inspiration of that earlier publication.[42] What distinguished Knight's magazine from any previous or contemporary periodical was the combination of the quality, variety, and abundance of its illustrations, its widely affordable price, *and* its profitability. Informed observers, such as publisher W. A. Chatto, thus acknowledged that the *Penny Magazine* was the earliest inexpensive serial publication to realize fully the commercial possibilities of mass-reproduced imagery.[43] Or, as Knight put it, wood-engraving had finally found its 'legitimate purpose'. In the magazine's October '1883 supplement, he explained to the readers that 'the circumstances dependent upon rapid printing . . . principally called forth by the great demand for the "Penny Magazine" have completely changed the character of the art of wood-engraving; and have rendered it peculiarly and essentially that branch of engraving which is applicable to cheap publications.'[44] In other words, illustration of high quality and low cost to the purchaser was now also efficient to produce and profitable for the publisher.

Knight's absorbing interest in his new publication thus arose not only from anxiety about the condition of English society but also from commercial motives and enthusiasm for the latest advances in printing technology. However, these concerns seem to have been the lesser motives behind his dedication to the magazine. Of greater signific-

[42] Knight, *Passages*, i. 244.

[43] W. A. Chatto, 'The History and Practice of Wood-Engraving', *Illustrated London News*, 22 June 1844, 405.

[44] 'Commercial History of a Penny Magazine', *PM* 2 (1833), 420; and see also Knight, *The Old Printer and the Modern Press* (London, 1854), 254–9.

ance and duration was his genuine belief in education as an ideal to which people at all levels of society should aspire.[45] As he had stated in his introduction to its first issue, the *Penny Magazine* not only aimed to be 'agreeable and innocent', but to enlarge the scope of the readers' factual knowledge. In addition then to conveying social and moral messages, the examples of art discussed above also introduced the readers to an array of cultural knowledge previously inaccessible to them. Reproducing art works in detail, often quoting authorities verbatim, these pictures and texts transmitted imagery, aesthetic theories, art history, and criticism with faithful exhaustiveness. Interested readers thus became acquainted with the working methods of Leonardo, Winckelmann's opinion on the date and provenance of the *Laocoön*, Hogarth's originality and sense of beauty, 'the sweetness, brilliancy, harmony and freshness' of the colour in Murillo's *Beggar*—and so on.[46]

The magazine also devoted countless other pictures and texts exclusively to the advancement of aesthetic and cultural knowledge. The key points of style in the work of Rubens and Correggio, Titian's use of colour, Rembrandt's 'management of the lights and darks, technically called chiaroscuro', the 'silvery brightness' of Guido's paintings, the 'golden . . . tone . . . the elegance and precision' of work by Teniers, the origins of 'the Bolognese School of Painting', and the 'progress' of manuscript illumination from the 'dark ages' to the Renaissance—this information and much more of a similar nature was summoned to aid those readers who wished to understand and enjoy art.[47] At least one of the magazine's articles explicitly encouraged this kind of informed appreciation:

> Pictures . . . must be studied as attentively as books, before they can be thoroughly understood, or the principles of art so established in the mind as to render those works which are truly sublime or beautiful the objects of admiration, in preference to those which catch the inexperienced eye by mere gaudiness or exaggeration of any kind.[48]

The same article also indicated that the central purpose of such study was not the viewer's social and moral improvement, but rather the

[45] Knight, 'Diffusion of Knowledge', n.p.; id., 'Education of the People', 7 and 13; and id., *Passages*, ii. 180 and *passim*.

[46] *PM* 1 (1832), 314; and 3 (1834), 92–4, 114, 124, and 127.

[47] *PM* 1 (1832), 100, 197–8 and 382; 3 (1834), 4 and 258; 4 (1835), 73; 8 (1839), *passim*; and 10 (1841), 53.

[48] *PM* 2 (1833) 67.

enhancement of his or her capacity to share in the emotional and intellectual rewards of aesthetic experience: 'the contemplation of works of art may afford one of the purest pleasures which a refined mind is capable of enjoying.'[49] Thus, whatever might have been the social fears and commercial motives behind the *Penny Magazine*, these did not preclude an apparently greater and sincere desire to foster art appreciation as an intrinsically worthwhile attainment —one, moreover, which should be brought within the reach of all classes, however humble.

Knight's reaction to criticism of his magazine also argues that he was deeply and genuinely committed to placing 'fine specimens of art . . . within the reach of thousands, instead of being confined to the cabinets of a very few'.[50] In the early years of its publication, a number of critics variously took exception to the magazine's social and intellectual content, its general format, and its use of art and imagery. For the most part this criticism left Knight relatively unmoved. But one writer's comment seems to have stung. The *Morning Chronicle*'s critic—an enthusiastic proponent of aesthetic and cultural exclusivism—had expressed 'bitterness and near-indignation' at Knight's 'mistaken view' that art could be removed from the domain of 'a comparatively small and gifted few, under the patronage of men of wealth and leisure'. 'ONCE FOR ALL,' this critic had thundered, 'as there is no royal road to mathematics . . . there is no *Penny Magazine* road to the Fine Arts.'[51] Knight responded to this criticism at some length, with considerable irony and increasing vehemence:

> We do not quite understand all this, [he began in apparently mild puzzlement], but we suppose it means, that the production of a picture or a statue for the exclusive gratification 'of men of wealth and leisure', is the sole end and object of the 'cultivation of the Fine Arts'; that it is a matter of the most absolute indifference whether the bulk of the people have any perception of the beauty of Art, or any knowledge of its principles; . . . that such men as Josiah Wedgwood, who introduced the forms of classic antiquity into our potteries, have adopted a most 'mistaken view of the case'; that the French government, who have Schools of Design for manufacturers . . . have adopted

[49] *PM* 2 (1833), 67.

[50] Knight, 'Commercial History of a Penny Magazine', 421.

[51] *Morning Chronicle*, 19 Oct. 1836, 3; for other criticisms and Knight's reactions to them, see Carter Hall, 'The Chartered Booksellers', *New Monthly Magazine*, 40 (1834): 72; Hansard, 3rd ser., 23 (1834), 1216; *Poor Man's Guardian*, 14 Apr. 1832, 353; and Knight, *Passages*, ii. 180, 182, and 236 f.

a most 'mistaken view of the case'; that our government, which has just established a School of Design . . . is labouring under the same delusion; and that, once for all, as there is 'no Penny Magazine road to the Fine Arts', the expenditure of Twelve Thousand Pounds upon the engravings of the 'Penny Magazine' has been an utter waste of capital with reference to the cultivation of Art, and the popular taste would have been as much advanced by . . . the manufacture of the old red and blue prints which are still scattered . . . amongst the cottages of the rural population, and [by] . . . green and yellow parrots . . . in ill-assorted company with Canova's Graces.[52]

Perhaps, more than any other available evidence, it is this uncharacteristic outpouring of verbal energy, sarcasm, and righteous indignation that argues for the sincerity both of Knight's dedication to popularizing art and his concept of the magazine as a pioneering effort to disseminate what had traditionally been restricted knowledge.

Additional evidence also suggests that Knight's 'sincere interest in the progress of knowledge' took precedence over other motives.[53] For reasons which will be noted later, after 1835 the magazine did not maintain its initial success. Knight nevertheless continued to publish it for another ten years—all the while making little or no profit.[54] It may be that he persisted with the magazine in the hope of re-establishing its original comfortable profit margin, but a decade of such persistence with a financially uncertain enterprise hardly seems to indicate single-minded commercialism. Rather, as the magazine's content during this period implies, Knight's perseverance was more likely an aspect of his continuing commitment to popular education.

In 1837, and again in 1841, he changed the magazine's editorial policy.[55] With each change, he reduced both the miscellaneous content and the number of short items that had typified the format before 1837. Thus, between 1837 and 1845, the magazine offered increasingly substantial contributions whose texts and pictures were loosely organized under a few general subject headings: Topography and

[52] 'Address to the Readers of the Penny Magazine', *PM* 5 (1836), 515–16.

[53] Knight's dedication to knowledge was noted in the SDUK's 'Address of the Committee on the Suspension of the Operations of the Society', Mar. 1846, reprinted in Smith, *Society for the Diffusion of Useful Knowledge*, app. C(v).

[54] Bennett, 'Revolutions in Thought', 245 and 256 n. 29.

[55] He announced the forthcoming initial change to the SDUK late in 1836 at the Publication Committee meeting (Minutes, 25 Oct. 1836).

Antiquities, Natural History, Trade, Manufactures and Commerce, and of course Fine Arts.[56]

The magazine's declining circulation was perhaps a factor in these changes. After 1836 reductions in the newspaper tax and the duty on paper both increased and facilitated the competition which had been progressively eroding the *Penny Magazine*'s market.[57] Knight may therefore have modified his policy to retain current readers or to recapture the magazine's one-time wider market. But it is also possible that he had a long-term educational strategy which required periodic adjustments of editorial policy—adjustments intended to coincide with the readers' advancement through successive stages of learning. This possibility is implied in Knight's comments on the changes. In 1836 he explained that the magazine had 'realized many [of] its objects' and could thus introduce 'some new features . . . to carry forward our readers in the same road we have so long travelled together'.[58] Later, recalling the further modification of the magazine's format in 1841, he wrote: 'I may truly say that the object of the change was to present to a public which had been advancing in education, a Miscellany of a higher character . . . The engravings were superior; the writing was less "ramble-scramble".'[59] Beyond these remarks, Knight did not elaborate his reasons for altering the magazine's format. But even allowing for some retrospective glossing of motives, the evidence indicates that educational objectives were high among the considerations that dictated his policy.

This adjusted policy encompassed not only the magazine's formal character but also, more significantly, its thematic content. At the same time as articles lengthened and subject-matter decreased, the once frequent textual and pictorial homilies on industry, self-

[56] See e.g. the lists of illustrations in *PM* 9 (1840) and 10 (1841). Knight would later modify this formula further in a new periodical, *Knight's Penny Magazine*, which had only a few illustrations and devoted itself to serious discussion of history, literature, and travel. It survived only the first six months of 1846.

[57] Knight, letter to Sir Alexander Duff-Gordon, 17 Mar. 1855, reprinted in Clowes, *Knight*, 226; and see also William Kennedy, 'Lord Brougham, Charles Knight and the Rights of Industry', *Economica*, NS, 29 (1962), 61. The changes in fiscal policy which facilitated competition were not comparably advantageous for the *Penny Magazine*: it had never been subject to the stamp tax, and the reduction in the paper duty was not sufficient to compensate for losses due to declining circulation; in fact, in *The Struggles of a Book against Excessive Taxation*, 2nd edn. (London, 1850), 12, Knight cited the paper duty as a central factor in the magazine's demise.

[58] 'Address to Readers', *PM* 5 (1836), 516.

[59] Knight, *Passages*, ii. 322.

restraint, and so on largely disappeared. In a wide sampling of issues from 1837, 1839, 1840, 1841, and 1844, it is possible to find occasional half-hearted references to the desirability of civilized and disciplined behaviour, but on the whole the magazine no longer embodied the kind of social and moral perspective that had dominated its earlier issues. Now, with only a few exceptions, portraits of exemplary people became an infrequent feature, and representations of painting and sculpture inspired only what was for the time the most dispassionate visual analysis and art criticism.

Knight's new editorial position may well have been the reflection of a corresponding ideological shift. For, at some time during the mid-1830s, anxiety about the stability of English society ceased to be a motivating force in his educational thought and activities. There is no direct evidence to show precisely when and why he might have experienced such a shift—his autobiography is not markedly introspective. It may, however, be more than coincidental that this change in his thinking occurred at about the same time as his business relations with the SDUK became strained. The initial rancour apparently stemmed from the secretary Thomas Coates, and other members who had by 1836 become resentful of Knight's financial and editorial control of Society publications. Commenting on this situation, Knight's friend M. D. Hill confided to Lord Brougham that 'the poor fellow [Knight] feels it bitterly'.[60]

Whether or not his difficulties with the Society were a factor, it is certain that Knight's earlier view that education should entail the inculcation of a restrictive set of social virtues was not a lifelong conviction. When he looked back some thirty years later on his educative endeavours of the 1820s and early 1830s, his tone was that of one who recollects an old enthusiasm, long since past, but still able on occasion to evoke embarrassment. It now seemed to him 'something like hypocrisy' that he had once believed that those of 'humble station' could, and for their own good should, cultivate 'the happiness peculiar to the course of peaceful labour', learn to appreciate being 'masters of their own possessions, however small', and so come to 'view the difference of ranks without envy.' In the same passage, perhaps in self-justification, he added: 'I followed in the wake of men most anxious for the welfare of the lower classes, but who were at

[60] Coates to Brougham, 21 Jan. 1836; Hill to Brougham, 2 Mar. 1836, Brougham correspondence, University College London Library; and Coates to Knight, 19 Aug. 1837, SDUK letter-book, 20.

that time convinced that the first and greatest of all popular exhortation was to preach from the text of St. James, "Study to be quiet".'[61]

Knight's disaffection with this narrow view of social relations must have been formative by the early 1830s. For, as this discussion has tried to make clear, his magazine had never been primarily, nor even consistently, devoted to overt moralization or embedded social content. The wealth of factual, straightforwardly presented cultural knowledge contained in even the earliest issues indicates that Knight's educational idealism had already begun to offset his fears about social unrest. Thus for most, if not all, of the magazine's publication life he was, as he purported to be, genuinely and above all 'anxious to carry information into the dwellings of the peasant and artisan, and to excite the curiosity of those who have been unaccustomed to think upon any subject connected with art and literature'.[62]

V

In according Knight his deserved credit for promoting the education of the people and popularizing art, we must not wholly lose sight of the power relations that were enacted through the *Penny Magazine*'s content. Its tone was at times painfully condescending and the values it promoted unquestionably served the interests of those in positions of social, economic, and political authority. To recognize this aspect—and it would be naïve not to do so—is not to fall back on the consensus interpretation of the magazine as a philistine exercise in social control.[63] On the evidence we have, it seems more appropriate to characterize the magazine as one of the many cultural forms through which society's advantaged and powerful asserted their leadership informally and not necessarily consciously or maliciously.[64] Thus, however altruistically intended, Knight's endeavour

[61] Knight, *Passages*, i. 247.

[62] 'Commercial History of a Penny Magazine', *PM* 2 (1833), 420.

[63] See, among others, Fox, 'Political Caricature', 239 and 245; Harrison, *Learning*, 28–9; Hollis, *Pauper Press*, 137 f., 296, and *passim*; Brian Maidment, 'Magazines of Popular Progress and the Artisans', *Victorian Periodicals Review*, 17 (1984), 87; and Webb, *Working Class Reader*, 77 f.

[64] For the theoretical grounding of this view, see Introduction, n. 8 on Antonio Gramsci; here again I use the term 'leadership' in the sense of Gramsci's concept of hegemony.

to disseminate knowledge cannot, and should not, be entirely divorced from the social and economic privilege that he both enjoyed and represented. Equally, though, as the previous discussion of his educational and commercial motives has argued, the obligation remains to acknowledge that it was not one, but a complex of mixed interests that shaped the magazine's character.

This effort to reach beyond the simplistic notion of control leads to a reconsideration of the historiographical commonplace that has most persistently dogged the *Penny Magazine*: the argument that it was an expression of the 'middle-class' point of view.[65] This argument clearly has little explanatory value when applied to the greater part of the magazine's content, which aimed to be broadly informative. But even when we turn to its embedded social themes, the term 'middle-class' does not provide an adequate description. For there is no substantial body of empirical evidence that establishes the existence of a monolithic set of social, cultural, political, and moral values that can be uniformly, persistently, and exclusively associated with the middle class in the early nineteenth century.[66] Knight for one did not consider himself, his activities, or his outlook to be middle-class. Rather, he seemed to believe himself to be part of a social and intellectual vanguard, capable of unusual and advanced insights into the relationship of knowledge, morality, and society. As he put it, he and other social and educational reformers were not just 'educated and intelligent' men; they were also the representatives of 'high thinking' and dedication to 'duty not pleasure'.[67] In this, he stressed, they were distinct from members of the middle class. It seems then to be an over-simplification to equate the *Penny Magazine* with the dissemination of middle-class values (if in fact such values could be identified and isolated). Knight's apparent goal was the more ambitious one of delimiting an ideal, not necessarily class-specific, system of social, moral, and cultural values—a system which he believed would foster the improvement of individuals at *all* levels of society.[68]

[65] Harrison, *Learning*, 29 and 89; Hollis, *Pauper Press*, 106; id., Introduction to the reprint edn., *Poor Man's Guardian* (London, 1969), p. xxviii; Maidment, 'Magazines of Popular Progress', 87; and Webb, *Working Class Reader*, 80.

[66] For a similar view, see Raymond Williams, 'Minority and Popular Culture', in Michael Smith, Stanley Parker, and Cyril Smith (eds), *Leisure and Society in Britain* (London, 1973), 22, 24, and 26.

[67] Knight, *Passages*, iii. 325–7; and see also ibid., i. 124–5.

[68] Ibid. iii. 80–1.

The question of the magazine's readership also needs to be reconsidered. Clearly the intended readership was working people. The consensus has however been that radical consciousness dictated the wholesale working-class rejection of the magazine, and that it drew its readers instead from other social groups.[69] Letters to Knight and the SDUK indicate that this view is partially correct and that the readership did indeed include shopkeepers, clerks, some professionals, and country gentry.[70] But there is also reason to believe that the magazine attracted a wide and faithful working-class following. Among the suggestive evidence for this view are the *Penny Magazine*'s print-orders.[71] Normally these print-orders closely matched actual circulation, since profitability was dependent on such a match. In 1833 Knight's print-orders averaged 187,000, a figure which agrees closely with his claim that the magazine's circulation was 200,000. This figure becomes all the more compelling when we consider that the circulation of the supposedly representative working-class paper, the *Poor Man's Guardian*, was at the most 15,000 in the same year, and would decline to 3,000 by 1835.[72] The *Penny Magazine*'s impressive circulation indicates that it must have reached and been read by some significant number of working people.[73] As we will later see, other evidence supports this suggestion: letters from workers to the SDUK, working-class autobiographies which favourably mention the magazine, its distribution in working men's coffee-houses—and, no doubt, the appeal of its many fine engravings and their ability to communicate to both the well-read and the unlettered. It thus appears that the opinion of one contemporary observer was quite correct, and that the *Penny Magazine* did indeed 'meet with great sale among the class for which it was principally intended'.[74]

[69] Fox, 'Political Caricature', 239, 241, and 245–6; Harrison, *Learning*, 29–30; Hollis, *Pauper Press*, 20–1, 88–9, and 139–40; Smith, *The Society for the Diffusion of Useful Knowledge*, 12, 32, 40, and 41; and Webb, *Working Class Reader*, 78–80.

[70] e.g. James Greenwood to the Publication Committee, 27 Nov. 1837; C. Jacomb to Sir J. W. Lubbock (SDUK member), 17 Apr. 1832; James Nelthorpe to Coates, 13 Dec. 1832; Josiah Riddle to Knight, 23 May 1832; Edward Strutt to Coates, 6 Dec. 1835; J. B. Tenniel to Coates, 15 Jan. 1841: all SDUK correspondence.

[71] Scott Bennett has compiled a table of these from Society records in combination with Knight's memoirs: see Bennett, 'Revolutions in Thought', 236; my argument is greatly indebted to this seminal essay and the data it presents.

[72] Hollis, Introduction to the *Poor Man's Guardian*, p. xxv.

[73] James, *Fiction for the Working Man*, 15, has made this suggestion previously; and see also Bennett's discussion of the creation of mass markets, 'Revolutions in Thought', 249–53.

[74] J. Rowland to M. D. Hill, 11 May 1832, SDUK correspondence.

VI

In the 1830s and early 1840s the popularity of the *Penny Magazine* engendered a host of imitators. Of these the longest-lived was the *Saturday Magazine* (1832–44), published by John Parker and sponsored by the Society for Promoting Christian Knowledge (SPCK). This organization's General Literature Committee had been quick to note the growth and influence of penny publications and determined to enter the market with their own 'Weekly Magazine of useful and interesting knowledge'.[75] Trading upon the *Penny Magazine*'s successful formula, Parker and the SPCK also used steam power and the process of stereotyping to produce a low-cost illustrated miscellany —but one which, unlike its model, would represent the interests of religion and the Church of England. Thus, the *Saturday Magazine* sprinkled its general information with stories from the Scriptures, Church histories, portraits and biographies of religious men, Biblical illustration, scenes from the Holy Land, and pictures of churches and cathedrals (figure 20).[76]

With a circulation at times as high as 80,000, the *Saturday Magazine*, in combination with numerous other penny 'Journals', 'Storytellers', and 'Gazettes', weekly 'Visitors' and 'Miscellanies', progressively cut into the *Penny Magazine*'s market. Its circulation thus reduced to an unprofitable 40,000, it ceased publication in 1845. Looking back to the last days of his magazine, Knight recollected that there were at that time no fewer than 'fourteen three-halfpenny and penny miscellanies and thirty-seven weekly sheets'. And, as he further recalled, the *Penny Magazine*, 'popular as it once was . . . could not hold its place'.[77]

But although it inevitably gave way under the weight of imitative competition and, as we will see later, the public's changing taste, Knight's magazine has a none the less unique cultural significance. In

[75] Report of the General Literature Committee, 21 May 1832, and Committee Minutes, 3 June 1834, SPCK archive, London; see also W. O. B. Allen and E. McClure, *Two Hundred Years: The History of the SPCK, 1698–1898* (London, 1898), 192–4; Altick, *Common Reader*, 393; *Bookseller*, 1 June 1870, 491–2; W. K. L. Clarke, *History of the SPCK* (London, 1959), 182–3; *DNB*, under 'Parker, John W.'; and James, *Fiction for the Working Man*, 16.

[76] See, e.g., *Saturday Magazine* 1 (1832), 33, 105–6; 2 (Jan.–June 1833), 1–2, 17, 59, 136, 208; 3 (July–Dec. 1833), 49–50, 201; 4 (1834), 41 and 65.

[77] Knight, *Old Printer*, 279–80; and see also Knight, *Passages*, ii. 322; and Bennett, 'Revolutions in Thought', 256 n. 29.

THE

Saturday Magazine.

COMMITTEE OF GENERAL LITERATURE & EDUCATION

No. 59. JUNE 1st., 1833. { PRICE ONE PENNY.

UNDER THE DIRECTION OF THE COMMITTEE OF GENERAL LITERATURE AND EDUCATION, APPOINTED BY THE SOCIETY FOR PROMOTING CHRISTIAN KNOWLEDGE.

VOL. II. 59

20. Worcester Cathedral, *Saturday Magazine*, 1833

its innovative use of technology and illustration, consistently wide distribution, and appeal to more than one social class, it provided the impetus for the development of a new, increasingly visual mass culture—became, in fact, that culture's first artefact. Beyond this, it was an unprecedented and enlightened attempt to introduce the theories and imagery of art into everyday life. By today's standards this might seem to be a far cry from the democratization of knowledge. To Knight and his contemporaries, though, it represented the reversal of a tradition that had confined high culture to the domain of the economically and socially privileged.

It was thus on two counts that Knight would later reflect proudly on his magazine. For not only had it transformed the face of popular publishing and illustration; it had also narrowed dramatically the distance between the Academy exhibition room and the pictorial experience of the people. It was this dual achievement that justified the claim that Knight made in his memoirs—indeed, as he put it, the *Penny Magazine* had produced 'a revolution in popular art'.[78]

But in one respect this revolution was to be short-lived. Those who followed in Knight's wake increasingly directed their efforts away from serious education, and towards light or sensational entertainment. The high culture that had only just entered the popular domain thus began a retreat back to its old position of exclusivism. The signals of this retreat are to be found in the pages of the *Penny Magazine*'s most popular successors: the three magazines that would next come to dominate the field of pictorial publishing—through the mass circulation of the new printed image.

[78] Knight, *Passages*, ii. 223.

3

The Business of Imagery: The Second Generation of Pictorial Magazines

1845–1860

IN 1855, in a letter to a friend, Charles Knight remembered the early days of the *Penny Magazine* and the large readership it had then attracted. He next observed that three current magazines had achieved similar or higher sales. Four years later, when the *British Quarterly Review* ran an article on 'cheap literature', the author likewise remarked upon the 'prodigious circulation' of certain 'miscellaneous pennyworths'.[1] In each case the same three publications had excited comment—the *London Journal*, *Reynolds's Miscellany*, and *Cassell's Illustrated Family Paper* had become the new flagships of mass-circulation pictorial publishing.

In noting the success of this second generation of illustrated penny miscellanies, our commentator on 'cheap literature' made the following observation:

> It was reserved for the present time to see very low-priced publications realizing very large pecuniary profits. Where we reckoned before by thousands, we now reckon by tens of thousands. The struggling benefactor of the masses, who long laboured in vain at the establishment of a useful and entertaining serial for the working multitude, is now displaced by the wealthy projector who has carved a handsome fortune out of a penny miscellany, and who contemplates a seat in parliament at least, as the crown of his golden toils.[2]

There is no evidence that those who operated the *Journal*, *Miscellany*, and *Paper* had political ambitions of the kind that the commentator supposed; nor does it appear that any of these proprietors

[1] Knight to Sir Alexander Duff-Gordon, 17 Mar. 1855, reprinted in A. Clowes, *Charles Knight* (London, 1892), 226; 'Cheap Literature', *British Quarterly Review*, 29 (1859), 321 and 329 ff.

[2] Ibid., 329.

became immensely wealthy. Nevertheless our expert on 'cheap literature' identified the crucial factor that distinguished the new magazines from their prototype and, indeed, from its main pictorial competitor, the *Saturday Magazine*. That is, although all five of these magazines were operated as sole proprietorships or partnerships for all or much of their publication lives, the three new miscellanies were from the start, and remained, independent of any outside sponsoring body. The second generation of proprietors was thus entirely free to make business and editorial decisions without having to accommodate—or even, as in Knight's case, nod in the direction of—the policies and ideals of any such association as the SDUK or SPCK. This is not to say that those who operated the *Journal*, *Miscellany*, and *Paper* did not sometimes use these publications to air their personal concerns or promote the causes of certain organizations, such as those advocating temperance, for example. This was especially true in the case of John Cassell. But more often than not, social issues did not figure prominently in the second generation of pictorial miscellanies.

Unlike Knight, who had catered more and more to a market of serious self-educators, the new breed of proprietors did not let their commitment to any social cause divert their attention too long from the greater part of the market-place. They allowed themselves to be guided largely by their perception of the most widespread public taste; and, as the magazines' consistently high circulations attest, their perception was usually accurate. It had not escaped their notice that by the 1840s people increasingly looked to magazines for light entertainment, and it was this demand to which proprietors of the second generation catered. Their miscellanies thus purported to offer the same blend of amusement and instruction that had been the *Penny Magazine*'s staple provisions, but what they actually served up was rather different. They provided a saleable main course of light amusement and little of the sustenance of art—for, as their proprietors well appreciated, this was now the way to prosper in the business of imagery.

I

The *London Journal* was the earliest of the three magazines to begin publication. It made its appearance on 1 March 1845 and, at a penny per weekly issue, offered what would become its standard fare: a collection of informative articles, anecdotes, aphorisms, short stories, serialized novels, and—accompanying it all—numerous fine wood-engravings. Published by the printer George Vickers, the *Journal* was the inspiration of its proprietor, a former engraver for the *Illustrated London News*, George Stiff. During his proprietorship, Stiff employed a succession of editors: the well-known author of sensational fiction George W. M. Reynolds (1845–6); a classicist and regular contributor to the *Journal*, John Wilson Ross (1846–9); and the popular serialist J. F. Smith (1849–55).[3]

Despite these changes in its editorship, the *Journal*'s overall character remained remarkably uniform during the first dozen years of its operation. This was apparently due to the 'active zeal' with which, Stiff claimed, he always superintended both the correspondence page and the magazine's 'literary departments'.[4] In the period covered here, however, there was one notable shift in the *Journal*'s editorial policy and the general cultural level of its fiction. This occurred towards the end of 1857 when Stiff sold the magazine's copyright to the proprietor of the *Illustrated London News*, Herbert Ingram. Ingram and his newly appointed editor, the playwright Mark Lemon, abandoned the *Journal*'s characteristically florid fiction and imagery, introduced instead a more elegant style of illustration, and ran as the feature serials two Walter Scott novels, *Kenilworth* and *The Fortunes of Nigel*. This foray into somewhat higher than usual cultural ground resulted in an alarming and steady decline in the magazine's sales during the period 1858 to 1859. Ingram at this point sold the *Journal* back to Stiff, who immediately took measures to restore its former character and circulation. He

[3] On the *London Journal*, see 'Cheap Literature', 330, 340–1, and 345; Margaret Dalziel, *Popular Fiction One Hundred Years Ago* (London, 1957), 22–3; Francis Hitchman, 'The Penny Press', *Eclectic Magazine*, June 1881, 842–3; Louis James, *Fiction for the Working Man* (Oxford, 1963), 45–9; id., 'The Trouble with Betsy: Periodicals and the Common Reader in Mid-Nineteenth-Century England', in Joanne Shattock and Michael Wolff (eds.), *The Victorian Periodical Press* (Leicester, 1982), 360–5; and Sally Mitchell, 'The Forgotten Woman of the Period: Penny Weekly Family Magazines of the 1840s and 1850s', in Martha Vicinus (ed.), *A Widening Sphere*, (Bloomington, Ind., 1977), 31–7, 41, and 46 ff. On Stiff, see *Bookseller*, 1 Dec. 1874, 1109; and H. Vizetelly, *Glances Back Through Seventy Years*, 2 vols. (London, 1893), ii. 9–13; on Reynolds, see n. 7 below; on Ross, see *Athenaeum*, June 1887, 739; F. Boase, *Modern English Biography*, 1965 edn., under 'Ross, John Wilson'; and T. Cooper (ed.), *Men of the Time* (London, 1884), 943–4; and on Smith, see Boase, under 'Smith, J. F.'; and 'An Old Printer' [John Forbes Wilson], *A Few Personal Recollections* (London, 1896), 91–2.

[4] Stiff, 'Notice to the Trade', *London Journal* [hereafter *LJ*], 4 (1846), 128.

dropped Scott and replaced Lemon with Pierce Egan (the younger), a popular writer whom Stiff had hired as a serialist prior to the *Journal*'s sale. But, according to the *Bookseller*'s somewhat cryptic account, before Stiff could 'fully mature his plans, the periodical was sold to Messrs. Johnson of St. Martin's Lane', who ran it from 1860 into the 1870s.[5] Egan remained as editor and serialist until his death in 1880.[6] The magazine never again enjoyed the circulation it had reached in Stiff's time; none the less it continued to sell hundreds of thousands of copies per issue, and survived into the early years of the twentieth century.

The fall in circulation that the *Journal* experienced in the late 1850s may not have been wholly due to the misjudgement of Lemon and Ingram. Increasingly, it had faced competition from a number of new, similar publications that must have eroded its market. One principal source of this competition was the *Journal*'s own one-time editor, G. W. M. Reynolds. In the issue of 15 August 1846 the notices at the end included a brief announcement that Reynolds was 'indisposed' and had therefore been unable to carry out his editorial duties during recent weeks. Whatever the nature of his illness, it was undoubtedly of short duration and did not prevent him from appreciating the potential viability of a rival for the *Journal*'s readership.

On 7 November 1846 he brought out his own version of an illustrated penny weekly. First entitled *Reynolds's Magazine*, it became *Reynolds's Miscellany* with the issue of 5 December 1846. In addition to its mix of pictures, stories, and non-fiction along the lines of the *Journal*, the first number of the *Miscellany* also included the portrait of a particularly robust-looking Reynolds. Indeed, despite any real or spurious 'indisposition', he was by all accounts a man of noteworthy energy. Not only was he the prolific author of many highly successful romantic novels, but he also wrote the *Miscellany*'s feature serials. Beyond that he was its editor and proprietor until it ceased publication in 1869.[7]

In the first few weeks of his magazine's operation, Reynolds had

[5] *Bookseller*, 1 Dec. 1874, 1109.

[6] For biographical information on Egan, see Boase, *Modern English Biography*; and the *Dictionary of National Biography*, under 'Egan, Pierce (1814–1880)'.

[7] For a miniature version of the portrait mentioned in the text, see figure 29; on Reynolds's various literary and editorial activities, see E. F. Bleiler, Introduction to the Dover edn. of Reynolds, *Wagner, the Wehr-Wolf* (1846–7; reprint edn., New York, 1975), pp. vii-xi and xiii-xviii; *Bookseller*, 3 July 1879, 600–1; Thomas Clark, *A Letter Addressed to G. W. M. Reynolds . . .* (London, 1850), 19 ff.; Dalziel,

employed the *Journal*'s printer, George Vickers. But early in 1847 he made a permanent change to John Dicks, then a small publisher in Warwick Square.[8] The combination of Reynolds—whom the *Bookseller* would deem 'the most popular writer of our time'—and Dicks—who would become one of London's largest publishers—was clearly a fortunate one. The *Miscellany*'s readership grew steadily in the 1840s, and by 1855 Reynolds's success in the field of low-cost illustrated periodicals was only surpassed by the *Journal* and one other publication.

This was *Cassell's Illustrated Family Paper*, whose first number appeared on 31 December 1853. Like its two established competitors, the *Paper* came out every Saturday afternoon; and, like the *Journal* and the *Miscellany*, it provided its own pennyworth of the now familiar, still widely appealing array of serialized fiction, short stories, factual information, and a generous amount of illustration.[9] The *Paper* was originally the publication of the tea and coffee wholesaler John Cassell. In the late 1840s he had entered the publishing business with such small enterprises as the *Standard of Freedom*, a weekly paper begun in 1848. His activities quickly expanded to include a number of more ambitious serial publications, and by the early 1850s, in addition to the *Paper*, he had brought out *John Cassell's Library* and the *Working Man's Friend* (both begun in 1850), the *Illustrated Exhibitor: A Tribute to the World's Industrial Jubilee* (1851), the *Popular Educator* (begun in 1852), and the *Illustrated Magazine of Art* (begun in April 1853).[10]

Although Cassell was a seasoned publisher by the time he launched

Popular Fiction, 35–45; Anne Humpherys, 'The Geometry of the Modern City: G. W. M. Reynolds and the *Mysteries of London*', *Browning Institute Studies*, 2 (1983): 69–80; D. Kausch, 'George W. M. Reynolds: A Bibliography', Transactions of the Bibliographic Society, the *Library*, 5th ser., 28 (Dec. 1973), 321–5; Victor E. Neuburg, *Popular Literature* (Harmondsworth, 1977), 157–62; and Montague Summers, *A Gothic Bibliography* (London, 1940), 146–59. On the *Miscellany*, see 'Cheap Literature', 339; James, *Fiction for the Working Man*, 45–9; and Q. D. Leavis, *Fiction and the Reading Public* (London, 1932), 175–7.

[8] On Dicks's publishing career, see *Bookseller*, Mar. 1881, 231; and Neuburg, *Popular Literature*, 174 ff.

[9] For general remarks on the *Paper*, see 'Cheap Literature', 337–9; and Simon Nowell-Smith, *The House of Cassell* (London, 1958), 40–4.

[10] On Cassell, his career and publications, see *Bookseller*, 29 Apr. 1865, 225, and 31 May 1865, 291–2; Henry Curwen, *A History of Booksellers* (London, 1873), 267–74; Thomas Frost, *Forty Years' Recollections* (London, 1880), 226–8; Neuburg, *Popular Literature*, 205–10; Nowell-Smith, *House of Cassell*, 3 ff.; and 'Old Printer', *Recollections*, 66–72.

his *Family Paper*, he was purportedly unbusinesslike in his methods.[11] Thus, despite its initial popularity and ongoing regular circulation of 250,000 or more, the *Paper* soon fell into financial difficulty. To meet credit obligations, Cassell sold it in 1855 to the printing firm of Petter and Galpin, who in turn sold it to magazine distributors W. Kent and Company. Shortly after, however, Petter and Galpin took up their repurchase option with Kent, and the *Paper* stayed in their hands until Petter's retirement in 1883.[12] By virtue of his name, Cassell became a senior partner in 1858 and remained so until his death in 1865.

The *Paper*'s first editor was John Tillotson, a popular writer of miscellaneous non-fiction and stories for boys.[13] Tillotson left the *Paper* in 1855 when it changed hands. At that time Cassell himself took over as editor and remained in that capacity until the autumn of 1859 when he resigned to make an extended visit to America and open a New York branch of the business. After Cassell's resignation, William Petter became the magazine's editor and attempted to follow his predecessor's policy of combining entertainment and instruction. Thomas Galpin, however, pressured his partner to make changes, and after 1860 the *Paper* devoted itself increasingly to purely escapist amusement, to the exclusion of more informative but less saleable material.

II

The three main figures who edited and operated the *Journal*, the *Miscellany*, and the *Paper* between 1845 and 1860 evinced different kinds and levels of commercial and social interests. The case of the *London Journal*'s proprietor, George Stiff, is the most straightforward, since there is no evidence to suggest that he was professionally motivated by any concerns other than those related to commercial success. He seems in fact to have been a model of the nineteenth-century entrepreneurial spirit in its purest form.

[11] Nowell-Smith, *House of Cassell*, 28 and 51.

[12] The publishing firm was then incorporated as Cassell and Company, with Thomas Galpin as chairman and managing director, and the one-time Islington printer Robert Turner as general manager. The *Family Paper* became *Cassell's Magazine* in 1867; it underwent various other such name changes between 1874 and 1932, when it finally ceased publication. On the *Paper*'s publishing history, see ibid. 42, 51–7, 73, 77, 87, and *passim*.

[13] On Tillotson, see Boase, *Modern English Biography*, under 'Tillotson, John'; and Frost, *Forty Years'*, 232–8.

The most detailed evidence on his career comes from a contemporary publisher, Henry Vizetelly.[14] According to this source, Stiff initially was noteworthy only for his incompetence as an engraver. But, apart from this purported artistic failing, his was a success story. Early experience in the engraving department of the *Illustrated London News* had undoubtedly awakened him to the commercial potential of pictorial serial publishing. After leaving his position as an engraver he noted the large circulation of a non-pictorial weekly, the *Family Herald*; and, as Vizetelly put it, 'Stiff puzzled his brains how he could best cut into this. Finally, he determined upon bringing out a somewhat similar sheet with illustrations, and thereupon planned the subsequently well-known "London Journal".'[15]

At this point, without either capital or credit, he demonstrated his entrepreneurial panache. Through 'pleading and cajolery' he obtained several thousand pounds in credit and loans from a number of engravers, wholesale stationers, and a printer (presumably Vickers). Thus supplied with the necessary printing machinery, paper, and illustrations, he then pursued 'his one set purpose—the increasing of the sale of his publication'. This he did by a judicious tailoring of the *Journal*'s content to what he perceived to be the tastes of his potential market. In addition to the magazine's staple fare of wide-ranging miscellaneous subject-matter and generous illustration, he added short stories and cliff-hanger serial novels by such best-selling writers as Reynolds and J. F. Smith. As Stiff related to Vizetelly, 'weekly circulation used to rise as many as 50,000' when the conclusion of one of these exciting serials approached.[16] Thus, by 1855 the *Journal*'s sales had reached 450,000; its annual profit in some years was as high as £10,000; and in 1857, on its sale to Ingram, the copyright was worth the then substantial sum of £24,000.[17] All of this was no small achievement, for, as the *Bookseller* recognized on his death in 1874, 'Mr. Stiff pushed the *London Journal* into a, then, unprecedented sale, [and] he may be regarded as one of the principal pioneers of illustrated literature in its present popular form.'[18]

Another such pioneer, Stiff's one-time editor turned competitor,

[14] Vizetelly, *Glances Back*, ii. 9–13. [15] Ibid. 10.

[16] Ibid. 12; and see also James G. Bertram, *Some Memories of Books, Authors, and Events* (London, 1893), 140.

[17] Vizetelly, *Glances Back*, ii. 9; Dalziel, *Popular Fiction*, 22; and Mitchell, 'Forgotten Woman', 37.

[18] *Bookseller*, 1 Dec. 1874, 1109.

G. W. M. Reynolds, was also undoubtedly interested in commercial success. As reputedly 'the most popular writer' of his day, Reynolds had already enjoyed considerable financial returns on his work by the time he began the *Miscellany*. It thus seems probable that he, like Stiff, had a keen sense of popular taste and an eye for the sort of publication that would both satisfy this taste and potentially turn a profit. There are no surviving records to show the exact state of the *Miscellany*'s finances. We do know, however, that its circulation climbed steadily, from a fairly modest initial figure of 30,000–40,000, to 200,000 in 1855.[19] Thus, after *Cassell's Paper*, the *Miscellany* was the chief contender for the *Journal*'s dominant position in the field of mid-century pictorial publishing.

But however much Reynolds's commercial competitiveness might have rivalled that of Stiff, the motives dictating his activities as the *Miscellany*'s proprietor were not likely to have been simply a matter of business. Although he came from an upper middle-class military family, he had early in life abandoned an army career in favour of writing, publishing, and the promotion of various social and political causes. He was a sympathizer with European revolutionary movements of the 1840s, an advocate of temperance and various kinds of social reform, and, from 1848 to 1851, a prominent spokesman for Chartism.[20] Reynolds's social and political concerns were often reflected through his fiction, but they found their most direct expression in two of his periodical publications: the *Political Instructor*

[19] Knight to Duff-Gordon, in Clowes, *Knight*, 226; and Neuburg, *Popular Literature*, 157. There was, however, a brief slump in 1848 when Reynolds for a short time stopped writing for the *Miscellany*. He attributed this lapse to the stress caused by his personal financial difficulties—for despite having made money on his novels, he was apparently somewhat financially feckless and had declared personal bankruptcy several times between 1835 and 1848: see Clark, *Letter*, 13–14. How exactly this last bankruptcy affected the *Miscellany*'s finances is not clear, but it was at this time that Reynolds sold the copyright to the engraver, Edward Cooke (Clark, *Letter*); the latter does not, however, appear to have taken an active part in the operation of the business, and Reynolds continued as the magazine's proprietor.

[20] On Reynolds's social and political activities, see J. O. Baylen and N. J. Gossman (eds.), *Biographical Dictionary of Modern British Radicals* (Brighton, 1984), under 'Reynolds, G. W. M.', by Curtis W. Wood; Bleiler, Introduction to *Wagner, the Wehr-Wolf*, pp. xi–xiii; Joyce M. Bellamy and John Saville (eds.) *Dictionary of Labour Biography* (London, 1972–76), under 'Reynolds, G. W. M.', by L. James and J. Saville; R. G. Gammage, *History of the Chartist Movement* (London, 1894), 294–5, 308–9, 352, and *passim*; Reynolds, letter to George Holyoake, quoted in Joseph McCabe, *Life and Letters of Holyoake*, 2 vols. (London, 1908), i. 139; and see also ibid. 217.

(1849–50), whose main purpose was to promote Chartism; and *Reynolds's Newspaper* (begun in 1850), which proclaimed itself to be a 'Journal of Democratic Progress and General Interest'.[21]

Reynolds's commercial appeal and the sensational content of much of his writing have prompted some scholars to question the depth of his political commitment and the sincerity of his radical viewpoint.[22] One literary historian, however, has taken a slightly different approach and argued that the sincerity or insincerity of Reynolds's radicalism is not the most significant issue. It is more important simply to recognize that his career combined a popular political outlook with an unerring ability to pinpoint what was saleable entertainment, and that this combination was the source of his continuing popularity. Reynolds's work 'came to rest, as it were, on the fine point in the popular mind where escapism and activism touch'; in other words, 'his contradictions were the contradictions of the audience he was writing for'.[23] This perception seems particularly applicable to the *Miscellany*. For, as later discussion will attempt to show, it judiciously blended stimulating escapist entertainment with a certain amount of topical, mildly radical material. And this combination not only satisfied Reynolds's dual social and commercial purposes but—as the *Miscellany*'s high circulation argues—the tastes and interests of the reading populace were also well served.

John Cassell's was a somewhat different case from that of Reynolds and Stiff. As already indicated, he did not display the latter's level of business expertise. This was not necessarily owing to any native inability, but rather, as the historian of Cassell's publishing house has suggested, it was because Cassell's 'reforming enthusiasms' sometimes led him to neglect the tedious financial details of his business.[24] Certainly, in comparison with Reynolds and

[21] On the *Political Instructor*, see Anne Humpherys, 'G. W. M. Reynolds: Popular Literature and Popular Politics', in Joel Wiener (ed.), *Innovators and Preachers*, (New York, 1985), 8–9 and 13 ff.; on *Reynolds's News*, see Virginia Berridge, 'Popular Journalism and Working Class Attitudes, 1854–1886', Ph.D. thesis (London, 1976), 327 ff.; ead., 'Popular Sunday Papers and Mid-Victorian Society', in G. Boyce, J. Curran and P. Wingate (eds.), *Newspaper History*, (London, 1978), 247–64; and ead., 'Content Analysis and Historical Research in Newspapers', in Michael Harris and Alan Lee (eds.), *The Press and Modern Society* (London, 1986), 208 ff.

[22] See, e.g. R. D. Altick, *The English Common Reader* (Chicago, 1957), 344; Berridge, 'Popular Sunday Papers', 264; and Neuburg, *Popular Literature*, 159–60.

[23] Humpherys, 'G. W. M. Reynolds', 10 and 19.

[24] Nowell-Smith, *House of Cassell*, 51.

Stiff, he was the one who most displayed the kind of reformist spirit that had characterized Charles Knight's publishing career.

The son of Manchester working people, Cassell was as a child employed in a cotton mill and then a velveteen factory; he was next a carpenter's apprentice until the 1830s, at which time he became an itinerant missionary for the National Temperance Society.[25] In 1841, with the help of his wife's money, he established himself as a tea and coffee merchant, purveying what was in his view a wholesome alternative to intoxicating beverages. His first publishing venture, the *Teetotal Times* (begun in 1846), also reflected his commitment to temperance. However, the crusade against alcohol was by no means the only social cause that Cassell's career embraced. In another of his early publications, the *Standard of Freedom*, he aligned himself with 'Religious, Political, and Commercial Freedom throughout the world', while opposing 'Intolerance, the Gibbet, Intemperance, War, and all other systems which degrade, demoralize, brutalize, and destroy Mankind'.[26] But like his publishing predecessor, Knight, Cassell found his most consuming interest to be the social and intellectual advancement of working people. He was an outspoken opponent of the newspaper stamp and paper duty not merely because they encroached on the profits of his business, but because he believed sincerely that these were indeed 'taxes on knowledge'. Like Knight he also deplored what he considered to be the generally poor quality and 'immoral tendency' of much of the popular literature of his day. He therefore conceived the *Family Paper* and most of his other publications as vehicles for promoting education and counteracting 'low tastes' and extreme sensationalism.[27] 'I entered into the publishing Trade', he once said, 'to advance the moral and social well-being of the working classes.'[28] Thus, compared with the *Journal* and *Miscellany*, the *Paper* was the most serious in its underlying intent. Even so, we must remember that it was still a commercial enterprise; it was in competition with other such

[25] On Cassell's early life and involvement with the temperance movement, see G. Holden Pike, *John Cassell* (London, 1894), 5–59.

[26] *Standard of Freedom*, 1 July 1848, quoted in Nowell-Smith, *House of Cassell*, 17.

[27] Pike, *Cassell*, 116; on Cassell's efforts toward the abolition of the stamp and paper duty, see C. D. Collet, *History of the Taxes on Knowledge*, 2 vols. (London, 1899), i. 126–8; and Nowell-Smith, *House of Cassell*, 27–8.

[28] Quoted by Nowell-Smith, *House of Cassell*, 22, without giving the original context of the remark.

publications, and, like them, it had no formal associational ties to honour. Cassell, moreover, was no Knight in one significant respect: he never let his high social aims colour his view of what most of the public wanted. The people, he insisted, 'will not take what is termed namby-pamby'.[29] He made sure that the *Paper* contained much that would be highly entertaining, and he achieved the expected result: as a contemporary observed, 'popular appreciation was immediate'.[30]

III

For all the diversity in background, character, and motives among Stiff, Reynolds, and Cassell, their magazines did not differ markedly in overall appearance and content. Moreover, in using wide-ranging subject matter the second generation of pictorial miscellanies also recalled the varied content of the *Penny Magazine*. The *Journal*, *Miscellany*, and *Paper* thus included much that was 'pleasing to all orders of the community', but like their predecessor their major purpose was to appeal 'particularly to the industrious classes'.[31] Accordingly, in all three publications a significant portion of the overall content addressed itself to working people's widening intellectual interests and increasing literacy. For instance, in a random sampling of issues of the *Journal* and the *Miscellany*—from the periods 1845 to 1846 and 1853 to 1854—the dedicated reader would have encountered numerous articles, featured series, and short items treating travel and geography, contemporary life and new inventions, history and archaeology, and noteworthy people of the past and present. Similarly, in its first number of 31 December 1853, and in all subsequent issues, the later entry into the field, *Cassell's Paper*, also offered its readers 'every matter of interest to the public': for example, biographies of 'those who lived before us', accounts of 'far distant lands', and information on 'the onward march of civilisation'.[32]

The *Journal*, *Miscellany*, and *Paper* also followed the *Penny Magazine*'s lead in their use of mechanized stereotype printing for the inexpensive mass reproduction of quality wood-engravings. Like Knight before them, Stiff, Reynolds, and Cassell placed illustration high amongst the most attractive and saleable features of their publications. Never half-hearted in the promotion of his own enterprise,

[29] Nowell-Smith, *House of Cassell*, 22. [30] Pike, *Cassell*, 116. [31] *LJ* 5 (1847), 16.
[32] *Cassell's Illustrated Family Paper* [hereafter *CIFP*], 1 (1853), 1.

Stiff declared that the *Journal*'s pictorial department produced 'the most beautiful illustrations ever issued from the press'; his two rivals, meanwhile, contented themselves with inserting an occasional, more modest notice to the reader about the number and quality of engravings in the *Miscellany* and *Paper*.[33]

All three men took pains to secure the services of talented artists and engravers. Hablot K. Browne ('Phiz') occasionally contributed to the *Journal*, as did Cruikshank to the same publication and to the *Paper* as well; John Gilbert, the prominent historical painter and engraver, did occasional work for both the *Journal* and the *Miscellany*, and he designed the *Paper*'s first headpiece (figure 21). For the most part, though, the three magazines employed illustrators and engravers who are now less generally well-known but who attained at least a degree of prominence in their own day through their work for popular fiction publishers like Dicks, and for periodicals such as *Punch* and the *Illustrated London News*. Among others, there were W. Corway, Louis Huard, and T. H. Wilson of the *Journal*; Henry Anelay and E. Hooper who illustrated much of the *Miscellany*; and such contributors to the *Paper*'s pictorial department as Kenny Meadows, T. H. Nicholson, and G. F. Sargent.[34]

With such a pool of draughtsmen and engravers the second generation of pictorial magazines was able to dispense imagery whose stylistic competence rivalled and at times surpassed that of the *Penny Magazine*'s engravings. Thus, in these later publications, textual instruction in science, geography, history, and current affairs had as its complement technical illustration, scenes of foreign lands and monuments, representations of historical events, portraiture, and images of the modern world.[35]

But if the new magazines emulated their prototype in the variety of their instructional content and generosity of illustration, they also added much that was innovative in low-priced pictorial magazines. They offered, for example, accounts of such current events as the 1848 French revolution, the Crimean war, and conflicts in India; and to offset such sobering material they introduced as well theatrical

[33] *LJ* 1 (1845), 16; *Reynolds's Miscellany* [hereafter *RM*], 10 (1853), 64; *CIFP* 1 (1853), 1.

[34] On the magazines' artists, see Rodney K. Engen, *Dictionary of Victorian Wood Engravers* (Cambridge, 1985); and Simon Houfe, *Dictionary of British Book Illustrators and Caricaturists* (Woodbridge, Suffolk, 1978; revised edn., 1981).

[35] For representative examples, see *LJ* 3 (1846), 37; 17 (1853), 53; *RM* 1 (1847), 389; 14 (1855), 200; *CIFP*, NS 3 (1859), 232.

21. Headpiece, *Cassell's Paper*, 1853–7

22. Fashion illustration, *Reynolds's Miscellany*, 1853

anecdotes and reviews, riddles and other short humorous items, and an unprecedentedly generous amount of light poetry, treating nature, love, family life, work, war, and patriotism.[36] In addition, at the end of every issue of each magazine, 'Notices to Correspondents' answered readers' questions on a vast range of topics and concerns: the literary achievement of Chaucer, the history of Spanish wars, and the origins of the almanac; how to enter into apprenticeship and when to leave; what to do for baldness, bad skin, and general debility; where to obtain a marriage licence, how to get a divorce, and when to kiss a lady.

Beyond this array of information and advice, the *Paper* additionally solved chess problems and provided 'Hopes and Helps for the Young'. Moreover to show that 'the ladies are not to be forgotten', it also included recipes, ideas for needlework projects, and fashion news. The *Journal* and the *Miscellany* were similarly interested in attracting a female readership and they too reported on fashion, dispensed household hints, and printed 'useful receipts' and guides to beauty. In addition, they frequently ran short biographies of notable—and, sometimes, notorious women: Jenny Lind and other contemporary performers, Shakespeare's mother, Florence Nightingale, Catherine of Russia, and the beauties of the court of Charles II.[37]

Whether they aimed specifically at women or youth, or addressed themselves to a wider cross-section, many of these new texts demanded imagery that was also new to the field of inexpensive publishing. In the *Paper*, for instance, stitchery patterns and game-board diagrams clarified needlework instructions and chess problems, while representations of performers, plays, and scenery accompanied theatrical news in the *Journal* and the *Miscellany*. The same two also included portraiture to complement their accounts of women's lives, and in all three magazines depictions of stylish ladies and their ribbons, laces, feathers and fringes enhanced reports on the latest in Continental fashion (figure 22).[38]

[36] This observation and the comments that follow are based on a sampling of issues from *LJ* and *RM*, 1845–6, 1848–9, 1853–5, and 1860; and from *CIFP* 1853–5 and 1858–60.

[37] For representative examples of content aimed at women, see *LJ* 1 (1845), 31 and 264; 8 (1849), 322; 18 (1853), 264; and 19 (1854), 200; *RM* 10 (1853), 78; 14 (1855), 56; and 24 (1860), 59; *CIFP* 1 (1854), 328; and NS 1 (1858), 95.

[38] For typical illustrations, see *LJ*, 7 (1848), 353; *RM* 14 (1855), 121; *CIFP* NS 1 (1858), 95; and figure 38.

In many, perhaps most, cases the magazines' artists designed engravings specifically to accompany written material. This had also been the predominant practice in the *Penny Magazine* and was a departure from the earlier mode of illustrating inexpensive publications by loosely matching stock images to texts. Sometimes, though, editorial policy required yet another innovation, and in these instances texts had to be composed to suit illustrations, rather than the other way round. Thomas Frost, an occasional contributor to the *Paper* and sub-editor of *Cassell's Popular Educator* and *Magazine of Art*, recalled one such incident, which must have occurred early in November 1854. The *Paper*'s editor, John Tillotson, had asked Frost to write an article to accompany one of the illustrations in an ongoing series of images of the Crimea—scenes, for example, like the 'Battle of Alma', reproduced in figure 23. As Frost recollected it, Tillotson's request for a complementary article was both forthright and commercially pragmatic:

> You know the sort of thing we want. The popular claptrap about British valour, and a compliment to the Emperor [Napoleon III], you know. It has all been said before, but we must say something about recent events; for our war illustrations are exceedingly popular, and that is the key that our accompaniments must be played in.[39]

But, popular as they were, war illustrations and their descriptions could not match the wide and lasting appeal of one other feature which distinguished the *Penny Magazine*'s successors from their prototype. This was the exciting fiction that dominated the content of the *Journal*, *Miscellany*, and *Paper*. Week after week through the 1840s and 1850s, these magazines captured the collective imagination of their readers with an array of short stories expressly conceived to titillate, intrigue, or pleasurably horrify all those who made up the ever-growing market for entertaining fiction. In 1855, for example, the *Journal* offered such stimulating fare as 'The Haunted Mirror', 'Hearts are not Playthings', 'The Pirate's Three Visits', and 'The Lover's Grave'; meanwhile the *Miscellany* thrilled its readership with tales like 'Tower of Terror', 'The Living Corpse', 'Love's Young Dream', and the 'Drugged Chalice'; and, in its turn, the *Paper* provided comparable stimulation with 'The Fatal Pleasure Trip', 'Bandit's Captive', and 'How Lucy was Cured of Flirting'.[40]

[39] Frost, *Forty Years'*, quoted by Nowell-Smith, *House of Cassell*, 43.

[40] These titles are drawn from the respective tables of contents of *LJ* 21, *RM* 14, and *CIFP* 2 (all 1855).

23. 'Battle of Alma', *Cassell's Paper*, 1854

All of this, however, was no more than an entrée to the fictional main course: the serialized novel. Unfailingly, throughout their publication lives the three magazines featured at least one long-running serial each. And with good reason, for such works were immensely popular. One bookseller, James G. Bertram, remembered the 'enormous demand' for the *Journal* and its competitors on account of their serials. He recalled too that some of his customers not only read works such as '"Kenneth", an exciting story published in *Reynolds's [Miscellany]*', but they also became 'so much interested in the fate of the characters that they used to visit my shop in the course of the week to chat about the story'.[41]

The wide appeal and ready marketability of serialized fiction made it profitable for the magazines' proprietors to employ the most accomplished popular writers of the time. In this Reynolds, himself a notably successful author, had a distinct advantage, for he was able to feature his own highly saleable work and thus avoid the competition to engage similarly talented authors. His steady output of such enthralling material as *Wagner, the Wehr-Wolf* (1847), *The Coral Island: Or, the Hereditary Curse* (1848–9), and *The Massacre of Glencoe* (1852–3) was undoubtedly a central factor in the *Miscellany*'s commercial success.[42]

On the other hand Stiff and Cassell, not having Reynolds's narrative capabilities, were forced to vie aggressively for the services of other prolific and saleable writers of fiction. One such was J. F. Smith, the *Journal*'s editor and chief serialist after Reynolds's departure. As noted before, Smith's serials—for example, *Minnigrey* (1847), *The Will and the Way* (1853), and *Woman and Her Master* (1854)—did much to build the *Journal*'s circulation to its unprecedented number. And this did not pass unnoticed: in 1855 Cassell lured Smith from the *Journal* with the offer of a higher salary.

The memoir of the contemporary publisher Henry Vizetelly provides an entertaining account of how the serialist effected his transition from the one magazine to the other:

Smith, who always wrote his weekly instalment of 'copy' at the 'London

[41] Bertram, *Memories*, 139.

[42] The works named here are only a few of the many that Reynolds wrote for the *Miscellany* between 1846 and 1859: for a complete list of titles and dates, see Summers, *Gothic Bibliography*, 150 ff. In 1859 Reynolds gave up his position as the *Miscellany*'s leading serialist to James Malcolm Rymer ('Malcolm Errym'), author of the popular *Varney the Vampire*; see Bleiler, Introduction to *Wagner*, p. xi.

Journal' office, chanced to be in the middle of a story for Stiff at the moment he had chosen for abandoning him. In this dilemma he decided upon bringing the tale to a sudden close, and to accomplish this artistically he blew up all the principal characters on board a Mississippi steamboat, and handed the 'copy' to the boy in waiting. Then, proud at having solved a troublesome difficulty, he descended the office stairs, and directed his steps . . . to take service under his new employer.[43]

Never confounded for long, Stiff quickly replaced Smith with the equally popular Pierce Egan (who would later become the *Journal*'s editor). Vizetelly remembered that Egan 'ingeniously brought about the resurrection of such of [Smith's] characters as it was desirable to resuscitate, and continued the marvellous story in the ''London Journal'' for several months longer'.[44] Smith in the meantime began a new serial, *The Soldier of Fortune*, the first of many such stories that he would write for the *Paper* in the late 1850s and early 1860s.

Smith's serials and those which Reynolds, Egan, and others produced for the three magazines are myriad, and the concern here is neither to list titles nor to describe plots. Nevertheless we can take note of a nineteenth-century commentary or two, and from these gather the generally gripping tone and content of the serialized fiction that contributed so greatly to the popularity of the *Journal* and its two main competitors. The most saleable examples of such fiction were, as Vizetelly put it,

lengthy and exciting stories, telling how rich and poor babies were wickedly changed in their perambulators by conniving nursemaids, how long-lost wills miraculously turned up in the nick of time, and penniless beauty and virtue were 'led to the hymenal altar by the wealthy scion of a noble house', after he had gained the fair one's affections under some humble disguise.

Writing in a similar vein, another commentator offered this description of the successful serial's characterization and plotting:

The villains were generally of high birth and repulsive presence; the lowly personages were always of ravishing beauty and unsullied virtue. Innocence and loveliness in a gingham gown were perpetually pursued by vice and debauchery in varnished boots and spotless gloves. Life was surrounded by mystery; detectives were ever on the watch, and the most astonishing pitfalls and mantraps were concealed in the path of the unwary and of the innocent.[45]

[43] Vizetelly, *Glances Back*, ii. 12–13. [44] Ibid. 13.
[45] Ibid. 11–12; Hitchman, 'Penny Press', 842. Both quotations concern the

But it was not such verbal stimulus alone that the three magazines used to draw their readers. Adding to the appeal of weekly serial adventures were the boldly styled engravings that gave visible form to characters and events. Writing in 1859, the *British Quarterly Review*'s expert on 'cheap literature' aptly remarked upon the typical content and overall effect of serial fiction's pictorial accompaniments:

> the illustrations . . . with few exceptions, are of a violent or sinister character. There is usually either a 'deed of blood' going forward, or preparations for it. If there be not a dishevelled villain in a slouched hat shooting a fair gentleman in lace and tassels, or a brawny savage dragging an unprotected female into a cavern by the hair of her head, we may reckon at least upon a man in a cloak watching from behind a rock, or a 'situation' of thrilling interest, in which the figures look as of they had been taken in a spasm, and were suddenly petrified. The art employed upon these pictures is proper to the subject. The effects are broad, bold, and unscrupulous. There is an appropriate fierceness in the wild cutting and slashing of the block; and the letter-press always falls short of the haggard and ferocious expression of the engraving.[46]

Clearly images similar to those reproduced in figures 24–26 must have prompted this description. As these plates show, Reynolds's highly-coloured tales of romance and intrigue lent themselves well to the kind of stylistic and iconographic excesses that so bemused the *Review*'s commentator. Similarly, representative illustrations from the *Journal* and the *Paper* (figures 27 and 28) make it plain that Smith's stories also inspired their share of slashing diagonals, frenzied cross-hatching, melodramatic lighting effects, and sinister shadows.

Together figures 24 to 28 additionally show that the illustrations accompanying serial fiction frequently occupied a conspicuous position on the front pages of the various issues in which they appeared. Normally a half-page or more in size, often set below a given magazine's title, these pictures were apparently meant to attract the notice of those who browsed at the windows and stands of booksellers and news-vendors. And without doubt they did so. For who but the most strong-minded reader, determinedly bent on self-improvement in its purest form, could have failed to respond to the lure of vivid depictions of jousts and duels; gripping portrayals of murders

Journal's serial fiction, but the descriptions are equally applicable to the serials in *RM* and *CIFP*. See also 'Cheap Literature', 333 ff.

[46] 'Cheap Literature', 333.

REYNOLDS'S MISCELLANY

Of Romance, General Literature, Science, and Art.

EDITED BY GEORGE W. M. REYNOLDS.

[A]UTHOR OF THE FIRST AND SECOND SERIES OF "THE MYSTERIES OF LONDON," "FAUST," "THE DAYS OF HOGARTH."

[N]o. 62. Vol. III.—New Series.] FOR THE WEEK ENDING SATURDAY, SEPTEMBER 15, 1849. [Price One Penny.

[T]HE BRONZE STATUE; OR, THE VIRGIN'S KISS.

[B]Y GEORGE W. M. REYNOLDS.

CHAPTER LII.

[A] CONVERSATION ON A THRILLING TOPIC.

W[e] preceding chapter we have narrated the [meet]ing of Gloria and Sir Ernest de Colmar at [the so]uthern gate of Prague ; and we have like[wise e]ndeavoured to afford the reader an idea of [the] feelings which the Knight experienced when [thus a]gain exposed to the witching influence of [the la]dy's superhuman beauty. But we did not [paus]e to interrupt our narrative in order to [notice] the effect which Gloria's presence produced [upon] the youthful page Ermach.

[We] must therefore now observe that when the radiant being threw back her veil and thus made all the sun-lit glory of her charms burst upon the dazzled eyes of Sir Ernest de Colmar,—at that moment Ermach, who had reined in his steed beneath the shade of a wide-spreading oak on the way-side, gave utterance to an ejaculation of amazement as he caught sight of the resplendent countenance of Gloria.

But this expression of wonderment on his part escaped the ears of the rest : for the Knight had spurred his steed towards the lady as she issued from the outer gates—and the two grooms had halted with their sumpter-horses at a little distance. Thus the surprise of Ermach at thus beholding Gloria, passed unnoticed : but from beneath the deep shade of that friendly oak did he contemplate the beauteous creature with a strange and profoundly earnest attention, as she extended her hand to the Austrian Knight, whose feelings as he touched it with his lips we have already described.

The cavalcade now arranged itself in travelling order. Sir Ernest de Colmar and Gloria went first, the Knight riding on the lady's left hand, according to custom :—then came Linda and Beatrice, between whom the young page Ermach placed himself with a due observance of courtesy ;—and the two grooms brought up the rear.

But we must observe that while these arrangements were making,—or rather, while all the members of the party thus fell into their proper places, in the procession,—Gloria did not happen to take any notice of Ermach : therefore whether she would recognise him on any future occasion when she could not help observing him, was a matter of doubt to the young page, defying all conjecture as to the issue.

There was another circumstance which we must mention in connexion with this meeting at the southern gate of the city of Prague : namely, the mingled surprise and vexation which Linda and Beatrice experienced when the timid and furtive

24. Scene from Reynolds's *The Bronze Statue*, *Reynolds's Miscellany*, 1849

REYNOLDS'S MISCELLANY

Of Romance, General Literature, Science, and Art.

EDITED BY GEORGE W. M. REYNOLDS,

AUTHOR OF "THE MYSTERIES OF LONDON," "FAUST," "MASTER TIMOTHY'S BOOK-CASE," &C.

No. 22. Vol. I. SATURDAY, APRIL 3, 1847. Price 1*d*.

WAGNER: THE WEHR-WOLF.

BY THE EDITOR.

CHAPTER LII.

THE GREEK PAGE.—SONG OF THE GREEK PAGE.—A REVELATION.

THREE months had now elapsed since Ibrahim-Pacha had risen to the exalted rank of Grand Vizier, and had married the sister of Solyman the Magnificent. The Sultan daily became more attached to him; and he, on his part, rapidly acquired an almost complete influence over his Imperial Master. Vested with a power so nearly absolute that Solyman signed without ever perusing the hatti-sheriffs, or decrees, drawn up by Ibrahim,—and enjoying the confidence of the Divan, all the members of which were devoted to his interests,—the renegade administered according to his own discretion the affairs of that mighty empire. Avaricious and ever intent upon the aggrandizement of his own fortunes, he accumulated vast treasures; but he also maintained a household and lived in a style unequalled by any of his predecessors in office.

Having married a sister of the Sultan, he was not permitted a plurality of wives;—but he purchased the most beauteous slaves for his harem, and plunged headlong into a vortex of dissipation and pleasure.

25. Scene from Reynolds's *Wagner, the Wehr-Wolf*, *Reynolds's Miscellany*, 1847

REYNOLDS'S MISCELLANY

Of Romance, General Literature, Science, and Art.

EDITED BY GEORGE W. M. REYNOLDS

AUTHOR OF THE "MYSTERIES OF LONDON," "FAUST," "MASTER TIMOTHY'S BOOK-CASE," &C.

No 18. Vol. I. SATURDAY, MARCH 6, 1847. Price 1*d.*

WAGNER: THE WEHR-WOLF.

BY THE EDITOR.

CHAPTER XLII.

THE TEMPTATION.—THE ANACONDA.

In the meantime Fernand Wagner was engaged in the attempt to cross the chain of mountains which intersected the island whereon the shipwreck had thrown him.

He had clambered over rugged rocks and leapt across many yawning chasms in that region of desolation,—a region which formed so remarkable a contrast with the delicious scenery which he had left behind him.

And now he reached the basis of a conical hill, the summit of which seemed to have been split into two distinct parts; and the sinuous traces of the lava-streams, now cold, and hard, and black, adown its sides, convinced him that this was the volcano, from whose rent crater had poured the bituminous fluid so fatal to the vegetation of that region.

Following a circuitous and naturally formed pathway round the base, he reached the opposite side; and now from a height of three hundred feet above the level of the sea, his eyes commanded a view of a scene as fair as that behind the range of mountains.

He was now for the first time convinced of what he had all along suspected—namely, that it was indeed an island on which the storm had cast him.

26. Scene from *Wagner*, *Reynolds's Miscellany*, 1847

THE

LONDON JOURNAL:

And Weekly Record of Literature, Science, and Art.

No. 483.—Vol. XIX.] FOR THE WEEK ENDING MAY 27, 1854. Price One Penny.

[ATTEMPTED ASSASSINATION OF DICK VERNON, AT RIO DE JANEIRO.]

WOMAN AND HER MASTER.

CHAPTER CX.

Man is a child of sorrow, and this world
In which we breathe has cares enough to plague us;
But it hath means withal to soothe these cares;
And he who meditates on others' woe
Shall in that meditation lose his own. CUMBERLAND.

It is the last drop which makes the cup run over. The touch of sympathy will wake the chord mute to ruder hands. The kindness and deep feeling evinced by the young Englishmen to the unhappy husband of Clara Briancourt broke the seal of silence so long imposed upon his sorrows, and the pent-up waters flowed afresh.

During the many years he had spent in the prison of Rio, he had encountered nothing but the brutal jests, the heartless mockeries, and fierce oaths of the herd of wretches by whom he was surrounded, till at length his crushed soul had taken refuge in that sullen apathy which hides the wound—not heals it.

"Why are you here?" inquired Dick, with sailor-like frankness; "I feel assured you have not committed any crime!"

"Crime!" repeated the old man, in a tone of bitterness; "you judge with the confidence of your age—in ignorance of the world and its harsh laws! My crime was the heaviest man could be charged with—a crime," he added, "which palsies the energy of manhood—reduces genius to ashes—glides like a spectre between love and the object of its choice—draws an impassable circle round the garden of life—condemning the guilty wretch to its briars and deserts!"

"Murder?" faltered Fred, with a look of horror.

"Worse—much worse!" said Mr. Stanley.

"Worse!" exclaimed both the young men.

"*Poverty!*" continued the prisoner; "the only crime which earth knows or punishes with unrelenting hate—all other ills are called misfortunes! Murder! Pah! There is sympathy for the murderer—justice may be hoodwinked—bribed—even the angel Mercy will ofttimes plead for him: her voice is dumb for poverty alone!"

What a martyrdom of suffering did these brief words imply—a blight which had fallen upon the heart, and scathed it.

Bitter as was the explanation, it was a relief both to Fred and Dick to find that the being in whose misfortunes they had taken so sudden and deep an interest was guilty of no worse crime than being poor.

"Your tale must be a sad one!" observed the lieutenant.

"So sad," said Mr. Stanley, "it might have drawn iron tears from the stern eyes of Destiny! Shall I tell you all that I have endured? It is not often that I am garrulous—but there is something in your youth and words which inspires confidence! The world," he added, "has not hardened you yet!"

"I was young," he continued; "I cannot tell how many years have elapsed since my hair was of the same raven hue as yours, and my heart beat high with energy and hope; but it seems ages—ages! I loved and won the love of a fair girl—one of those rare beings which at intervals appear on earth to convince mankind that Eden was something more than a tradition! You may well gaze upon me!" he added, with a sigh; "is it not strange to think that the withered, decrepid being before you was ever gazed upon with eyes of affection—that his ears ever heard from the lips of beauty the avowal of a passion pure as the breath which uttered it? Believe or doubt it as you will—but it was so!"

His listeners assured him that it required no great stretch of credulity to give faith to his assertion.

"She I loved was rich," resumed the old man; "my sin, I have already told you, was poverty! Her mother hated me—why, I never could divine—for my name was ancient as her own! She was a proud, passionate woman—a worshipper of the world—and doubtless looked with contempt upon the herald's blazoned coat of arms, when the possessor's body-coat was threadbare! Despite her menaces, Clara and I were married! Her vengeance and her curse alike pursued us!"

Overcome by his recollections, the speaker paused and pressed his hand to his forehead, to veil his emotion—perhaps to hide a tear. Neither Fred nor his companion broke the silence which ensued. They felt that sympathy at such a moment would sound like mockery.

"I thought I had been transformed to stone—stone!" muttered the prisoner, bitterly; "but find some portion still is human!"

"We were steeped to the neck in poverty," he added; "yet, strange to say, were happy—happy in our love—happy in each other! My young wife at last became a mother—presented me with an image of herself—a tender, helpless girl!"

"The birth of my child awoke me from my dream of life! I felt for the first time the necessity of exertion, and I resolved to meet the spectre reality face to face! I was a ripe scholar, and offered to teach—none would employ me! Men feared to trust their sons to a tutor in a threadbare coat, lest poverty should prove infectious! I wrote a book—a poem—I scarce remember the subject! The publishers smiled when I offered it for sale! I solicited employment—*labour*—anything: my prayer was rejected! I had none to recommend me—the fact of my being a *scholar and a gentleman* told against me!"

"Is it possible?" said Dick, deeply moved; "is the world so hard?"

"So selfish?" added Fred.

George Stanley looked at them for an instant with surprise, as if he fancied that they were mocking him. He could not comprehend a doubt so utterly at variance with his own experience.

"Is it hard—is it selfish!" he repeated; "it is like the mountain whose tall crest shadows the plain beyond the city! The *surface* is soft enough, but the heart—*the heart is granite!* At last," added the speaker, "I found a friend!"

"You were fortunate!"

"Ay, as the child who finds a viper, and hides it in his bosom!" said the old man; "in my blindness, I trusted him—for his hairs were white with age, and his words were those of kindness! From time to time he assisted me, and finally proposed a situation in the house of a relative, as he said, in Rio: he supplied me with the means of reaching it, promising at the same time to guard my wife and child from want, till by my industry I had acquired sufficient money to send for them. The rest is soon told. I had not been in this accursed city more than three months, when a letter arrived from the clergyman of the village where I had left them, informing me they were both dead—of fever! Fever!" he repeated, with a laugh; "the fever of starvation!"

"For weeks I was a maniac. When I recovered, I had but one wish—one thought: to return to England—to visit their graves—to sit by the low, grassy mound

27. Scene from J. F. Smith's *Woman and Her Master*, *London Journal*, 1854

[THE RIGHT OF TRANSLATION AND REPUBLICATION IS RESERVED.]

NEW SERIES. VOL. I.—No. 10.] LONDON, SATURDAY, FEBRUARY 6, 1858. [PRICE ONE PENNY.

SMILES AND TEARS:

A Tale of our own Times.

BY J. F. SMITH,

AUTHOR OF "PHASES OF LIFE," "DICK TARLETON," ETC.

CHAPTER XIX.

I dwell amid the city,
And hear the flow of souls!
I do not hear the several contraries,
I do not hear the separate tone that rolls
In art or speech,
For pomp or trade, for merry-make or folly
I hear the confluence and sum of each,
And that is melancholy!
Thy voice is a complaint, O crowned city,
The blue sky covering thee like God's great pity.

ELIZABETH BROWNING.

WE cannot conceive a more desolate abode than London for those who, without kindred, friends, or some engrossing pursuit, seek to find a home in it. It is animation without life, the world seen in a camera, a mart to spectators who have nothing to buy or sell, who soon tire of taking an interest in the interests of others—a raree-show where curiosity flags and repetition palls, a tinsel spectacle leaving the heart like a tired bird without one green bough to rest upon.

In London—as in most great cities—the affections and sympathies require to be well endorsed before humanity will discount them. The only bills which invariably possess a certain value are those drawn by the passions: there is little difficulty in cashing them. If first-class they are done in the bank parlour of society, and at a moderate premium. When the names are not quite so good, or doubtful, a heavier one has to be submitted to, frequently cent. per cent. —paid either in *suffering*, *character*, or *self-respect*. Some desperate speculators may always be found to dabble in such securities, even when they flood the market, gorging it to repletion.

London to the stranger is indeed a desert. In the proper acceptation of the word, it is impossible to find a home in it, and it takes years to make one. Can anything be more cheerless than the sitting-room of one of its lodging-houses? the faded drugget with patches of grease as numerous as the spots in the skin of the leopard; the gaudy hearth-rug, regulation number of chairs, horse-hair sofa, dirty blinds, tawdry mirror over the chimney-piece, the half-dozen ill-washed glasses, and odd decanters—facetiously called a pair—on the rickety chiffonniere, to say nothing of the old moreen curtains with yellow fringe, and brass rings which set the inmate's teeth on edge as they rattle along the lacquered poles.

Then the beds, the—but no, we will not take our readers even in imagination *into them;* it would be a *biting* return for the years of kindness we have experienced at their hands; besides, not being a disciple of the Radcliff school, there are horrors into which we really cannot go.

Sometimes the wretched pariah who has no other shelter than one of these dens, rushes desperately into

LILLIAN STRUCK FOR THE FIRST TIME.

28. Scene from Smith's *Smiles and Tears*, *Cassell's Paper*, 1858

attempted and maidens imperilled; glamorous scenes of the elegant gatherings and sumptuous surroundings of court and high society; affecting tableaux of love lost and found, betrothals, marriages, and family reconciliations; provocative images of the scantily clad victims of war, abduction, and white slavery; and the pictorial drama of eleventh-hour rescues from burning buildings, watery graves, and assorted villains' seamy haunts.[47] In other words, such illustrations not only added to the interest of every thrilling instalment that they pictured, but also helped to sell the magazines.

In their prolific use of fiction and its illustration, and in their introduction of other kinds of material largely new to inexpensive pictorial publishing—fashion news, recipes, chess problems, and so on—the three magazines professed merely to offer the necessary leavening to offset their more serious and specifically educational content. The *Journal* declared itself to be 'devoted to the amusement and instruction of the people'; the *Paper* vowed that 'to unite amusement with instruction—one of the happiest marriages on earth—will always be attempted'; and similarly the *Miscellany* aimed to 'steer the medium course' between 'too much light matter' and 'another set of periodicals [which] are too heavy'.[48] Not content with a verbal statement alone, this publication also expressed its aim pictorially. Figure 29 reproduces the title-page to the *Miscellany*'s first volume, where at centre-top the image of Reynolds benignly presides—midway between instruction, personified in the guise of Science, and entertainment, represented in the persona of Romance.

But, as we might gather from the contrast between the comparative slenderness of Science and the buxom robustness of Romance, the *Miscellany*'s purported balance between the serious and the amusing was in fact weighted in favour of the latter. Moreover, as if in confirmation of this tendency, Reynolds's gaze turns away from Science and her sober accoutrements, toward the more blatantly enthralling (and saleable) charms of Romance. The content of the

[47] For some representative examples, see *LJ* 19 (1854), 113, 193; 20 (1854), 161; 21 (1855), 177, 193, 321; *RM* 1 (1847), 337; NS 1 (1848), 145, 161, 289; 15 (1855), 113, 305; and *CIFP* 1 (1854), 329; NS 5 (1860), 161; NS 6 (1860), 65. Among these three magazines, it was the *Journal* that initiated the practice of placing a dramatic serial illustration on the first page; it first did so with the opening instalment of Reynolds's *Faust*, *LJ* 1 (1845), 47 (issue of 4 Oct.).

[48] *LJ* 17 (1853), 64; *CIFP* 1 (1853), 1 (and see also Cassell to Brougham, 4 Sept. and 30 Sept. 1858, Brougham correspondence, University College London Library); *RM* 1 (1846), 16.

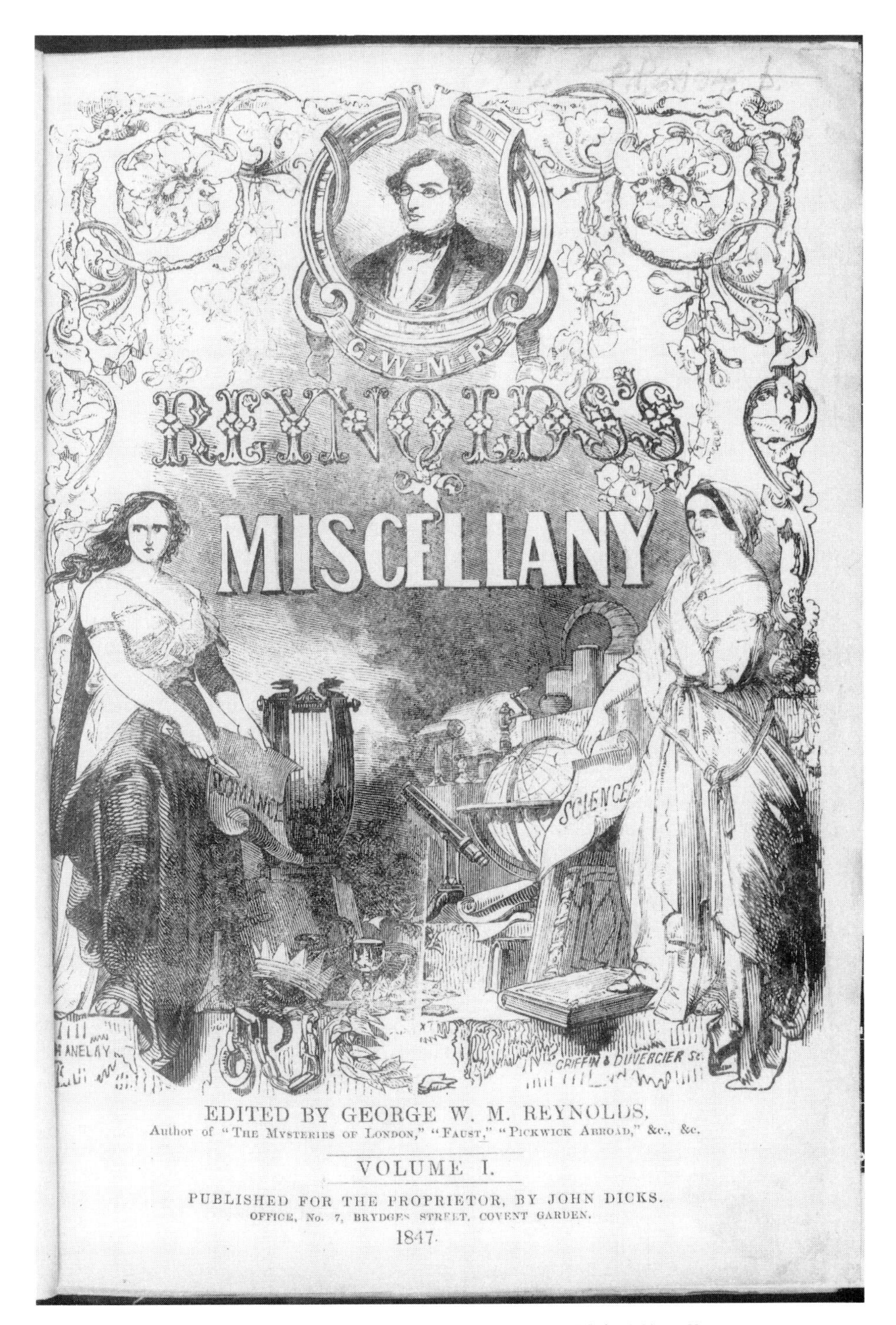

29. Title-page with portrait of Reynolds, *Reynolds's Miscellany*, 1846–7

Journal and the *Paper* reflected a similar bias, as both magazines, like the *Miscellany*, emphasized readily marketed entertainment over more purely instructional fare.[49] With their overall editorial efforts thus directed towards providing light diversion, the second generation of pictorial miscellanies could not offer the same quantity and kind of high-minded material that had characterized the *Penny Magazine*. The clearest signal of this difference between the earlier publication and its three successors was the shift in treatment of one particular feature—Knight's innovative contribution to pictorial publishing—the discussion and reproduction of works of art.

IV

It is only a mild exaggeration to say that just before the first stirrings of the 'art for art's sake' movement became discernible, the three new magazines espoused an opposing credo of 'art largely for entertainment's sake'. For, while the *Journal* on occasion included a serious discussion of painting or sculpture,[50] its general policy, like that of the *Miscellany* and the *Paper*, was to treat art as just another sundry amusing item in an array of such material, all of which stood subordinate to the main selling point, fiction. Or, putting it another way, in the second generation of pictorial miscellanies there are indications that, in its visual forms at least, high culture had begun to retreat from the popular domain, back towards the tradition that the *Penny Magazine* had briefly interrupted: what Knight had described as 'art's long reign of exclusiveness'.

In place of their predecessor's rich tapestry of art history, theory, and imagery, the *Journal*, *Miscellany*, and *Paper* offered a homelier,

[49] The distinction between entertainment and instruction is of course not entirely clear-cut: educational material could be entertaining; and fashion news, humorous items, and fiction could equally have a substantial instructional dimension. If, though, for the sake of argument we take the magazines' fiction as a gauge of the extent to which they devoted themselves to entertainment, the text's generalization about the relative weighting of light and serious matter is convincingly enough borne out. For example, in two representative issues of the *Miscellany*, 12 Feb. and 20 May 1848, 74% and 60% of total text space were respectively allotted to fiction; the *Paper* devoted 59% and 61% of its text space to fiction in issues for 11 Sept. 1858 and 28 Jan. 1860; and the *Journal* allocated 48% and 43% of its issues for 11 Mar. and 1 Apr. 1848 to fictional content. (In each case, total available text space has been calculated exclusive of illustrations, correspondence columns and advertising.) For a more detailed content analysis of the *Journal* using a larger sampling of issues, see James, 'Trouble with Betsy', 361–2.

[50] See, e.g. the article on Michelangelo's *Moses*, *LJ* 25 (1857), 168.

patchwork version of art for the people. Rather than a feature, art was now frequently a filler, as short, often unillustrated paragraphs on the 'Fine Arts' interposed themselves as if in afterthought between columns labelled 'Miscellaneous' and the end-of-issue 'Notices to Correspondents'.[51] The *Journal* on occasion omitted even abbreviated discussion of the fine arts and solved the problem of excess space simply by inserting an appropriately cropped image without additional explanatory comment. In such cases the reproduced works of Raphael and Correggio, for example, became visual *non sequiturs* amongst unrelated 'Gems of Thought', snippets of poetry, statistics, 'Facetiae', and 'Useful Receipts'.[52]

When layout space permitted the inclusion of both a reproduction and some accompanying text, all three magazines tended by their focus and presentation to trivialize both the art and its production. The *Miscellany*, for instance, published an engraving of Van Dyke's painting *The Virgin* but, beyond a few brief and generalized remarks about the artist's style, offered little in the way of informative art history and criticism. Instead, the reader learned that Van Dyke always began work in the morning, frequently invited his model to lunch, and then, with appetite but not creativity sated, finished the picture in the afternoon.[53] Similarly, the *Miscellany*'s commentary on a reproduced genre scene by the contemporary painter Robert McInnes (figure 30) told the reader nothing about the artist and provided only a word or two on the picture's 'life-like effect'. In this case the major concern of the literal-minded critic was to assure the reader that although 'we Londoners are scarcely in the habit of taking our children to the cloisters of old cathedrals to give them a bath, this . . . detracts nothing from the merits of the picture'[54]

The *Paper* took a similarly trivializing approach to art, but frequently added its own distinguishing touch of cloying sentimentality. For example, in 1858 it ran a reproduction of the painter Frederick Goodall's *Swing*, a genre picture of eleven impossibly

[51] See, e.g. *LJ* 7 (1848): 346; and see also 'Whims and Devices of Painters', *CIFP* 2 (1855), 83.

[52] See, e.g. the reproduction of Correggio's *Infant St John the Baptist*, *LJ* 27 (1858), 376.

[53] *RM* 14 (1855), 312. For a similar sort of example, involving an unidentified Dürer engraving of children, see *RM* 3 (1848), 417–22; in this case the image was a marginally related adjunct to the commentator's highly romanticized account of an apocryphal meeting between Dürer and Raphael.

[54] *RM* 14 (1855), 408.

ENFORCING THE SANITARY LAWS.

THIS picture, by Mr. Robert Mc Innes, is one of those happy ideas which, however well or ill painted, are pretty sure to find their way into the print-shop windows. Fortunately for the public, in this case, the painting is a good one, independent of the pictorial pun in which its humour consists. The struggling boy in the hands of his determined nurse, or mother, vainly attempting to resist the application of clean water and rough towel, is an incident familar to us all,—though not, perhaps, associated with fountains of such decorative beauty—for we Londoners are scarcely in the habit of taking our children to the cloisters of old cathedrals to give them a bath. This, however, detracts nothing from the merits of the picture, but rather the reverse. We remember an old fountain attached to the cathedral of many a venerable city, where the good wives fill their buckets at all hours of the day, and the weary wayfarer quenches his thirst in hot summer weather; aye, and many a long deep draught has the poor man taken at the pleasant spring, thanking God for giving him so sweet a liquor.

But to return to Mr. Mc Innes' picture. The little child to the right, shivering from the effect of *his* recent ducking, is extremely well delineated; and the whole picture has a life-like effect, quite refreshing to behold. Mr. Gilks has quite caught the spirit of the artist, and transferred the picture to wood in the most satisfactory manner.

THERE is no selfishness where there is a wife and family. There the house is lighted up by mutual charities; everything achieved for them is a victory; everything endured is a triumph. How many vices are suppressed, that there may be no *bad* example! How many exertions made to recommend and inculcate a *good* one!

SUNLIGHT CHASING THE SHADOW.

BY FANNIE MORETON.

THE shadow is deepening and casting a lengthening shade over Bessie Irvin's life. For months—months has she toiled in that little attic room. The sunshine has greeted but dimly that weary form. The window—the *only one*, is too small to admit but a feeble ray reflected from yonder stone mansion. Yet it enters *there*, and tiny feet leap joyfully and play in its beams, and little hands fling down book and toy, and try vainly to clasp its merry light. But poor Bessie! there she sits toiling on—oh! how wearily. The soft brown hair is parted on as pure a brow as eyes ever looked upon. The delicate features are beautiful in their contour. The form is as graceful as that of Lady Emma reclining on her velvet couch in that sumptuous mansion yonder. Aye! and her step was *once* as light; and her voice, though ever sweet and gentle in its carolling, spoke of joy and *lightness* within. She has lost none of her guileless innocence, though sorrow has cast her withering bane over Bessie's young heart. Father, mother, brothers, sisters, all gone. She has bid, perhaps, an eternal adieu to the vine-covered cottage with its pleasant fields, and clear, running brook, and the little portico, with its wealth of flowers and gay singing birds.

Her flowers may bloom as beauteously, her birds warble as sweetly, and the little brook flow on in its unceasing gentle ripple—but Bessie hears them not. The sounds that greet her ears now are those of carts and freighted omnibuses, and luxurious carriages rolling on with unceasing din.

Once too she loved. But he, who had sworn to be hers, had been called away to distant climes; and the ship in which he had sailed had never been heard of more. Oh! poor Bessie! yours is a hard lot seemingly—

30. Reproduction of a painting by R. McInnes, *Reynolds's Miscellany*, 1855

pretty children displaying improbable amicability over the sharing of a single tree swing. The magazine's commentator expressed the view that 'our picture describes itself'; then, with art criticism thus neatly disposed of, he or she proceeded to the main point: 'Children at play are a pleasant sight . . . Children soften the heart; foster kindly feelings; recall the pleasant passages of our own childhood'—and so on in comparable vein.[55] It was perhaps the same sentimental critic who had previously described another genre scene published in the *Paper*, a reproduction of a painting entitled *The Grandfather's Watch* (figure 31).[56] The picture shows a cottage room, in which is seated a pleasant-looking elderly man who holds his pocket watch to the ear of a small girl. Meanwhile, leaning on the back of the old man's chair, the child's mother looks fondly down upon the pair. All of this the readers could have noted for themselves. But had they wished further enlightenment about the painting or its artist, they would have been disappointed; for, rather than explaining the theories and practice of art, the *Paper*'s critic was more concerned with expanding upon kindly grandfathers, winsome children, maternal solicitude, and the marvels of horology.

The insubstantial treatment of art which characterized the *Penny Magazine*'s three successors did not arise from any particular animosity towards the subject on the part of the magazines' editors and proprietors. Cassell, in fact, had by 1853 gained a reputation as one of the foremost contemporary popularizers of art with the publication of his *Magazine of Art* (1853–6); and the replacement for Reynolds at the *Journal*, John Wilson Ross, eventually became editor of a periodical conceived to promote popular knowledge of design, the *Universal Decorator*.[57] Nothing is known about the attitudes to art of Stiff, Reynolds, Smith, and others closely associated with the production of the three magazines. There is, however, no evidence to suggest that any of these men were actively ill-disposed towards either art or its dissemination to the people. They merely emphasized what had become more readily saleable imagery than art reproduction—imagery which, as we have already seen, accompanied works of fictional narrative.

[55] *CIFP*, NS 1 (1858), 392.

[56] *CIFP* 4 (1857), 284; the original was painted by Walter Goodall, brother of Frederick.

[57] Nowell-Smith, *House of Cassell*, 42; the *Decorator* ran 1858–63; Ross was a contributor in the 1850s and editor 1860–3.

never weary of the repetition. And Meggy's mother, looking over the back of the chair, is as interested in the child as the child is in the watch, and no learned philosophers were ever more intent upon their work than this little group on the "ticking" of that marvellous piece of horology. The painter has made a capital scene. It is so natural, so thoroughly like real life, that sympathy is immediately enlisted, and you are interested in the child and the old man beyond that which is commonly called forth by a picture. The fact is, the artist has given us a truthful delineation of an every-day occurrence, and such productions are sure to find admirers.

"SPANISH GIPSIES."

There is an old saying which tells us that "no washing will turn the gipsy white." The gipsy is unchanging and unchangeable. He preserves his natural characteristics everywhere, and, instead of blending with other people, falling into ordinary customs, and adopting common practices, he steadfastly maintains his singularity with a pertinacious spirit worthy of a better cause.

In Russia the gipsies are styled Zigani; in Turkey, Zingarri; in Germany, Zigeuner; in France, Bohémiens; in England, Gipsies; and in Spain, Gitanos. Their peculiar physiognomy distinguishes them from all other people; and whether you meet them amid the freezing snows of Russia, or on the burning sands of India, you recognise immediately their common relationship.

In Spain the gipsies are, as we have already mentioned, generally known as Gitanos, a word equivalent to Egyptians. It is regarded as a term of infamy and reproach, and is never employed by the people themselves. Their first appearance in Spain dates from the early part of the fifteenth century. They are described by an author of that period as coming from Egypt; he tells us "they had their ears pierced, from which depended a ring of silver; their hair was black and crispy; and their women were sorceresses, who told fortunes." They were first noticed in France, where they were regarded as a curse and a scandal, and from which they were driven with a cruelly relentless persecution. Terrible laws were enacted especially against them, and hanging, burning, drowning, mutilating, and scourging, were the penalties freely dealt out by the hand of the magistrates and people. Under these circumstances the Gitanos looked around for a place of safety; some fled to the plains of Hungary, and others to the forests of Bohemia; but the majority found refuge in the mountains of the Spanish peninsula. At the time when the Gitanos settled in Spain, the condition of that country was admirably adapted to their predatory habits. They had but to thieve and murder—for they were in nowise particular—and if they had gold enough to bribe the officers, the stoutest halberdier and most sapient alcade would shut their eyes to their enormities. Thus wandering over the plains and mountains, with little of the fear of man and nothing of the fear of God before their eyes, these Gitanos led their strange life for many a long year. It was the age of wild adventure, and numerous romantic stories are told of the doings of these nomadic people. They trafficked in horses and mules, and were accounted excellent blacksmiths, having their smithies in the heart of the mountains; but their real trade was plunder, and they were ever ready to throw aside the hammer and quit the anvil to engage in a less laudable branch of industry.

The condition of gipsy life in Spain has naturally, in the lapse of centuries, undergone considerable modification. They are not what they were. "The roads have ceased to be infested by them, and the traveller is no longer exposed to much danger on their account. They at present confine themselves, for the most part, to towns and villages; but if they occasionally wander abroad, it is no longer in armed bands, formidable for their numbers and carrying terror and devastation in all directions." But different in its manifestation, gipsy life is the same in principle. They are bound together by a feeling of kindred which renders them averse to mingle with other races. They are accounted as the vilest of the people, and have, therefore, little to hope for in the sympathy of their oppressors. They number forty thousand in the Peninsula, and some of them are reported to be exceedingly wealthy.

The gipsies represented in the painting are of that class which can do almost anything except cultivate the earth or enter regular service. The bright-eyed Gitano who sits in the middle of the picture, is possibly a horse jockey or a mule dealer; perhaps he could make the anvil ring with the blow of his hammer, and, to employ a beautiful Gitano metaphor, produce at one time more than a hundred lovely daughters, fiery as roses — daughters that expire the same moment they are born. Perhaps he manages to do a little bit of plunder now and then—a few eggs, a side of bacon, a duck or a fowl—but nothing on a very extensive scale. Then these dark-eyed women are sibyls — that one especially, who is beating the tambourine and singing, doubtless, a gipsy song. She professes to trace your destiny by the lines on your hand, can sell you a love philter, or give you a charm against the evil eye. That they are merry and light-hearted is evident enough. They have an intense affection for the life they lead, and are not so desperately wicked as some people suppose.

THE GRANDFATHER'S WATCH. FROM A PAINTING BY W. GOODALL, CONTRIBUTED TO THE ART TREASURES EXHIBITION BY C. PEMBERTON, ESQ.

31. *The Grandfather's Watch*, by W. Goodall, *Cassell's Paper*, 1857

The focus on entertainment through story-telling was particulary pronounced in the *Miscellany*, and frequently it managed to recreate art as romantic narrative. In one such instance a short commentary on Verheyden's genre painting *The Peasant-Girl's Return* transformed the picture into a visual short story whose ending was the usual one of romantic fiction:

We may fancy that the young peasant girl has gone forth to sell her eggs, her butter, and her poultry, and has brought home a good store of fruit, flowers and vegetables in her ample basket and in the folds of her apron. She knocks at the door, saying, 'It is I!'—and thereupon a kind mother or worthy old father rises and opens for her admittance. A little later in life, and when she knocks at some other cottage-door, saying, 'It is I!' a watchful husband will be ready to give her ingress.[58]

In another case a reproduction of a Fragonard painting of a young woman engaged in correspondence also became an implied narrative as the commentator speculated about the contents of the pictured letter, exclaimed over 'the world of loving thoughts' in the writer's mind, and inventively evoked scenes of 'whispered conversations in crowded rooms', 'the gentle pressure of hands when they meet in the mazes of the dance' and 'long moonlit wanderings in shady lanes . . .'.[59] For those who were *aficionados* of art as well as romance, the author remembered to include a brief addendum which named the painter and engraver of the picture and assured the reader that 'it has never before been rendered in wood'.

In a more notable and somewhat different kind of example, there was no need to weave a whole new story around the work of art. Instead, Reynolds simply applied his own inimitable style to a highly-coloured reworking of the narrative originally associated with a well-known series of images. One-time readers of the *Penny Magazine* perhaps might have recognized the opening scene of *Industry and Idleness* now reproduced on the front page of the *Miscellany*'s issue of 12 June 1847 (figure 32). Unlike the earlier magazine's image, this version was not an illustration for long quotations from Charles Lamb's seminal essay on Hogarth; and it was no longer strictly a visual homily on civilized behaviour. Along with reproductions of other engravings in the series, it had become part of the pictorial accompaniment to one of Reynolds's typical works of serialized fiction. Running for several weeks in mid-1847, this was a florid tale of

[58] *RM* 10 (1853), 76. [59] *RM* 14 (1855), 376.

REYNOLDS'S MISCELLANY

Of Romance, General Literature, Science, and Art.

EDITED BY GEORGE W. M. REYNOLDS,

AUTHOR OF "THE MYSTERIES OF LONDON," "FAUST," "PICKWICK ABROAD," &c. &c.

No. 32. Vol. II. SATURDAY, JUNE 12, 1847. Price 1*d*.

THE DAYS OF HOGARTH:

OR, THE MYSTERIES OF OLD LONDON.

BY THE EDITOR.

CHAPTER V.

THE TWO APPRENTICES.

It has been well said that man is the noblest work of God; but it is not equally easy to decide which is the noblest work of man. Though in contrast with all the wondrous achievements of Almighty Power, the efforts of the human race are as nothing,—though the most complicated, the most perfect results of mortal ingenuity are mean and contemptible when placed in comparison with the stupendous creations of the Divine Architect,—nevertheless, the earth is covered with monuments, which excite our astonishment and our admiration at the intelligence, the power, and the perseverance of Man!

But of all the arts which, in their application, constitute the distinctions between social and savage life—between a glorious civilisation and an enduring barbarism,—that of Weaving is decidedly one of the chief. For though the savage may affect the finery of shells and flowers—though he may study external adornment by means of the natural products most pleasing to his sight—and though he may even conceal his nakedness with leaves, or defend himself from the cold by the hides of animals,—yet it is only in

32. *Industry and Idleness*, *Reynolds's Miscellany*, 1847

THE

LONDON JOURNAL:

And Weekly Record of Literature, Science, and Art.

No. 436.—Vol. XVII.] FOR THE WEEK ENDING JULY 2 1853. [Price One Penny.

[OLD MARTIN POINTING OUT THE MURDERER OF SIR WILLIAM MOWBRAY.]

THE WILL AND THE WAY.

BY THE AUTHOR OF
"THE JESUIT," "THE PRELATE," "MINNIGREY," ETC.

CHAPTER CVI.

There is a judge from whose all-seeing eye
Man cannot hide himself. He needs
Nor witness nor confession—in secret
He prepares the punishment reserved
For crime—bursts on him in a thunder-cloud,
And he is gone.
Old Play.

No sooner had the Khan succeeded in performing the operation which was to restore old Martin to reason, than he left him to the care of the medical men, whose presence had in some degree sanctioned the hazardous experiment: under their care, the patient gradually recovered his memory. At first his recollections were confused and indistinct as some hideous dream which had oppressed his sleeping hours; but the second day they returned with terrible reality. The scene of the murder—the victim and his assassin—all were remembered; and a second time the reason of the faithful and attached domestic all but sank beneath the excitement they produced.

After a consultation with the surgeons, it was decided by Colonel Butler and the rector, that he should be questioned magisterially before them.

A note was accordingly dispatched to General Bouchier and Sir Jasper Pepper—who were both in the commission of the peace for the county—to attend.

The library at the rectory was accordingly arranged for the occasion. A table and seats were placed for the magistrates, and Dr. Orme's large easy chair for the witness.

Colonel Butler, who presided, opened the proceedings, by reminding his brother magistrates of the mysterious death of the late Sir William Mowbray, and added, "that evidence had been unexpectedly obtained, to bring the murderer to justice." The minutes of the coroner's inquest were then read, as well as the verdict of "Wilful murder against some person or persons unknown," returned by the jury.

At this stage of the proceedings Will Sideler was led into the room, in charge of Joe Beans, the sexton, and the village constable. The countenance of the ruffian was haggard—terror, remorse, and despair had ploughed deep furrows in his iron visage—his glance, usually so bold and fierce, was humble and subdued. He evidently felt like a man over whom tardy but sure-footed justice had visibly suspended her avenging glaive.

No sooner did Henry Ashton, who was standing close to the chair of the rector, behold the man by whose hand the thread of his benefactor's life had been so rudely sundered, than his countenance became suddenly flushed, and his eyes lit with a fire which betrayed the feelings of hate, disgust, and indignation which took possession of his soul; those of the warrener sank beneath his avenging glance.

"William Sideler," said the presiding magistrate, in a tone which fell like the sound of a death-bell upon the assassin's ear, "you are brought before us to answer the accusation of murder—cruel and deliberate murder—perpetrated upon the person of your late master, Sir William Mowbray. It is my duty to warn you that any statement you may choose to make will be taken down, and used as evidence upon your trial."

"I have nothing to state," answered the prisoner doggedly, "but that I am innocent! This is an idle accusation trumped up against me by a madman and my enemies!"

"Whom do you consider your enemies?" demanded General Bouchier.

"Joe Beans and that young man!" exclaimed the ruffian, pointing at the same time to our hero—who noticed the accusation only by a calm but bitter smile.

"And the madman?" inquired Sir Jasper.

"Martin the groom," replied the warrener; "from boys we were enemies—we both loved the same girl. It was my quarrel with him which drove me from my service with—with ——"

The ruffian hesitated. He could not bring himself to pronounce the name of Sir William Mowbray.

"Your victim!" added Henry Ashton, for the first time breaking silence. "No wonder that his name falters on your tongue; it was his image which haunted you upon the pier at Calais—it will stand beside you at the hour of death, and accuse you at the judgment-seat of heaven!"

The prisoner shuddered so visibly, that a similar feeling ran through the veins of the magistrates. The sensation was like to that which the sight of some loathsome reptile produces the first time that it meets our sight.

"You are well acquainted with Carrow Abbey?" observed Colonel Butler, resuming the examination.

"Yes."

"Are you aware of any secret passages or entrances to the house or apartments?"

"No."

"How came this gibern, then," exclaimed Dr. Orme—"which twenty witnesses can prove to have been yours—to be found in a vaulted chamber, at the end of a passage or recess opening from the library, the scene of the murder?"

Every eye was bent upon him; twice the warrener essayed to speak, but the words died away upon his tongue.

"You cannot answer!" continued the speaker. "The letters it contains, prove how long and foully you have conspired against the honour and happiness of the generous man whose bread you had eaten from childhood!"

"I know not how they came there!" said the accused, endeavouring to assume a firmness which his whole demeanour gave the lie to; "but it is my firm belief my enemies placed them there to blacken me!"

"Whom do you mean by your enemies?"

"Joe Beans and Henry Ashton," was the reply.

No sooner had the ruffian pronounced the name of Joe Beans, than the honest rustic, indignant at the villany of such a charge, burst out in a passionate but unnecessary denial.

"It be a lie!" he exclaimed; "a wicked, infernal lie—and will not serve thee, Will! Till the night I accompanied poor old Martin and the sexton, I wor never at abbey twice in my life—once when a boy and once since! Thee wor always a bad, revengeful man, but I never had concern or quarrel with thee! I would not raise my hand against a dog, unless he deserved it—much less a fellow-creature! Ask Chettleborough, your worship," he added; "he will tell 'ee how we found the bag: it's my belief it wor the finger of God—not our poor wits!"

The deep earnestness with which these few and simple words were uttered, must have convinced his hearers—even if they had previously entertained any doubt upon the subject—that he had spoken nothing but truth

33. Scene from Smith's *Will and the Way*, *London Journal*, 1853

love and licentiousness, gallantry and degradation, virtue outraged, vice rampant, horrible crime, dissipation and depravity, duelling, drinking, dancing, and gambling—all in Old London at the time indicated in the title: *The Days of Hogarth*. Needless to say, apart from its title and illustrations, this story had little to do with the history and theory of fine art.

In other encounters between art and serial fiction, the former in no way inspired or played a key role in the narrative. For the most part it had relinquished all claims to centre-stage and now served as a backdrop to more readily saleable imagery. In one typical engraving a faintly delineated picture of the Madonna and Child hangs in a 'well-appointed' ship's cabin and overlooks the much larger and bolder figures of two dashing characters from Reynolds's *Massacre of Glencoe*. This was a historical tale of gripping adventure and dubious accuracy which featured in several issues of the *Miscellany* early in 1853. *Cassell's Paper* similarly included many illustrations in which art hung in the background of dramatic fictional scenes. In one such case a staple of parlour art—a painted seascape—took second place to the affecting vignette beneath it: the reunion of a mother and her long-lost son, from an episode of J. F. Smith's 1858 serial *Smiles and Tears*. Not to be outdone, the *Journal* had some years earlier run an illustration containing no fewer than three pairs of painted eyes to witness 'Old Martin Pointing Out the Murderer of Sir William Mowbray' (figure 33), from another Smith serial, *The Will and the Way*, published in 1853. In short, as these and other such examples indicate, by the 1850s the *Journal*, *Miscellany*, and *Paper* had reduced art to a subservient position in a new popular realm where high drama, high intrigue, and high romance had deposed high culture.[60] And in such a domain there was little place for the Academy exhibition room and all that it stood for.

But however much the new pictorial miscellanies diverged from the *Penny Magazine* in their light approach to fine art, they followed in the wake of their prototype in one important respect. As we will see, the second generation also managed to contribute its share to the dissemination of the civilizing values associated with individual virtue and social stability.

[60] For the illustrations cited in the text and a few of the many other similar examples, see *LJ*, 28 (1858), 193; 32 (1860), 737; *RM* 10 (1853), 81; 13 (1854), 1; 14 (1855), 17; 20 (1858), 17 and 313; *CIFP* 2 (1855), 57 and 97; NS 1 (1858), 321.

4
The Civilizing Image: The Second Generation and Social Virtue
1845-1860

As our now familiar commentator on 'cheap literature' prepared his review and perused his copies of penny miscellanies, he made the following observation: 'As to the matter of wisdom in the conduct of life, the control of the passions, and the regulation of the temper . . . the axiomatic sentences, or, as they are called in the *London Journal*, the ''Gems of Thought'' . . . are notoriously inexhaustible'.[1] This was yet again an instance of our commentator's astuteness. For, in abandoning a *Penny Magazine*-style programme of serious education in fine art and other subjects, the *Journal* by no means wholly neglected the matter of its readers' social and moral instruction. Similarly, despite all their efforts to subordinate high culture to entertainment, the *Miscellany* and *Paper* also found ways to transmit a set of civilized values and civilizing exhortations along with their thrilling fiction and spirited illustration: improve yourself; practise discipline; work hard; exercise moderation. As they had been in the *Penny Magazine*, these ideals of social virtue were the catch-phrases that promoted social stability and thus served the interests of those in positions of privilege and power.[2] Frequently the three magazines confined themselves to conveying generalized messages about the nature, and value for all, of civilized behaviour. But at times they also managed to suggest that the meaning of 'civilized' was fluid, that it shifted in relation to an individual's position and role in society. In other words, from the standpoint of the second generation of pictorial miscellanies, the ideals of social virtue permitted variations on their main themes, variations specific to class and gender.

[1] 'Cheap Literature', *British Quarterly Review*, 29 (1859), 330.

[2] For the theory underlying this line of argument, see Introduction, n. 8 on Gramsci.

I

In an 1846 editorial the *Journal* dedicated itself to the spread of 'light, useful truth and moral improvement'.[3] From time to time the *Miscellany* and *Paper* made similar avowals; and each of the three magazines offered its share of short homilies on the merits of patience, perseverance, and self-improvement; scientific facts on the healthful benefits of mildness of temper; essays on etiquette and politeness, the hallmarks of civilized society; headlines such as 'Industry Its Own Reward'; and dire warnings against the evils of intemperance.[4] Indeed such civilizing material was so extensive that even Charles Knight, a relative purist in these matters, somewhat reluctantly had to admit that 'for all their bad taste', the three magazines and their like demonstrated 'partial and manifest utility in some portions . . . In the whole range of these things we can detect nothing that bears a parallel with what used to be called "the blasphemous and seditious press".'[5]

But it was not solely non-fictional material that promoted the virtues of work, self-reliance, and moderation in all things. As exciting, even titillating, as the magazines' fiction was, it too tended to be moralistic in tone and directly or indirectly supportive of much the same sort of values as had characterized the *Penny Magazine*. In other words, in the communication of a particular social outlook conducive to the maintenance of social stability, the difference between the earlier magazine and its new counterparts was a matter more of ostensible form rather than embedded content.

John Cassell for one clearly recognized the social utility of the kind of entertaining fiction that sold his magazine. In an 1858 letter to Lord Brougham he wrote:

Without professing to be a champion of Fiction, I may be allowed to state my opinion that novels may be rendered something more than mere books of amusement. That they may be made appropriate vehicles in the conveyance of useful lessons, inculcating good morals, cultivating the best affections of the heart, kindling the noblest aspirations, awakening inert ambition, inci-

[3] J. W. Ross, 'Address to Readers', introduction to *LJ* 4 (1846).

[4] For these and other similar examples, see *LJ* 2 (1845), 119; 3 (1846), 215–16; 5 (1847), 270; 6 (1847), 190–1; *RM* 1 (1846), 92; 14 (1855), 88, 231, 302, 334, 381, 391, 398; *CIFP* 1 (1854), 19, 22, 95; 2 (1855), 91, 103, 111, 119, 135, 167; NS 1 (1858), 46 and 133–4.

[5] Charles Knight, *The Old Printer and the Modern Press* (London, 1854), 284–5.

ting to enterprise and exertion, and thus advancing the Moral and intellectual welfare of the People at large.[6]

Consistent with this philosophy, the *Paper*'s chief serialist, Smith, managed to reconcile a racy, readable style with 'high moral tone', so that, as one commentator (possibly Cassell) put it, 'he never panders to vice, nor paints the brutal and abandoned in attractive colours'.[7]

Similarly, however sensational the fiction in the *Journal* and *Miscellany* might at times become, it also preserved and promoted a standard of civilized behaviour. Even Reynolds, whose stories for the *Miscellany* were comparatively tolerant of excess, particularly in sexual matters, frequently made sure that greed, profligacy and all forms of social irresponsibility came to a bad fictional end—even if they had managed to have a good, long, graphically entertaining run for their money in earlier chapters. Indeed, what Reynolds claimed for two of his most famous stories—*The Mysteries of London* (1845–8) and *The Mysteries of the Court of London* (1848–56)—might be said of several other examples of his fiction: they were collectively a 'moral document' conceived with a strong notion of social and personal right and wrong.[8] In one such story, *The Seamstress*, which ran in the *Miscellany* in mid-1850, the aristocratic villains of the piece variously die unpleasant deaths not only for their persecution of seamstresses and others in their employ, but also for such personal vices as idleness, dissipation, and greed.

We have less explicit information on how Stiff might have felt about the importance of redeeming social and moral content in the fiction featured in the *Journal*. It is however suggestive that that writer of incomparably 'high moral tone', Smith, was the *Journal*'s chief serialist for several years before he joined the *Paper*. Other examples of the *Journal*'s fiction are also telling. A random sampling of stories from 1848 shows the kind of moral underpinning that was part of a wider cultural concept of the individual behaviour necessary for a stable, civilized society. One such story, a tale of young love and marriage, was also a scarcely veiled lecture on fiscal responsibility

[6] Cassell to Brougham, 29 Sept. 1858, Brougham correspondence, University College London Library.

[7] *CIFP*, NS 1 (1858), 386.

[8] For further commentary, see E. F. Bleiler, Introduction to the Dover edn. of Reynolds, *Wagner* (1846–7; reprint edn. New York, 1975), pp. xv–xvi; *The Mysteries of London* was published by Vickers in weekly penny numbers and monthly sixpenny parts; *The Mysteries of the Court of London* was similarly published by Dicks and excerpted in the *Miscellany*: see, e.g. *RM* 5 (1850), 300.

and the folly of trying to live beyond one's means and station in life; another example, a story of thwarted love and tragic death, was intended to show the reader 'the valuelessness of every personal grace and accomplishment' if passion and temper are 'allowed to run riot with the will'; and still another 'romance', with the intriguing title 'Scandal', charted the path to madness taken by a beautiful and charming young woman who was regrettably prone to frivolity and indulgence in scandalous gossip, the behavioural aspects of her real vice—idleness.[9]

With the three magazines' fiction and non-fiction alike so blatant in their promotion of civilized and civilizing values, there was not much need for further clarification through illustration, and indeed many non-fictional items and short fictional pieces had no accompanying pictorial material. Where illustration was added, it had little to do but provide general reinforcement for the textual messages. For instance, portraits of deserving individuals usually accompanied biographies extolling their subjects' individual virtues and achievements in the interest of civilized society.[10] In another kind of example, the *Journal* ran an engraving entitled 'The Ruined Family', which showed a homeless mother, father, and three children all bearing the sartorial traces of one-time gentility, but now brought down by what the adjacent essay referred to as 'the evil effects of drinking'. The following issue continued the theme with a series of illustrations by Cruikshank and commentary by the *Journal* contributor R. S. Mackenzie, both of which traced another family's descent into degradation via 'The Bottle'.[11] Additionally, in all three magazines the illustration of fiction echoed the texts' social and moral messages with sympathetic renderings of the tribulations and triumphs of virtuous factory-girls and their like, compelling images of other worthy characters who prosper both economically and emotionally, and equally graphic pictures of the villains, wastrels, and drunkards who meet different, deservedly unpleasant fates.[12]

In rare instances the imagery and discourse of fine art also helped to promote civilizing values and behaviour. Apart from any other

[9] 'The Dower Debt', *LJ* 7 (1848), 261–4; 'The Lost Pearl', ibid. 245–8; 'Scandal', ibid. 54–5.

[10] See e.g. the illustrated biography of Lord Brougham, *CIFP*, NS 3 (1859), 232; and for additional examples, *LJ* 21 (1855), 149; *RM* 24 (1860), 59; and *CIFP* NS 1 (1858), 385–6.

[11] *LJ* 6 (1847), 161 and 180–1.

[12] See, e.g. *LJ* 5 (1847), 65 and 111; *RM* 3 (1849), 249; and *CIFP* , NS 2 (1858): 321.

effect, the most notable example of this sort might well have induced a sense of *déjà vu* in some older readers of the *Journal*. In 1848 it ran a short essay on a work of art once reproduced in the *Penny Magazine*: the morning-after scene from *Marriage à la Mode*. Here, a decade and a half later, was art criticism in the grand style of the earlier magazine—a verbatim denunciation of 'withering satiety', 'poison in the cup', and 'the ruin which has overwhelmed thousands'.[13] But, in contrast to the *Penny Magazine*'s version, the *Journal*'s illustration of this 'useful lecture on morality' signalled art's regained exclusivism: the engraving provided was a fold-out supplement available only to regular subscribers.

With or without an accompanying reproduction, however, the above case was something of an anomaly. Generally speaking, the bland examples of genre painting and the trivial commentary that were most characteristic of the three magazines' treatment of art had little power to convey or even reinforce civilizing values—their cultural content was simply too sparse.[14] This is not, however, to imply that there no longer existed a prevalent belief in the capacity of fine art to elevate the viewer. This tradition had in fact persisted and by mid-century had developed an industrial variant. That is, amongst the many reformers, writers, social critics, and others who considered the matter, it was not from exposure to the old masterpieces of painting and sculpture that the working class would most benefit. Rather, for their own moral and aesthetic development, and the wider good of preserving social stability and improving English manufactures, working people ought to learn more about the principles of design and their practical application to the production of household objects and so-called 'minor' art forms—woven goods, brass work, silver plate, china, and the like. For, as one of its proponents argued, such education would have 'an Economic, a Moral, and a Social value, for, it tends to increase production, it produces healthy feelings of content, and it renders men disinclined to disturb Law and Order'.[15]

[13] *LJ* 6 (1848), 301.

[14] *Cassell's Family Paper*, though, may provide a few exceptions. As its title indicated, it was a strong, self-styled advocate of the ideal of stable family life, and it thus may be argued that pictures like *The Grandfather's Watch* embodied a cultural message which reiterated that ideal.

[15] W. C. Taylor, 'On the Cultivation of Taste in the Operative Classes', *Art Journal*, 11 (1849), 4; and see also Clive Ashwin, *Art Education: Documents and Policies, 1768–1975* (London, 1975), 11–13, 18–21, and *passim*; J. W. Ross, Preface,

The *Journal*, *Miscellany*, and *Paper* also embraced the cause of practical design education and incorporated numerous discussions and engravings of tapestry screens and chair covers, silver celery bowls, porcelain jugs and salt-cellars, glass vases, brass door-knockers, and cast-iron boot-scrapers.[16] The illustration of a silver wine-cooler in figure 34 is typical of its kind and, additionally, inspired the author of the accompanying article to interject a moralizing word or two about the dangers of intemperance. But the major concern of this and other such articles was to disseminate knowledge about design and so aid the progress of English manufacturing.

In texts of this sort and their associated pictures there was undoubtedly a connoted message. For, in emphasizing design and its applications over painting and sculpture, the three new magazines helped to validate the prevailing view that there were two kinds of aesthetic experience: for the privileged, the history, theory, and imagery of fine art; and for the people, the principles and exemplars of practical design. The refrain of the *Journal*, *Miscellany*, and *Paper* was thus a variation on the old *Penny-Magazine* theme of improvement through art. Only now it had become a culturally depleted, if still somewhat familiar, chorus: work hard; improve yourself; learn design skills; increase English productivity—in short, be civilized according to your station.

While thus encouraging artisans and factory-workers to cultivate social virtue through practical design, the three magazines also managed to provide guidance for what was perhaps an even larger group—their female readers.[17] As mentioned earlier, the *Journal*, *Miscellany*, and *Paper* regularly included many items directed specifically toward women. Combined with other, general-interest content, this material too had its embedded social and moral values to impart. And, if civilized social virtue was a desirable trait in the

Universal Decorator, NS 1 (1860), n.p.; the evidence of various witnesses before the Select Committee on Arts and Manufactures, 1835–6, *Report*, vol. 5, 391 ff.; 415, item 500; 417, items 582–3; 465, item 1195; 475, items 1354–6; and vol. 9.1: 157 ff., items 334–8, 348, and *passim*; 'Reports and Documents of the State and Progress of the Head and Branch Schools of Design', *Report of the Select Committee on Industrial Design*, 1851, vol. 43, pp. 419 ff.

[16] See, e.g. *LJ* 7 (1848), 13, 57, 133; *RM* 14 (1855), 120; and *CIFP* 2 (1855), 208 and 376.

[17] There are no comparative figures that break down the magazines' circulation by occupation, age, sex, and so on. However, as Chap. 5 will show, other kinds of evidence allow for the speculation that a majority of readers may well have been female.

34. Silver-gilt casket and wine-cooler, *London Journal*, 1853

35. Portrait of a Reynolds heroine, *Reynolds's Miscellany*, 1850

readership at large, it was even more particularly a female imperative. Amongst numerous contributors to all three magazines there was a consensus that women should be patient and forbearing, gentle and nurturing, cheerful and temperate, dutiful and hard-working. Beyond all this, it need hardly be said, the ideal woman was as innocent of mind as she was pure in body. For, as more than one writer was apt to point out, 'woman's true beauty' lay in her ability to embody at once both social and sexual virtue.[18]

But at the same time as they enthused over this lofty and somewhat abstract ideal of female beauty, these and other writers energetically promoted a more earthbound and physical notion of beauty in women. For this, moreover, the suggested criteria were often uncompromisingly explicit. In the view of one expert, for example, the essential elements of female attractiveness were long and luxuriant hair, a 'speaking eye', 'even and well set rows of teeth', a delicate hand, 'finely-rounded arms', and a 'well-formed figure'. And, concluded this aesthetic tyrant, only these particular attributes 'constitute physical beauty, and nothing less than these deserves the name'.[19] Not everyone was quite so dogmatic, however, and many contributors not only acknowledged that physical beauty admitted some variation, but that 'artificial means of enhancement' were also permissible. The three magazines were full of long and short items, fashion reports and illustrations, and 'notices to correspondents', all of which advised readers on their dress, hair-styles, complexion, and figures. On this last subject there was general agreement, and most authorities considered a well-rounded shape to be a particularly important female asset. The *Miscellany* especially upheld this view and Reynolds and other contributors were inclined to dwell lovingly on 'undulating roundness and softness', 'voluptuous fullness', and 'heaving bosoms'—and, as figures 25 and 26 show, the latter had a tendency to spill generously out of the attire of agitated heroines.[20]

In short, in their overall textual and pictorial portrayal of women, the *Journal*, *Miscellany*, and *Paper* presented their female readers with a restrictive and essentially contradictory ideal image of them-

[18] See, among many other such examples, *LJ* 1 (1845), 53; 3 (1846), 235; and 21 (1855), 255; *RM* 14 (1855), 120, 174, 189, 197, and 376; and *CIFP* 2 (1855), 163.

[19] *LJ* 8 (1849), 322–4. For a generally confused, but occasionally perceptive, attempt to situate 19th cent. ideas of physical beauty in a wide cultural context, see Arthur Marwick, *Beauty in History* (London, 1988), chaps. 5 and 6.

[20] See e.g. *RM* 1 (1846), 54–5; and 1 (1847), 262; see also Margaret Dalziel *Popular Fiction One Hundred Years Ago* (London, 1957), 37–8.

selves. On the one hand, they were to epitomize the 'true beauty' of goodness; on the other, the lesser but culturally as highly valued beauty of face and form. More paradoxically still, the ideal woman was also to be at once sexually virtuous *and* sexually attractive. The serialized stories that contributed so much to the magazines' sales were replete with the fictional embodiments of this contradictory image. Once again the most compelling examples come from the *Miscellany*: there was the hard-working but exceptionally pretty seamstress; the equally industrious factory-girl whose innocent attractiveness drew the unwelcome attentions of more than one manufacturer with 'a lustful eye'; and, from a different social sphere, there was Lady Ellen, who was not only captivatingly beautiful, but so highly virtuous that the mere thought of dining with a morally suspect individual caused her to grow pale as death and fall into an artistic swoon with hair attractively disarranged and breasts pointing provocatively upwards.[21] But perhaps most arresting of all was the young woman pictured in figure 35, the heroine of Reynolds's *Mysteries of the Court of London*. As the accompanying text informed the reader, 'the annexed portrait is that of Louisa, the personification of virtue, innocence and every good quality'. It is of course possible that viewers saw Louisa's virtue reflected in her speaking eyes. But presumably they also would not have failed to take in the meticulously artless curls, exquisite gown, and, not least of all, a figure so pneumatic as to verge on deformity.

We do not have far to look to account at least in part for Louisa and her like. If the three magazines are any guide, then the fundamental dualities of the feminine ideal—goodness and beauty, innocence and sexual attractiveness—were high qualifications for that one thing which all women, regardless of class, were to desire and, if possible, attain. This was marriage, or, more precisely, a glossy version of it. For while the magazines denied most of its variegated reality, not to mention how individual women felt about that reality, they were none the less effusive in their view that marriage was the natural destiny, occupation, expectation, and reward of all but the most unworthy of women. The altar was of course the fate that awaited most good and beautiful heroines in the fiction of Reynolds, Smith,

[21] *RM* 3 (1849), 249; 4 (1850), 146–7 and *passim*; and 10 (1853), 65–6; see also *LJ* 5 (1847), 282 ff. and *passim*; 7 (1848), 5; 8 (1849), 346–7; and 32 (1860), 737; and *CIFP* NS 1 (1858), 214–15, 235; NS 2 (1858), 172, 186; for similar non-fictional examples, see *RM* 3 (1849), 40 and 248; and 14 (1855), 57.

Egan, and other contributors. Meanwhile, on the assumption that a similar happy ending was the lot of most real-life women, essays and poems on female virtue tended to conflate womanly and wifely: a good woman was also, or inevitably would be, a good wife.[22] Other items focused on the less romantic and idealistic side of marriage and simply urged women to develop their practical domestic skills.[23] And there were undoubtedly powerful genetic and social reasons for encouraging women in this way. For, as one authority explained it, women lacked men's superior 'faculty of reason' and were therefore 'out of place in the pulpit, at the bar, in the senate, or in the profession chair', while men conversely were 'out of place engaged in the drudgery of the kitchen, or in superintending the management of domestic affairs'. To suppose otherwise, he argued, would be to 'subvert the intentions of nature, and introduce disorder into the social system'.[24] This point of view together with the magazines' image of women was consistent with the social outlook embodied in their other kinds of content. So, in the pictures and texts that both treated and addressed women, there was an underlying message, the gender-specific version of an old familiar tune: work hard; improve your domestic skills; aspire to matrimony; be good but also good-looking—in other words, be properly, femininely civilized.

Thus, through their representation of women, through the discussion and illustration of practical design, through fiction and its illustration, and through various other miscellaneous items and images, the *Journal*, *Miscellany*, and *Paper* found ways to reiterate and foster an already widely current set of socially conservative values. As previous discussion has indicated, it is fairly clear that

[22] See e.g. *LJ* 1 (1845), 53; *RM* 14 (1855), 174; *CIFP* 2 (1855), 163; and see also Sally Mitchell, 'The Forgotten Woman of the Period', in M. Vicinus (ed.), *A Widening Sphere* (Bloomington, Ind., 1977), 51; Judith Rowbotham, *Good Girls Make Good Wives: Guidance for Girls in Victorian Fiction* (Oxford, 1989).

[23] See the numerous recipes, needlework patterns, and household hints, *LJ*, *RM*, and *CIFP*, *passim*; and see also *RM* 14 (1855), 189, on the need for better female education in domestic economy.

[24] John Dix, 'On the Comparative Intellectual Power of the Sexes', *LJ* 5 (1847), 40. There was an important class dimension to this issue of marriage and women's place. For middle-class women, a materially comfortable marriage was in a sense a job or career substitute—or, put another way, the only vocation open to most women. But for the many working-class young women who had to face a cycle of poverty, household drudgery, and work outside the home, the greatest aspiration would have been to marry comfortably enough not to have to work at a job—a hope encouraged by the great number of fictional stories whose theme was that good and beautiful girls might marry upwards.

such values were integrally bound up with a network of social and economic power relations, some based on class differences, others more purely on gender.

II

It would be unproductive to take our recognition of class inequality too far and thus misinterpret the three magazines' civilizing messages as instances of attempted social control through the popular press. There is no evidence that Stiff, Reynolds, Cassell, and others involved in the magazines' production were motivated by class fears for the stability of society. Stiff appears to have been a single-minded man of business, while Reynolds, we will recall, was a spokesman for Chartism, and Cassell, once a labourer himself, dedicated his efforts to the advancement, not the repression, of the working class. But even so it must be remembered that, whatever their beginnings, those who edited, operated, and wrote for the magazines enjoyed significantly more social and economic power than did the majority of their readers. Thus the material that they produced cannot be altogether divorced from the interests and perceptions of those in positions of privilege and leadership. In other words, as was the case with the *Penny Magazine*, the *Journal*, *Miscellany*, and *Paper* were amongst those cultural forms whose embedded values helped to maintain the authority and status of the economically and socially powerful. But the transmission and acceptance of these values did not occur through some process of imposition from above, but rather through the active consent of those who purchased, read, and looked at the magazines.[25] This, after all, is little more than a matter of common sense, for the magazines' large numbers of readers were such by choice, and the commercial success of the *Journal* and its two main competitors could only have been founded on a consensus of approval for their content. As Cassell pointed out to the parliamentary committee investigating newspaper stamps, those who read the *Paper* and like publications had no taste for condescending 'twaddle', but they did want 'freshness, vigour of thought, *and moral sentiment*'.[26]

[25] Here again the argument relies upon Gramsci: see n. 2 above and Introduction, n. 9.

[26] Cassell, Evidence given before the Select Committee on Newspaper Stamps, 16 May 1851, *Report*, vol. 17, 215, item 1322; and see also item 1325. The emphasis on the last phrase is mine.

Certainly the three magazines gave them all of that—and more. For, in comparison to the *Penny Magazine*, its successors more conspicuously offered their working-class readers values at least in part opposed to those of social conservatism.[27] That is, in addition to the kind of moralistic, socializing content described above, the magazines also included material that showed another view of reality or, in varying ways and degrees, represented the interests of workers and others in subordinate social and economic positions. This applies particularly to the *Journal*, which took an explicit stand on the matter and assured its readers that 'wherever we have allowed an undercurrent of political bias to agitate the surface of our columns', that tendency had been and would continue to be in favour of 'the real sinews of society'—'the industrious classes'.[28]

As a sampling from 1848 reveals, in line with its avowed position, the *Journal* took note of its readers' enthusiasm for a series of articles on the French Revolution, responded to their requests for more of the same, and launched two further pro-Gallic, pro-populist series, one on 'the grandest and most interesting features of the glorious popular outbreak of 1830', the other on the French Revolution of 1848, but spiced with references and comparisons to English Chartism.[29] In August of the same year it serialized *Gideon Giles the Roper*, the story of a poor man's 'struggles to obtain a living' written by a one-time working man, Thomas Miller; and at various times in the period sampled it ran items with such topical themes as the advantages of emigration and the need to reduce the hours in a working day.[30] A particularly striking instance of its treatment of current social issues was an indignant report on 'Destitution in the Metropolis', which condemned the 'shocking state' of several London workhouses. To drive home its point, the report included a number of illustrations. One of these was for emphasis by way of contrast and pictured a Literary Association ball on behalf of Poland. Set against this

[27] According to Gramsci, hegemony can only operate effectively to the degree that it is able to accommodate opposing class interests and values. For further comment and explanation, see Tony Bennett, 'Popular Culture and the Turn to Gramsci', in T. Bennett, C. Mercer, and J. Woollacott (eds.), *Popular Culture and Social Relations* (Milton Keynes, 1986), pp. xiv–xv.

[28] 'Address to Readers,' *LJ* 3 (1846), 16.

[29] See the announcement, *LJ* 7 (1848), 80; and for examples of the articles, ibid. 97–100, and 129–32.

[30] Ibid. 221, 345 ff.; 8 (1848), 23; and see also Louis James, 'The Trouble with Betsy', in J. Shattock and M. Wolff (eds.), *The Victorian Periodical Press* (Leicester, 1982), 364; and Mitchell, 'Forgotten Woman', 33.

sumptuous scene with its well-dressed people, chandelier, statuary, and richly ornamented walls, the adjacent images became all the more tellingly graphic in their depiction of the overcrowding, bleakness, and misery of the East and West London Unions and Gray's Inn Workhouse (figure 36). It was perhaps no accident that the illustration showing the East London Union included a poster advertising Charles Cochrane's new *Poor Man's Guardian*, for there was a shade of that paper's crusading spirit in the *Journal*'s images and account of 'parochial abuses of power, more especially the huddling of the poor together like sheep'.[31]

The *Miscellany* and *Paper* did not generally engage in such straightforward social reportage. But they none the less offered their readers occasional alternatives to their predominant view of social virtue: for instance, items empathizing with the hardships of poverty, stories of workers and their troubles, portraits and accounts of reformers and radicals, and Reynolds's series of 'Letters to the Industrious Classes', in which he championed working people's right to improved education, political expression, and material well-being.[32] Sometimes, as a *London Journal* engraving from the *Mysteries of London* shows, even the illustration of fiction acknowledged that the hard-working and virtuous did not always end their days in middle-class comfort—let alone the lavish interiors of Gothic romance. For here instead was the image of abject poverty: huddled by an inadequate fire, 'The Aged Pauper'—an elderly woman with haggard face, tattered though much-mended clothing, and mismatched shoes—partakes of her meagre meal in a room no better than a squalid cell (figure 37).

But while the pauper woman represented an alternative view of social reality in one sense, in another she remained a personification of an entrenched outlook. For, according to the poem beneath her picture, until age and poverty took their toll, she had conformed well to the magazines' conventional female image: she had been an industrious worker, loving wife, happy mother, and, before all of that, an attractive enough girl to have been 'crowned the village-queen'.[33] The prevalence of this kind of image, and the fact that it

[31] *LJ* 6 (1848), 412–13.

[32] See e.g. *RM* 14 (1855), 200; *CIFP* NS 1 (1858), 46; *The Factory Girl*, *RM* 3 (1849); *The Seamstress* and *The Mysteries of the People, or, the History of a Proletarian Family*, both in *RM*, 4 (1850); *CIFP* NS 1 (1857), 10; portrait of Feargus O'Connor, *RM* 2 (1847): 305; and 'Letter to the Industrious Classes', *RM* 1 (1846), 199.

[33] *LJ* 1 (1845), 253.

36. Contrasting scenes from a charity ball and London workhouses, *London Journal*, 1848

37. Pauper woman, *London Journal*, 1845

can be identified in material whose main theme is not woman and her role, together suggest how we might structure our understanding of the portrayal of women in the three magazines. It seems that the female image they promoted was one of those informal cultural mechanisms through which were enacted power relations based, first of all, specifically on sexual difference, and only secondarily and incidentally on social and economic inequalities.[34]

To recognize the unequal nature of the power relations of gender is not to imply that the female image was simply inflicted upon women. For they, like so many others of the populace at large, chose to buy, and to keep on buying, the new magazines. Without doubt, this ongoing act signalled their generalized consent to the female image purveyed. But the returns on such consent were vast—for a conventionalized and restrictive ideal of themselves was only one aspect of all the information, entertainment, and sustaining escapism that women could now enjoy on an equal basis with men. For the time, this was no small gain: in their negotiations with the cultural representatives of authority, women had bargained well.

To their general gain, they could add one further concession. For the three magazines occasionally countered their usual female image with material that presented a somewhat less conventional view of women and their lives. For instance, in Reynolds's 1847 serial, *Wagner, the Wehr-Wolf*, the heroine, Nisida (figure 26), distinguished herself by her carefree abandonment of the ideal of chastity—and, moreover, she came to no worse end than old age, at which time she died peacefully and, we suspect, only mildly repentant. Other fictional heroines may have been less sexually liberated than Nisida, but they none the less showed exceptional enterprise, not to mention sartorial revolutionism, when they donned male disguise in order to facilitate some daring and suspenseful exploit.[35]

[34] In theoretical terms, we might describe the exercise of the power relations of sexual difference as gender hegemony, a hybrid of Gramsci's more generalized concept of hegemony. Gramsci himself appears to have recognized the possibility of gender hegemony but did not articulate it as a developed theory. He acknowledged, for instance, that uneven power relations existed among strata of one class, but did not explicitly relate this to gender. Elsewhere he expressed a rudimentary sense of the kind of contradictory female image identified here, noting that 'the "aesthetic" ideal of woman oscillates between the conceptions of "brood mare" and of "dolly"': Antonio Gramsci, *Selections from the Prison Notebooks*, ed. and trans. Quintin Hoare and Geoffrey Nowell Smith (London, 1971; reprint edn., 1986), 295 ff., 300, and see also 306.

[35] *Wagner* was serialized in *RM* 1 (1846 and the first few months of 1847); for

But not all alternative female images came from fiction. In one of its 1855 issues the *Paper* ran a large, showy engraving in which a composed-looking young woman, known as Mademoiselle Borelli the 'Beast-Tamer', efficiently held at bay several large lions, all fixed in attitudes of domestic cat-like docility—a symbolic reversal of the usual male-female power relationship. This did not pass unnoticed by the regrettably anonymous commentator who observed that 'the lions are her servants and feel her to be their mistress . . . Mmlle Borelli is prominent by the calmness of her attitude and the energy of her will'.[36] Both she and her career, though, were decidedly unusual.

The theatrical stage offered a less exotic but still of course uncommon way to bypass conventional domesticity. Large portraits and accompanying biographies of singers and actresses were a recurrent feature in each of the three magazines, but especially in the *Journal*. And, in contrast to the stereotypically dubious reputation of theatrical women, they invariably got 'good press'. A case in point is the biographical discussion and portrait of the actress 'Mrs Keeley' (figure 38). The text emphasized its subject's talent and career successes, while the accompanying picture showed a calm, pleasant-looking woman of perhaps young middle age, with normal figure development and, to quote the text, 'countenance intelligent'—all in all, a refreshing contrast to the artistically swooning Lady Ellen and the vapid, misshapen Louisa.[37]

Mrs Keeley, however, and other such alternative images were comparatively rare. Where they did occur, they were never quite free of the more conventional and restrictive image of virtue, domesticity, and beauty. Even *Wagner*'s Nisida, if not virtuous, was at least ravishingly beautiful. Mademoiselle Borelli was also a beauty and there was in addition no reason to doubt her virtue. The women who donned men's clothing somehow managed to be intrepid, yet properly gentle and mild; and of course when at last they emerged from their temporary male guise, they were always stunningly, femininely beautiful. With the exception of Mrs Keeley, whose appearance was apparently uncommonly distinctive, actresses and singers were usually accorded the description 'beautiful', and all in fact do look

commentary on Nisida, see Dalziel, *Popular Fiction*, 39. For the woman-in-male-disguise motif, see *RM* 3 (1849), 41; and *LJ* 5 (1847), 245.

[36] *CIFP* 2 (1855), 53.

[37] 'Mrs Keeley', *LJ* 7 (1848), 353; for other examples, see ibid. 273; and 6 (1848), 305.

LONDON JOURNAL;

And Weekly Record of Literature, Science, and Art.

1. Vol. VII.] FOR THE WEEK ENDING AUGUST 12, 1848. [Price One Penny.

MRS. KEELEY.

ris lady is the oldest daughter of a most re-table family residing in one of the eastern coun- and at a very early age exhibited that strong ilection for the stage which has since matured f into excellence in the peculiar line to which talent has been directed. The natural bias of Goward's inclination was not discouraged by friends; and when, therefore, she had arrived at t might have been considered the attractive t, she was introduced to a Thespian corps then ibiting in the Norwich circuit. In this company her youthful talent and lively disposition ensured her warm friends and much encouragement, and her success with the public was immediate and decisive. As a necessary consequence, an introduction to the metropolitan boards quickly followed the report of her provincial triumphs.

Miss Goward, then in her sixteenth year only, made her *début* at the Lyceum Theatre on Saturday, the 2nd of July, 1825, in the character of *Rosina*, in the favourite opera of that name. A novelty is at all times a powerful attraction to theatrical critics, and when it is presented in the person of a young and interesting female, it becomes doubly so. The celebrity Miss Goward had earned in her provincial engagement had been loudly echoed among the stage whispers of the Green Room in the London houses, and the public was gratified and delighted by the conviction that the report of the youthful *débutante's* merit had not "o'erstepped the modesty of truth." Her appearance was interesting—her countenance intelligent and pleasing, though, perhaps, not such as to warrant the term beautiful. Her *début* was marked with that irresistible charm of unaffected timidity which, in a young actress, never fails to awaken the better sympathies of even the most

38. Portrait of an actress, Mrs Keeley, *London Journal*, 1848

conventionally attractive in their pictures. Moreover, possibly because the three magazines advertised themselves as family publications, those who wrote the accounts of actresses and singers were always at pains to gloss over any real-life peccadilloes and present their subjects as women who never allowed their choice of career to compromise seriously either their obligatory female virtue or their social and biological destiny. Mrs Keeley for one was not only the blameless pride of a 'most respectable' county family, but was also the fond mother of two daughters—the issue of her legal and virtuous union with Mr Keeley.

Thus, for all that the *Journal*, *Miscellany*, and *Paper* might sometimes have shown women possibilities different from those within their own experience, the view was always limited by a generalized, not necessarily fully articulated, nor even conscious, perception of where authority would seemingly always rest. As one male writer, more enlightened than many, had declared with apparent sincerity: '[women have] an intelligence equal to our own . . . They deserve, therefore, the full enjoyment of every privilege that *it is in our power to confer on them.*'[38] A similarly limited vision structured the three magazines' forays into political commentary and social criticism. So, in general, the best that they could offer to counter the values of the status quo were empathy or compassion for the plight of the deprived or abused. There was little in the way of enlightened analysis of, or outright protest against, the unequal distribution of power that lay at the heart of social injustice.[39]

These, though, are criticisms from a present perspective; and, while it is important to make them, they should not distract us completely from a simpler approach to the lived past. To that end we need only remember that, whatever their shortcomings, the *Journal*, *Miscellany*, and *Paper* brought a high level of entertainment and escapism into lives that only a short time before had felt the want of such comforts. And if the popular experience of imagery was now much further removed from the Academy exhibition room than it had been just fifteen years earlier, that was not perhaps a matter of much concern to a majority of working people. For while their pictorial life had been depleted in one direction, along the lines of social and economic inequality, it had otherwise enriched and expanded itself. It

[38] *RM* 14 (1855), 120. The emphasis on the last clause is mine.
[39] Mitchell, 'Forgotten Woman', 50, has made a similar observation.

was not just practical design and the images of pots and boot-scrapers that had replaced affordable, high-quality, fine art reproduction —*The Dying Gladiator* had also given way to needlework patterns and game boards, fashion and war illustration, images of the theatrical world and its players, and, above all, to the teeming life and lines of the engraved illustration of popular fiction.

Of the readers and viewers who participated in and helped to shape this expanded pictorial experience only fragments of evidence remain. We can now do no more than repeat a few words, pick out a response or two, from all the vast number of individuals who chose to buy, read, and look at the second generation of pictorial miscellanies. Still, it is clear that these individuals made up a diverse group, a new kind of cultural formation which had begun with the readers of the *Penny Magazine*. They were together a social cross-section of women and men, the poor and the comparatively prosperous, the literate and the unlettered, the young and the not so, the middle and the working classes—they were, in a word, the mass.

5

The Printed Image and the Mass: The Illustrated Magazines and their Readership

1832–1860

BY the mid-1850s, Saturday afternoons were predictably busy in the shops and at the stands of those who sold popular magazines. For to mark the end of a week's work 'there now rushed in the schoolboy, the apprentice, the milliner, the factory girl, the clerk, and the small shopkeeper'—all intent on paying their pennies for the latest issues of the *London Journal*, *Reynolds's Miscellany*, and *Cassell's Paper*.

The commentator who had noted this weekend 'rush' was Charles Knight. As we would expect from one who was no merely casual observer of publishing trends, his was a fairly accurate and complete assessment of the range of people who read and looked at the new pictorial miscellanies.[1] Other contemporary observers also remarked upon the readership of these magazines and, like Knight, were of the opinion that the *Journal* and its two main competitors attracted a wide following among the 'lower middle and working classes'.[2] But it is not from such contemporary commentary that we gain our clearest sense of these readers. For that we need to turn to the magazines themselves and the pages containing their editorial correspondence.[3]

Before pursuing this source, though, a cautionary word or two is

[1] Charles Knight, *The Old Printer and the Modern Press* (London, 1854), 264. In the same passage, he also mentioned the non-pictorial *Family Herald*, whose 1855 circulation of 240,000–300,000 was indeed comparable to those of the *Journal*, *Miscellany*, and *Paper*. Chap. 6 will pursue the significance of the *Herald* somewhat further. For the circulation figures cited here and their sources, see R. D. Altick, *The English Common Reader* (Chicago and London, 1957), 394.

[2] 'Cheap Literature', *British Quarterly Review* 29 (1859), 329, 332, 344–5; and F. Hitchman, 'Penny Press', *Eclectic Magazine*, June 1881, 841.

[3] In its first issue of 1 Mar. 1845, the *Journal* announced its intention to have a regular page or two of 'Notices to Correspondents' and invited readers to send in

necessary, for the magazines' correspondents are by no means as accessible as we would wish. None of their letters survive in the original, nor were they reproduced in the magazines. All that we now have are the often cryptic printed replies addressed to individuals identified only by their place of residence, first names, sets of initials, or pseudonyms. As we will see, a few of these pseudonyms are telling, but others—'A Constant Reader', 'A Subscriber', 'A Sincere Admirer', and the like—reveal nothing about the correspondents' social class, sex, or age. To add to our difficulties, there are a host of terse and enigmatic replies that allow for no inference about the interest or query that they answered: 'Of course', 'He may', 'We cannot inform you', and so on.

The question of the authenticity of the correspondence is also of some concern. That is, it may well be that those who answered readers' letters occasionally filled space with made-up replies to non-existent queries—or, worse, perhaps there were no correspondents at all, only fabricated answers.[4] But to adopt this view is to be overly sceptical, for all three magazines offer evidence that they did indeed attract a good deal of genuine correspondence. For example, at the end of most if not all issues, care was taken to provide potential correspondents with correct addresses and detailed instructions on directing specialized questions about chess or gardening to the proper respondents. In addition, it is possible to find frequent, sincerely fraught-sounding notices to the effect that letter-writers should stop sending their efforts to the 'private residence' of 'Mr. Reynolds' or 'Mr. Cassell' and address them instead to the appropriate office. Still other such notices begged correspondents to cease demanding immediate responses when the volume of their letters made two or three weeks the inevitable wait for a printed reply. Then there was

their comments and queries. The other two magazines followed this lead when they commenced, and the correspondence section remained a regular feature in all three publications throughout the period considered here.

[4] Whether or not the 'Notices to Correspondents' were genuine, we do not have much of an idea who wrote them. With typical bombast, the *Journal*, 1 (1845), 16, announced that 'several writers, eminent in literature, science, and art' would answer readers' queries: Anne Humpherys, 'G. W. M. Reynolds: Popular Literature and Popular Politics', in J. Wiener (ed.), *Innovators and Preachers* (New York, 1985), 16, argues convincingly that Reynolds, with some assistance from others, wrote most of the *Miscellany*'s replies; similarly, in the first years of the *Paper*'s operation, Tillotson handled its editorial correspondence: T. Frost, *Forty Years' Recollections* (London, 1880), 233; afterwards, presumably, Cassell as editor supervised this aspect of the publication.

also the noteworthy occasion when the *Miscellany* was forced to admit to the loss of all of the mail for 15 December 1849, and to request that any who may have written around that time re-submit their letters.[5] Taken together, all of this seems to represent disproportionate effort merely to authenticate spurious correspondence—after all, the magazine's editors and staff had every right to compose such letters if they wished. It thus seems probable that the notices to correspondents were genuine replies to real letters. But if they were not, or if legitimate answers were occasionally spiced with an interspersed fabrication or two, we still have a useful source here—for even faked replies could at least give us a sense of the kinds of readers that the magazines' producers expected to attract. And that in itself would be valuable, for as the magazines' success argues, Stiff, Reynolds, and Cassell were all well aware of where their market lay. In other words, those that they expected to reach and those that they did reach were not vastly different.

I

Bearing in mind, then, their limitations and drawbacks, we can now see what remains to be inferred from the magazines' correspondence pages.[6] First of all, many of the pseudonyms are not as ambiguous as those noted above. One group of correspondents, for example, chose to identify themselves by the types of work that they did. From this we can gather that those who wrote to and, by extension, all of those who read the magazines came from several social, occupational, and economic levels—with perhaps a majority comprising clerks, shopkeepers, and the more prosperous strata of the working class.[7] The

[5] *RM* 3 (1849), 415; for the other examples mentioned, see *RM* 13 (1854), 15; *LJ* 3 (1846), 416; and 28 (1858), 192; *CIFP*, NS 1 (1858), 144.

[6] This section of the discussion is based upon the following sampling of correspondence pages: *LJ* 1 (1845), 208; 3 (1846), 416; and 4 (1846), 192; *RM* 1 (1847), 336; 2 (1847), 64 and 304; 3 (1849), 48 and 415; 4 (1850), 143, and 5 (1850), 303–4; *CIFP* 4 (1857), 7, 23, 31, 39, and 55; NS 1 (1858), 16 and 144; and NS 3 (1859), 224. The overall character of the readership does not appear to have significantly altered over the period covered here. There seem, however, to have been shifts in the proportion of categories of readers. For example, women correspondents were more in evidence in the late 1850s than they were earlier, which suggests that the female sector of the readership was larger than it had been in the 1840s.

[7] For a similar assessment of the readership of the *Journal*, see Sally Mitchell, 'The Forgotten Woman of the Period: Penny Weekly Family Magazines of the 1840s and 1850s', in M. Vicinus (ed.), *A Widening Sphere* (Bloomington, Ind., 1977), 33–4.

readership in general does not seem to have taken in more than a scant number, if any, of those in high-status professions—such as law or the Church—nor does it appear to have included many whose incomes were much beyond moderate.

Thus at the most genteel end of the scale of significant groups of readers were schoolmasters—none of whom gave details as to where or what they taught. Their number was exceeded by the many others who were law clerks, civil servants in clerical positions, or simply undifferentiated clerks or junior clerks. Then there were all of those who aspired to such positions. Among these hopefuls was one Frank Mildmay, but, sadly for his ambition, the *Miscellany*'s respondent informed him dampeningly that his 'handwriting should be clearer for a clerk's situation'. The unnamed keepers of unspecified shops constituted another conspicuous group of correspondents, to whose number we might also add the several who identified themselves as drapers or publicans, and the occasional milliner and confectioner who also had concerns to express. Still others indicated that they were in one of two kinds of service: a few soldiers wrote in, although none gave his rank or regiment; and from time to time those in domestic service sent in their queries; there was, for instance, the manservant seeking a change of scene and a new situation as valet to some ship's captain, and the dairymaid who, for reasons unexplained, wanted to know how to make Bologna sausages.

Apart from servants, the magazines' correspondents took in various other members of the working class. Letters signed 'An Apprentice' were particularly abundant, and most were queries about the terms of their authors' indentures or complaints about their treatment at the hands of their masters. One writer 'suffered' from a want of proper instruction and supervision in the workplace, while another justifiably felt 'discarded' because without his consent he had been assigned by one master to another. Others had managed to survive the trials of apprenticeship, and the magazines' correspondents also included a journeyman tailor or two, several mechanics, a few hand-loom weavers, the occasional carpenter, and a brassfounder. Finally, there were the many who signed themselves simply 'A Working Man' or 'A Labourer'.

Women also contributed their share to the magazines' correspondence pages. A few we know by pseudonyms that suggest their occupations—'A Housekeeper', 'A Milk Maid', 'A Mother'—but most went by first name. Among those who sent in their queries were several Annies, Janes, Kates, and Fannies, a few Claras, Rosas, Louisas, and Sophias, as well as Catherine, Laura, Matilda, Adeline, and Angela. This range of names from the humble Annies to the elegant Angela suggests that these women correspondents came from more than one social class—although it must be remembered that some names might have been fictitious (expressions perhaps of wishful thinking).

Amongst readers of both sexes—in cases, that is, where we can establish gender—there was widespread anxiety over complexion problems, notably blushing, and questions relating to courtship and appropriate behaviour with the opposite sex. From all of this we might gather that many of those who read and wrote into the magazines were adolescents or young adults—an impression which is confirmed by numerous pseudonyms such as 'A Juvenile Subscriber', 'A Young Grammarian', 'A Youth of Fifteen', and 'A Young Girl'. In addition there were all of those apprentices mentioned above and a number of women who candidly admitted to ages in the range of 18 to 23.

About other correspondents whose age and sex are not obvious (although sometimes inferable) we can gather different kinds of information. A few, for example, used pseudonyms that signalled the direction of their political leanings: 'A True Republican', 'A Tory', 'A Democratic Socialist', 'A Chartist'; regrettably, though, none of these writers were forthcoming about their income or occupation. One or two others, such as 'A Protestant', indicated their religious tendencies, but on the whole the letters do not reflect any generalized interest in doctrinal issues. Still other correspondents, by the nature of their queries, indicated that theirs was a comparatively prosperous lifestyle. For, presumably, in order to want hints on removing scratches from varnished tables and dressers, or cleaning stains from carpets, correspondents must have owned such items—although it remains possible that some of these enquiries were made by servants for the benefit of their employers' furnishings. But if a few at least of the writers enjoyed an adequate level of material comfort, others apparently did not. The numerous queries about how to emigrate and pseudonyms such as 'Poor but Industrious', 'A Destitute Orphan', 'A Poor Carpenter', 'A Poor Weaver', 'A Poor Man', and 'A Starving Workman' together suggest that many who troubled to submit their questions were anything but well-off. Finally, from yet a different set of correspondents, we gain a sense of the geographical diffuseness of the magazines' readership. For, to help differentiate their replies to those designated only by initials, the magazines' editors helpfully added a bracketed reference to the writers' place of residence. Thus we find reflected in their correspondence the whole sphere of the magazines' distribution, as readers wrote in from all over London, from Manchester, Birmingham, Newcastle upon Tyne, Liverpool, Salford, Nottingham, and Preston, from Oxford, from Dublin, from Paisley, Dundee, Glasgow, and Edinburgh, and from countless small towns and villages all around Great Britain.

Regardless of where they came from, whatever their sex, age, occupation, or income, a significant number of the magazines' correspondents were overridingly concerned with self-improvement. Some wished to better themselves vocationally and wrote to find out how to obtain a certain job or what form of education would enhance their qualifications. Many more, though, sought intellectual improvement for its own sake, and the magazines' correspondence pages are replete with replies to all manner of questions. What is the climate of Egypt? Or the value of a Queen Anne farthing? How do they manufacture gunpowder? And matches? And electroplate? Where can you acquire an inexpensive home library? Learn English composition? Or French grammar? How do you pronounce 'sauerkraut'? When was Socrates born? And so on.

Where they identified themselves according to their work, the authors of these and other such questions ranged along the occupational spectrum from clerks to labourers. Only one group appeared to participate with less than the generalized enthusiasm in this spirit of enquiry: schoolmasters, not too surprisingly, were more interested in imparting information of their own or correcting the errors of others. In the sampling used here, the youngest writer in pursuit of information was a 12-year old boy who wanted to know about silkworms and Charlemagne. Others, judging by their occupations, were adults, but there is nothing to suggest their exact ages. It seems safe to assume, though, that those who sought intellectual improvement were of various ages. Many, it is clear, were male, but many others failed to leave clues about gender. Some of these, presumably, were women who shared all the widespread interest in acquiring general knowledge. For, as a member of the *Journal*'s staff told a certain Helen B., who wished to further her schooling, 'Young ladies are apt scholars.'

Other correspondents were not of course so avowedly intent on intellectual self-improvement, and wrote in instead for advice on health problems and patent medicines, legal difficulties, and romantic or domestic relationships. But whatever were their specific interests or questions, those who troubled to send letters to the three magazines were clearly a varied lot. Thus the correspondence pages sampled here both support and elaborate Knight's and others' impression that the *Journal*, *Miscellany*, and *Paper* attracted readers from a large cross-section of society.

This was not, however, a brand-new achievement. For such a socially diverse cultural grouping—the mass—had initially formed itself around the *Penny Magazine*.[8] Although it had never included correspondence pages, the magazine did attract at least a few letters, usually addressed to some representative of its nominal sponsor, the Society for the Diffusion of Useful Knowledge. From this correspondence we begin to gain a sense of the different kinds of people and interests that this then pioneering publication served. J. B. Tenniel, illustrator of Carroll's Alice books, enjoyed it as a young man; an aspiring drawing master also 'gave unfeigned thanks that such a publication should have been circulated'; one Adam Pele, a baker, also perused it with close, although not always uncritical attention; an amateur horticulturist apparently liked it, but wanted more articles on gardening; a Welshman was impressed with its positive effect on 'this uncultivated and illiterate part of the kingdom'; and a young father valued the magazine so highly that he

> laid it by for the use, and instruction of, my infant son (if it please God to spare him) when he arrives at Riper Years . . . [This] I conceive of more real value than a paltry annuity for life that might be squandered away; but the contents of the Penny Magazine when once read and treasured up in the mind can never be lost.[9]

From the general contents of their letters, most of the above correspondents would seem to have been fairly comfortably-off, and we can probably situate them somewhere within the middle class. As their names indicate, all were men, although we will subsequently see

[8] For related commentary, see Jon P. Klancher, *The Making of English Reading Audiences, 1790–1832* (Madison, Wis., 1987): 77 ff.

[9] Tenniel to Thomas Coates, SDUK secretary, 15 Jan. 1841; James Greenwood to the SDUK publication committee, 27 Nov. 1837; A. Pele to the editors of the magazine, 1833; Charles Jacomb to SDUK member J. W. Lubbock, 17 Apr. 1832; W. Johnson to Coates, 1834; and the long quotation is from Josiah Riddle to the editor, 23 May 1832; all letters cited are in the SDUK archive, University College London Library.

that the magazine may have had at least a small female following. The weight of the evidence from SDUK correspondence and autobiographies indicates that a majority or, at the least, a significant minority of the *Penny Magazine*'s readers were working people. The next section of this chapter will consider this group in some detail. For the time being we need only acknowledge that the readers of the magazine were not exclusively of one sex, locale, or class, but together comprised a large and varied, or mass, market. In the words of one contemporary commentator, the *Penny Magazine* offered amusement 'to every man, woman, and child who takes it up. Its reception is consequently universal.'[10]

The magazine's wide-ranging popularity also came to the notice of another sort of cultural observer, the now anonymous artist who designed two satirical broadsides, published in 1833 by G. Purkess of Soho.[11] Both arranged like a modern page of comic strips, these broadsides regaled their purchasers with an array of humorous images of the *Penny Magazine*'s 'readers': a man who tramples a flower-bed while absorbed in an article on botany; an ancient lady who peers at an essay on antiquities; a large gentleman who consults an item entitled 'The Measurement of Solid Bodies', all the while being fitted for a suit by his tailor; a drunkard, who reads the magazine in a bottle-strewn gutter; the man in the moon, who studies a treatise on astronomy; and many, many more such vignettes. In fact, in the view of the satirist who created these images, so universal was the magazine's appeal that even animals, such as monkeys and owls, liked it. Of this group, perhaps the most interested reader of all was a large pig whom we see about to dip into a weighty essay illustrated with the minuscule image of yet another pig. And the essay's title? 'Bi-hog-raphy, for the Swinish Multitudes'.

II

In taking satirical note of the *Penny Magazine*'s varied following, our broadside artist had not failed to include humorous depictions of a street hawker, a sweep, a farm-labourer, and other working-class readers. As an earlier chapter's discussion indicated, many historians

[10] [Carter Hall?], *New Monthly Magazine*, Aug. 1835, 491. See also Edward Cowper, Evidence given before the Select Committee on Arts and Manufactures, 1836, *Report*, vol. 9.1, pp. 50–1, items 595–7.

[11] Both are in the Bodleian Library's John Johnson Collection, under 'Charles Knight', box 1.

have routinely insisted that the magazine had few, if any, such readers.[12] There is, however, no substantial evidence on which to base such insistence. Rather, almost without exception, what remains of correspondence and autobiographical commentary supports the opposite view that a great number of workers bought, read, looked at, and liked Knight's pioneering attempt to bring culture to the people.

These readers, most of whom we now can no longer identify, obtained the magazine in various ways: some were subscribers; others saved their pennies and purchased issues whenever they could; and a great many others had access to copies distributed in working-class coffee-houses, factories, workshops, and mechanics' institutes.[13] Among the identifiable working-class readers who managed to secure the magazine one way or another we find the radical tailor Francis Place; the factory operative turned poet John Plummer; the Colchester tailor Thomas Carter, who also became a contributor; the warehouse worker and Chartist sympathizer Adam Rushton; and one Richard Sheldon of Hull, 'a labouring man' who had had his 'share of misfortunes' and was 'shortly to be out of employ', but who none the less continued determinedly to read the *Penny Magazine*.[14]

Some who were devotees of the magazine found ways to incorporate its reading into a day's work. For example, a London footman, William Tayler, gave this account of his activities on New Year's Day, 1837:

> I got up at half past seven, cleaned the boys' clothes and knives [and] lamps, got the parlour breakfast, lit my pantry fire, cleared breakfast and washed it away, dressed myself, went to church, came back, got parlour lunch, had my own dinner, sit by the fire and red the Penny Magazine and opned the door when any visitors came.

[12] See Chap. 2, n. 69, above.

[13] See Altick, *Common Reader*, 342 and n. 63; Louis James, *Fiction for the Working Man* (Harmondsworth, 1974), 7; Charles Knight, *Passages of a Working Life*, 3 vols. (London, 1864), ii. 181.

[14] Place to T. Coates, 27 Nov. 1833, with enclosed circular from The Mechanics' Public Library; and Sheldon to Coates, 12 Apr. 1841, SDUK correspondence, University College London Library; John Plummer, *Songs of Labour, with Autobiographical Preface* (London, 1860), pp. xv ff.; Adam Rushton, *My Life as a Farmer's Boy, Factory Lad, Teacher and Preacher* (Manchester, 1909), 70–1 (Rushton later became a Unitarian minister in Manchester); and, for additional commentary on the magazine's readership, see also Altick, *Common Reader*, 335–7, and nn. 44, 49, and 50; Patricia Hollis, *The Pauper Press* (London, 1970), 139; James, *Fiction for the Working Man*, 15; and David Vincent, *Bread, Knowledge and Freedom* (London, 1981), 165 and n. 155.

And another working man, T. B. Clark, wrote this letter to SDUK secretary, Thomas Coates:

Honoured Sir
I hope you will excuse the liberty I am taking in addressing a gentleman of you rank. but Sir I have been a subscriber to the Penny magazine from the first copy to the last and on which I set the greatest value upon it as it comprises the principal portion of my Library and over which I pass away many a midnight hour in my Avocation as a Brickburner.[15]

For most readers, though, the magazine appears to have been part of the self-improvement programme with which they filled what little leisure time they had. This was the case with the Yorkshire stencil painter Christopher Thomson, who was particularly eloquent about the place the magazine held in his life, and the lengths to which he went to keep himself supplied with copies. He began with a description of the difficulties and expense associated with the acquisition of knowledge before that day when Charles Knight

unfurled his paper banners of free trade in letters. The 'Penny Magazine' was published—I borrowed the first volume, and determined to make an effort to possess myself with the second; accordingly, with January, 1833, I determined to discontinue the use of sugar in my tea, hoping that my family would not then feel the sacrifice necessary to buy the book. Since that period, I have expended large sums in books, some of them very costly ones, but I never had one so valuable, as was the second volume of the 'Penny Magazine'; and I looked as anxiously for the issue of the monthly part, as I did for the means of getting a living. I continued to be a subscriber up to the publication of the last number; and albeit, but an unit, out of the ten's of thousand's that have benefited by that work, I feel bound to tender my mite of gratitude to its spirited and enterprising publisher. The 'Penny Magazine' was the first intellectual mile-post put down upon the way-side, wherefrom coming ages may measure their progress towards a commonwealth of books.[16]

It is possible that upon the magazine's demise Thomson and many others of its readers might have become part of the mass who now read the *Journal*, *Miscellany*, and *Paper*. If so, then he did not acknowledge the fact—and nor did anyone else, with the exception of

[15] Diary of W. Tayler, excerpted in John Burnett (ed.), *Useful Toil* (Harmondsworth, 1984), 176; Clark to Coates, 15 Nov. 1842, SDUK correspondence, University College London Library. Peculiarities of spelling, capitalization, and punctuation in these passages have been transcribed as they appear in the originals.
[16] Christopher Thomson, *Autobiography of an Artisan* (London, 1847), 319.

just two of the autobiographers out of the sampling used here. One of these was the East London vellum-binder Frederick Rogers, who remembered that in his 'boyhood's days' he had been fond of the *London Journal*.[17] The other autobiographer was Thomas Burt, a Northumbrian pitman, later Labour MP, and he too recalled the *Journal* from his boyhood:

> When about fourteen years old a comrade lent me a few stray numbers of the *London Journal*, a highly-spiced periodical, which I read with great gusto. It was full of adventures of wild, romantic stories depicting duels and battles, deeds of daring, hairbreadth escapes by land and sea, the heroes being banditti, pirates, robbers and outlaws. This stirred the blood and excited the youthful imagination. When my father caught me reading it he gently chided me for wasting time on such rubbishy stuff. Wretched garbage no doubt it was, yet, after all, perhaps the time given to it was not wholly wasted. No useful information, indeed, was gained, but I was acquiring facility in reading, and laying hold of the golden key which would open to me the rich treasures of a great literature.[18]

In this passage we have a possible clue as to why we find so little autobiographical mention of the *Journal*, *Miscellany*, and *Paper*. Burt, his father, and, indeed, the vast majority of autobiographers belonged to that self-taught, self-improving faction of the working class, most of whom, like Burt's Methodist father, would have considered entertaining miscellanies to be 'time-wasting' and 'rubbishy stuff'. It thus seems quite likely that if any autobiographers had ever read and enjoyed the *Journal* and its like, it would have been a surreptitious affair. For to have admitted to such taste would have been to spoil the generally serious and industrious image in which most of these writers cast themselves. On the other hand, it may simply be that those who wrote their autobiographies genuinely did not care for and therefore did not read the second generation of pictorial miscellanies. But which of the two possibilities was more commonly the case, we will likely never know.

We can, though, recall the three magazines' correspondence pages and all those 'Apprentices', 'Mechanics', and 'Labourers' who wrote in and represented a wider readership of others much like themselves. There thus seems no reason to doubt the contemporary view that these miscellanies had a substantial working-class following. Here and there we get a further glimpse of some of these readers: for

[17] Frederick Rogers, *Labour, Life and Literature* (London, 1913), 118.
[18] Thomas Burt, *An Autobiography* (London, 1924), 114–15.

example, amongst Mayhew's labouring poor of London, there were the costermongers who were 'eager for . . . Reynolds' periodicals' and who would 'after their day's work or their rounds' read, or assemble to hear being read, the latest number of these or other such 'penny publications'. There were too all of those nameless others, in all the working-class districts of all England's urban centres, who regularly visited the shops and stalls and became part of that 'crowd of applicants' for their weekly issues of the *London Journal*, *Reynolds's Miscellany*, and *Cassell's Family Paper*.[19] But for a sense of what these magazines must have meant in many otherwise dreary and hopeless lives there is perhaps no more speaking image than one which comes down to us through Mayhew—a brief description of 'a rheumatic London crossing-sweeper crawling back to his cold, squalid room to pore over a copy of *Reynolds's Miscellany*'.[20]

III

On the basis of much of the evidence cited above, the working-class experience of the *Penny Magazine* and its successors might appear to have been a male prerogative. In fact this was not the case. As we already know from editorial correspondence, the three later miscellanies had an especially visible female readership; and this without doubt included working-class women. Indeed, when Thomas Wright, the 'Journeyman Engineer' and observer of working-class life, commented on 'working men's Saturdays', he was moved to remark that if any man 'has been unfortunate enough to get for a wife a woman who is . . . one of those lazy, lackadaisical *London-Journal*-reading ladies with whom working men are more and more curst, he will have to devote his Saturday afternoons to assisting in the woman's work of his own house'.[21] This observation aside, there is no reason to suspect that the *Journal* and similar publications actually contributed to any serious disruption of the routine or

[19] Henry Mayhew, *London Labour and the London Poor*, 4 vols. (London, 1851; enlarged edn., 1861–2, reprinted, London, 1967), i. 25; Josiah Williamson, examiner of unions, *Report of the Newcastle Commissioners*, 1861, 21: part. 2, 1, 405, cited by Virginia Berridge, 'Popular Journalism and Working Class Attitudes, 1854–1886', Ph.D. diss. (London, 1976), 53–4. Williamson's observation also included the *Family Herald*: see comment, n. 1 above.

[20] Altick, *Common Reader*, 11, citing Mayhew, *London Labour*, ii. 538.

[21] Thomas Wright, *Some Habits and Customs of the Working Classes, By a Journeyman Engineer* (London, 1867), 189.

necessitated the reallocation of weekend chores in most households—rather, as previous discussion has pointed out, the *Journal* and its like did their best to insist on domesticity as a specifically female obligation and virtue. But if Wright exaggerated a bit for effect, he was accurate in his main point that many women found the new pictorial miscellanies to be of absorbing interest. Charles Knight was another one who observed the many women readers of these 'penny journals'; and another contemporary publisher, Henry Vizetelly, noted that factory-girls were the 'great patrons' of the stories of J. F. Smith, which had first appeared in the *Journal* and later in the *Paper*.[22]

It was not necessarily only working-class women who read the new pictorial magazines. As the correspondence pages of the *Journal*, *Miscellany*, and *Paper* show, some women had preoccupations that signalled a style of life that might have been available to some daughters, wives, and sisters of the most prosperous artisans, but was perhaps more likely to have been the experience of those who were born or married into at least the lower levels of the middle class. For example, occasional comments or queries about the finer points of the etiquette of paying calls or taking leave at parties, as well as the occasional writer's claim to having had a boarding-school education, are suggestive (or at least mildly so) of a middle-class way of life.[23] In the majority of the letters from women, though, there are no clear or conclusive signals of social class.

What does come through strongly is a tendency that we have observed amongst the generality of correspondents: the desire to improve. Sometimes it was intellectual improvement that was the object and we can find a few replies to women who had enquired about some facet of history, science, or literature. More commonly, though, the women correspondents defined self-improvement in a restrictive sense that accorded well with the three magazines' female image. Thus, what most correspondents evidently sought was improvement (or, if not that, confirmation of adequacy) in the areas of personal morality, domestic skills, and physical appearance. How far, they wanted to know, could flirtation go before virtue was com-

[22] Knight, *Old Printer*, 284; Henry Vizetelly, *Glances Back through Seventy Years*, 2 vols. (London, 1893), ii. 12.

[23] These examples and the others given in this part of the discussion are from the following sampling of correspondence pages: *LJ* 1 (1845), 208; and 17 (1853), 64 and 256; *RM* 4 (1850), 143; 5 (1850), 303–4; and 10 (1853), 79; *CIFP* 4 (1857), 55, 63, 79, 87, and 119; NS 1 (1858), 144; and NS 3 (1859), 224.

promised? Could one, without impropriety, give a gift to a young man? Or walk home alone from church with him? Then, with these sorts of problems resolved, there came others to take their place. How do you dye wool? Or mend muslin? What is the best method to prepare mutton ham? Rich rice pudding? Vermicelli? Good butter cakes? Ratafia pudding? And tomato ketchup? But, most of all, the correspondents wanted information that would help them improve their appearance. Almost invariably their greatest concern was the state of their complexions and hair. They wanted to know about lotions to prevent wrinkles and remove freckles. They requested 'receipts' for facial cosmetics like elder-flower water and compound of milk and sulphur-flower. They worried that the hair on their heads was too dull, too thin, too short. Conversely, they were even more exercised that the hair on their arms and faces was too dark, too thick, too long. Those who wrote the replies tried their best to help all the unhappily hirsute like 'Poor Polly' and 'Superfluous'. Always, variously expressed, they made the same recommendation: 'we know nothing better than a razor'—a piece of aesthetically disastrous advice that could only have come from a man.

The correspondents' involvement with the magazines' female image of good looks, good behaviour, and good housekeeping found its single most complete expression in one kind of letter that many of them wrote. By the early 1850s the *Journal* and *Miscellany* had begun to print queries from men in search of wives. To take just one example, a young man named Roderick had written to the *Miscellany* with the information that he wished to marry and to that end would like to hear from suitable young ladies. To Roderick and the other men who had made similar requests, there was usually no shortage of replies. Without exception, the young women who answered attempted to demonstrate their suitability by aligning themselves with the magazines' female image. They thus tried to describe to advantage their wifely qualities, domestic capabilities, and, without stretching the truth too far, their physical attractiveness. The reply of one young woman of 23 to Roderick is typical:

> EMMA begs to introduce herself to the notice of 'Roderick.' She is not pretty, but good-looking, with nice black hair, good eyes, good figure, and altogether interesting. She can play on the piano a little, dance, is very domesticated, and has been told would make any kind man an affectionate and dutiful wife.[24]

[24] *RM* 10 (1853), 79; for similar examples, see *LJ* 17 (1853), 64.

Emma's and the other women correspondents' engrossment with their physical appearance and the tendency of this preoccupation to override or intermingle with other interests suggests that they and many other women readers studied closely, and compared themselves unfavourably to, the magazines' images of fashionable ladies, beautiful fictional heroines, and attractive actresses and singers. If so, then we have here an instance of the interaction of readers and imagery. But this is surmise for which there is no direct evidence. Janet Bathgate, the only female autobiographer in the sampling used for this study, did not mention the *Journal*, *Miscellany*, or *Paper* at all—let alone how she felt about or what she did with their illustrations.

We know even less about women's reaction to the *Penny Magazine*. Nor, indeed, can we determine much about the size or character of its female readership. There is no surviving editorial correspondence from women and our lone female autobiographer was as reticent about the earlier magazine as she was about its successors. We do know that the magazine attracted female contributors—the art historian Anna Jameson and Emily Shore, the teenage essayist on natural history.[25] We also know that the latter was a reader before she became a contributor, and possibly the same was true of Anna Jameson. Finally, we can point to items like an essay on corsets and, from such examples, speculate that Knight and those who produced the magazine had a rudimentary sense of directing material towards a female readership.[26] But such gender-specific content is rare in the magazine and we are left wondering whether or not it, or the other more general-interest subjects, attracted a female readership of any significant size.

IV

What remains to be glimpsed of the readers of the *Penny Magazine* and its three successors comes from exclusively male sources. These tell us something about reader interaction with the magazines' illustration and give an inkling of what the printed image meant in the lives of the mass. Unfortunately a great deal must also be left to surmise. This is particularly so when we consider the second generation of pictorial miscellanies. For, although there is no doubt whatsoever that these magazines enjoyed immense popularity, and that

[25] See Chap. 2, n. 16, above.

[26] *PM* 2 (1833), 80.

some of this popularity was due to the attraction of illustration, there is very little direct evidence from readers to this effect. Those who corresponded with the editors were apparently preoccupied with matters other than pictures when they sat down to compose their letters. And the two autobiographers who mention the *Journal* did not record what they thought of its illustrations. Thus, on people's responses to the three later magazines' imagery, we have only two sources of information—one famous, the other nameless.

The first is Robert Louis Stevenson, whose childhood's Saturdays were much taken up with the pursuit of the imagery in *Cassell's Paper*. His parents considered much of this imagery to be unsuitable for youthful consumption, so the young Stevenson was compelled to

> study the windows of the stationers and try to fish out of subsequent woodcuts and their legends the further adventures of my favourites. . . . The experience at least had a great effect on my childhood. This inexpensive pleasure mastered me. Each new Saturday I would go from one newsvendor's window to another's, till I was master of the weekly gallery and had thoroughly digested 'The Baronet Unmasked', 'So and So Approaching the Mysterious House', 'The Discovery of the Dead Body in the Blue Marl Pit', 'Dr. Vargas Removing the Senseless Body of Fair Lilias', and whatever other snatch of unknown story and glimpse of unknown characters that gallery afforded.[27]

But as replete as it is with detail and literary licence, Stevenson's description of his boyish fascination with the illustration in the *Paper* somewhat pales against the energetic enthusiasm with which Mayhew's costermongers approached the imagery in similar penny publications—in this instance, the *Miscellany*:

> 'The costermongers,' said my informant, 'are fond of illustrations. I have known a man what couldn't read, buy a periodical what had an illustration, a little out of the common way perhaps, just that he might learn from someone, who *could* read, what it was all about . . . Look you here, sir,' he continued, turning over a periodical, for he had the number with him, 'here's a portrait of Catherine of Russia. "Tell us about her," said one man to me last night: "read it, what was she?" Now here,' proceeded my friend, 'you see an engraving of a man hung up, burning over a fire, and some costers would go mad if they couldn't learn what he'd been doing, who he was, and all about him. "But about the picture?" they would say, and

[27] R. L. Stevenson, 'Popular Authors', chap. 7 in 'Random Memories and Other Essays', *Works*, Vailima edition (London, 1922), xii. 334–5.

this is a very common question put by them whenever they see an engraving.'[28]

The costermongers' enthusiasm for the imagery of the second generation of pictorial miscellanies was no greater, though, than the similar feelings that the *Penny Magazine*'s illustrations had aroused in others a few years earlier. For working men such as John Plummer and Adam Rushton the magazine's pictures were a gateway to greater knowledge and literacy. The latter remembered 'a rather fine view of the Castle of Chillon, accompanied with . . . lines from Byron' and how he had been inspired to 'learn more about the prisoner, and to read more of the writings of the poet'. Plummer recalled the first time that he had happened upon some stray copies of the *Penny Magazine* 'and other illustrated periodicals of a similar nature': 'No miser ever hugged his gold with a more jealous care, than I did those few old torn and soiled numbers which came into my possession. For hours I would gaze on the woodcuts, and strive to decipher the letterpress descriptions, in which I at last succeeded.'[29] But it was not just those from deprived backgrounds who had been stimulated by the magazine and its illustrations. Austin Dobson, author of studies of Bewick and Hogarth, offered this fond recollection:

It is difficult to understand nowadays what a revelation these . . . representations of far countries and foreign animals, of masterpieces of painting and sculpture, were to middle-class households fifty years ago. The present writer, though he can scarcely go back so far, still remembers with gratitude, that to Mr. Fairholt's careful copies of Hogarth's prints in the old 'Penny Magazine', he is indebted for an enthusiasm which has never since deserted him.[30]

The most detailed account of a reader's response to the magazine's imagery comes from W. B. Rands, who became a successful journalist, poet, and author of children's stories. But at the time of which he wrote Rands was a boy living in the home of his father, an impoverished tradesman with radical political leanings. The senior Rands's politics did not, however, stop him from subscribing to the *Penny Magazine* and thus, as his son put it, bringing 'an image of the mighty world' into a home that had previously been nearly barren of

[28] Mayhew, *London Labour*, i. 25.
[29] Rushton, *Life*, 70–1; Plummer, *Songs*, p. xv.
[30] A. Dobson, *Thomas Bewick and His Pupils* (London, 1884), 173, n. 1.

THE PENNY MAGAZINE

OF THE

Society for the Diffusion of Useful Knowledge.

142.] PUBLISHED EVERY SATURDAY. [June 21, 1834.

BOY EXTRACTING A THORN.

[Boy extracting a Thorn.]

This bronze statue is one of the best preserved among the monuments of Grecian art which have descended to our own times. It stood, many ages since, in the Roman capitol, and has been the subject of many tales, not only without foundation, but which the noble and simple style of the figure prove to be erroneously dated.

Vol. III. 2 H

39. *Boy Extracting a Thorn*, *Penny Magazine*, 1834

books and pictures. While his father enjoyed illustrations of cathedrals and foreign lands, the young Rands was drawn irresistibly to the reproductions of art. He 'pored over woodcuts from Raffaelle and Hogarth', 'doted on' the image of a statue of Apollo, and dreamed about the Belvedere Diana.[31] And he discovered in himself profound aesthetic feeling when he studied the image reproduced in figure 39: 'It did me unspeakable good to be familiarized with the human body as an object of beauty . . . There was a picture of the well-known lad extracting a thorn from his foot; and . . . [this] figure used to haunt me day and night with its beauty'.[32] Finally, we will give this same writer a few words more on the *Penny Magazine*. For from one simple statement we can gather fully the high position which that magazine held both in the affections and the home libraries of Rands and, we can presume, a great many others: 'I read my Penny Magazine all day and put it under my pillow at night, when I had not got a Bible or hymn-book there'.[33]

From this and other commentary on the *Penny Magazine*, from the correspondence pages of its three successors, and from the other scattered sources used here, one central fact persistently emerges. The *Journal*, the *Miscellany*, the *Paper*, and, indeed, their more serious predecessor all had much that was new, informative, and entertaining to offer those who had previously lacked ready and affordable access to such material—or such imagery. People in great number thus chose to buy, to read, and to look at these magazines. They chose, that is, to gather themselves into a socially diverse cultural formation of women and men, the youthful and the mature, the middle and the working classes. It was in this sense that the mass made itself. Working people had played a large part in this process, and they would continue to participate actively in the new culture that they and others had created.

[31] 'An Irreconcileable' [W. B. Rands], 'The Penny Magazine', *St. Pauls Magazine*, 12 (1873), 544–7.
[32] Ibid. 547.
[33] Ibid. 545.

6

The Transformation of Popular Culture: Working People in an Expanding Pictorial World

1832–1860

IN 1840 a commentator on the 'popular literature of the day' offered readers of the *British and Foreign Review* 'a collection of statistical notes' on the magazines and journals that then circulated amongst working people 'to an extent undreamed of' only a decade earlier:

> Seventy-eight weekly periodicals are enumerated, of which nearly two-thirds are issued at the price of one penny, none exceeding twopence: twenty-eight of these are devoted to miscellaneous matter; seven to more political subjects; fifteen to the publication of novels, romances and tales; sixteen to biography of celebrated individuals; four to scientific intelligence; three to drama; two to medicine; two are collections of songs, and one registers the progress of the Temperance cause. More than two-thirds of these have the attraction of illustrations.[1]

By 1859 such material had so greatly proliferated that our much-quoted contributor to the *British Quarterly Review* was moved to remark upon what had become a veritable 'flood' of 'cheap literature' and 'tempting' illustrations.[2]

This rapid and unprecedented growth in the number of inexpensive and, by 1840, usually pictorial publications was fundamental in expanding the common cultural experience of working people. And, because the expansion was dramatic, continuing, and wide-reaching in effect, we can with good reason think of it as the transformation of popular culture. The first phase of this transformation had begun in

[1] 'Popular Literature of the Day', *British and Foreign Review*, 10 (1840), 242–3; the *Wellesley Index to Victorian Periodicals* (3: 86, item 188) cites the article but does not identify the author.

[2] 'Cheap Literature', *British Quarterly Review*, 29 (1859), 316 and 329.

the early 1830s with the mass circulation of the *Penny Magazine* and one or two other publications such as the *Saturday Magazine* and the unillustrated *Chambers' Journal*. By 1860, with even higher circulations and wider appeal, the *London Journal*, *Reynolds's Miscellany*, and *Cassell's Paper* had brought this initial phase to its fullest development.[3] Illustrated miscellanies thus formed the nucleus of working peoples' experience of the printed image between 1832 and 1860. But other artefacts and their associated imagery also gained in number and importance during this period; and together with magazine illustration such imagery made up almost the whole of the English worker's expanding pictorial world.[4]

The transformation and expansion of popular culture was not just a matter of an increase in the quantity and kind of information, entertainment, and illustration available to working people. It was also a social shift whereby workers joined a wider cultural formation that was not restricted to a single age-group, gender, or class. As the previous discussion of magazine readership indicated, working people had by mid-century chosen to become part of a larger and more diverse group: the mass. In making this choice they indicated their consent to the conventional social values represented in many mass-circulation books and magazines. Such consent served their own purposes and did not negate developing class differences or the economic, social, and cultural inequalities from which these differences arose. As we will see, by the 1850s the printed imagery both of generalized social and political protest and of an emergent, although not fully formed, working-class consciousness existed side by side within the English worker's expanding pictorial world. Meanwhile that world held increasingly less of the imagery of power, privilege, and high culture: art and its printed reproduction was in rapid retreat from common experience.

[3] The decade or so following 1860 presents us with a different situation. The printed word and image of course remained of great importance to people's expanding cultural experience, but that experience also increasingly took in other forms of popular diversion such as music-hall entertainment.

[4] We should note in passing that this world would also have included the imagery of pavement painting, church interiors, the painted posters of fairs and circuses, theatrical scenery, and a few other such examples. However, as the text indicates, for the majority of working people the most accessible, regular, and reliable source of pictorial experience was the medium of print.

I

In trying to understand the place of the printed image in working people's lives after 1832 we find that our initial model of three kinds of popular experience—entertainment, religion, and radicalism—no longer adequately serves us. Certainly these cultural categories continued to have some bearing on people's lived experience at mid-century. However, in its pictorial forms at least, a transformed popular culture was more complex and multifarious than it had ever been before. Any one of the three main categories might now be divisible into multiple cultural levels, each of which might require separate attention and differing analytical approaches. For example, the kind of illustrated entertainment that from the 1830s proliferated in inexpensive magazines and books had become highly diversified in subject-matter and style, and covered a spectrum ranging from the respectable and moderate to the lurid and sensational. Moreover, the boundaries distinguishing entertainment, religion, and radicalism increasingly blurred as these different cultural categories found expression and intermingled in unpredictable ways in illustrated books and magazines and other forms of printed imagery.

The years after 1832 also saw the increase of types of illustration that tend to defy any effort to assign them conclusively to one of the three categories considered so far. Advertising is a case in point. As we have seen, before 1832 pictorial advertisements were rare enough to divert many an eye and amuse by virtue of novelty. We could thus with some justification situate the imagery of advertising within the popular culture of entertainment. From 1832, though, and especially after 1840, pictorial advertisements became so abundant and varied in content that we cannot with any accuracy label them simply entertainment or, indeed, assign them in entirety to any of the other two categories. It is of course possible that an illustrated playbill advertising a melodrama was in itself a minor form of entertainment; and presumably an advertisement for a book of sermons or a Sunday magazine had something to do with popular religious experience. But what about the increasingly greater number of advertisements for such household goods and personal products as furniture, clocks, and electroplate; and perfume, hair dye, and patent medicines? Certainly these had nothing to do with popular religion, nor likely with radicalism, and compared to an illustrated serial by Reynolds, they could hardly have ranked as entertainment. Rather, it seems that by 1860 advertising and its images were well on the way to becoming a distinct cultural category. The same also appears to have been true of certain other types of imagery: for instance, the illustration of current events, and the inexpensive prints which became widely available from about 1840, and which working people purchased and used to relieve some of the dreariness of their often otherwise comfortless homes.

Taken together, the complexities and confusions noted above indicate that when we consider popular pictorial experience after 1832, the use of a model is likely to be too restrictive and therefore inadequate for meaningful description and analysis. It seems to be more productive simply to acknowledge that the printed imagery which had become a common feature of most working lives was myriad in number, varied in form and content, and representative of several cultural levels, any of which might be present within a single artefact such as a magazine, or even within an individual illustration. Here, then, we can only sample a limited selection of the more commonplace kinds of popular printed image and in passing gather something about the diverse ways that such images reflected and combined with other forms of cultural expression and lived experience.

It seems clear that the bulk of the illustrated printed matter that became affordable and readily available for working-class consumption between 1832 and 1860 was either entertaining in a primarily escapist way, or factually informative but still in some measure diverting. For example, serial fiction belonged to the first group; fashion news, popular biography, and so on to the second. As we have seen, the offerings of the *Journal*, *Miscellany*, and *Paper* covered all, or nearly all, of the possible range of inexpensive pictorial entertainment. But, while these three publications achieved the highest circulations among weekly penny magazines, they by no means had that market all to themselves. Other similar miscellanies—all providing illustrated serial fiction, short stories, sundry anecdotes, poems, and informational items—proliferated from the mid-1840s especially. One such publication, the *Welcome Guest*, 'an illustrated journal of recreative literature', had an 1858 circulation of 120,000; meanwhile other comparable magazines like *Lloyd's Weekly Miscellany* and the *Home Magazine* did well enough to enjoy runs of several years. Their recipe for commercial success was the same as their three largest competitors: a sprinkling of mildly instructive nonfiction, and a generous measure of highly spiced stories and pictures of wronged serving-girls, beautiful and beset heiresses, evil poisoners, corpses, spectres, and chambers of death.[5] Apart from this sort of miscellany, there were also a number of other roughly contemporary weekly magazines that confined themselves to a more restricted range of subject-matter. There were, for example, illustrated magazines of fiction such as the *Weekly Novelist*, as well as several, often short-lived journals and gazettes of humour, horror, or crime with titles like the *Penny Satirist*, *Annals of Crime*, and *Calendar of Horrors*.

Inexpensive novels, many of which had at least one illustration, became widely available from the 1840s. Because they were commonly sold in penny parts, such works were now within the means of a large number of working people. One of the most popular of these was Stowe's *Uncle Tom's Cabin*, published in England in the early 1850s by two dozen or so different publishers. Three working-class autobiographers fondly recalled the story, and one of this group, the son of a Northumberland coal-miner, recorded that in 1852 *Uncle Tom's Cabin* 'was read aloud in our little family circle'.[6] During the 1840s and 1850s the works of Reynolds, Egan, and Smith (published in book form and penny parts as well as in magazines) also found a large readership. Reynolds, it seems, was the most popular of all, with tales such as his sensational *Mysteries of London* (1845) and its sequel, *The Mysteries of the Court of London* (1848–56), which was sold in penny parts and illustrated by Henry Anelay.[7] Charles Dickens was another successful author of this period and many of his works, such as *The Pickwick Papers* and *Nicholas Nickleby*, appeared in illustrated editions. It is uncertain, though, whether or not many working people read these or other stories by Dickens: he is not mentioned in any of the working-class autobiographies in our sampling; in addition, one-time editor for the house of Cassell, Thomas Frost, believed that Dickens did not become popular among

[5] The circulation figure for the *Welcome Guest* is from R. D. Altick, *The English Common Reader* (Chicago and London, 1957), 395; commentary on the content of this and other similar magazines is based on the following sampling: *Home Magazine*, 1–2 (1856–7); *Lloyd's Miscellany*, NS 1 (1850–2); *Welcome Guest*, NS 1 (1861).

[6] Thomas Burt, *An Autobiography* (London, 1924), 116; see also George Elson, *The Last of the Climbing Boys: An Autobiography* (London, 1900), 208–9; and R. Langdon, *The Life of Roger Langdon* (London, 1909), 33; for an illustration from an inexpensive edition of the story, see Victor E. Neuburg, *Popular Literature* (Harmondsworth, 1977), 185.

[7] Montague Summers, *Gothic Bibliography* (London, 1940), 147.

working people until the 1870s. Before then more than a few might well have purchased the cheaply produced and crudely engraved imitations that were about in the 1830s and 1840s: *The Penny Pickwick*, *The Sketchbook by 'Bos'*, *Oliver Twiss*, and *Nickelas Nickelbery*.[8]

If pirated versions of Dickens and the romantic outpourings of Reynolds lacked the uplifting tone and moral purpose of Mrs Stowe's tale of slavery, they none the less demonstrated a modicum of restraint in style and content when compared to another form of saleable fiction: the so-called 'penny dreadful'. The stories contained in examples of this type of small, inexpensive, paper-bound book invariably tended to dwell lovingly on crime, horror, and the seamier side of relations between the sexes. So, naturally, they attracted a substantial following of people in search of pleasurable terror, revulsion, titillation, and general escapism. After all, who but the most dedicatedly serious-minded reader could fail to respond to the lure of titles such as *Ada, the Betrayed, or, The Murder at the Old Smithy*, *The Apparition*, *Crimes of the Aristocracy*, *The Secret of the Grey Turret*, *The Death Ship, or, The Pirate's Bride*, and *Varney the Vampire*, also published as *The Feast of Blood*?[9]

An illustration from an 1847 edition of this last work (figure 40) provides as good an example as any of the kind of imagery that attracted readers with a penny to spend and a taste for the dreadful. Prominent in the centre of the composition is a horrifically bony and toothy vampire (Varney without doubt) whose lips are fastened on to the neck of a young female victim who flails her arms in agony. As she tormentedly arches her back, she thrusts her breasts upwards, thus providing Varney with a convenient place to rest a loving hand while he takes his nourishment. Here indeed was what our expert on 'cheap literature' called a '*pièce de résistance* for the strong stomach of the million.'[10] Astute publishers of such illustrated fiction were well aware of the popular appetite for graphic images of violence and horror. Edward Lloyd, one of the most prominent and successful of the penny dreadful publishers, was purported to have directed his

[8] Thomas Frost, *Forty Years' Recollections* (London, 1880), 323; on imitations of Dickens's works, see Louis James, *Fiction for the Working Man* (Oxford, 1963), 53.

[9] Titles are from the index to the Barry Ono Collection of . . . Bloods and Penny Dreadfuls, British Library. For commentary on this type of material, see W. H. Fraser, *The Coming of the Mass Market* (London, 1981), 225; Peter Haining, *The Penny Dreadful* (London, 1975); Neuburg, *Popular Literature*, 156 ff., *passim*.

[10] 'Cheap Literature', 332.

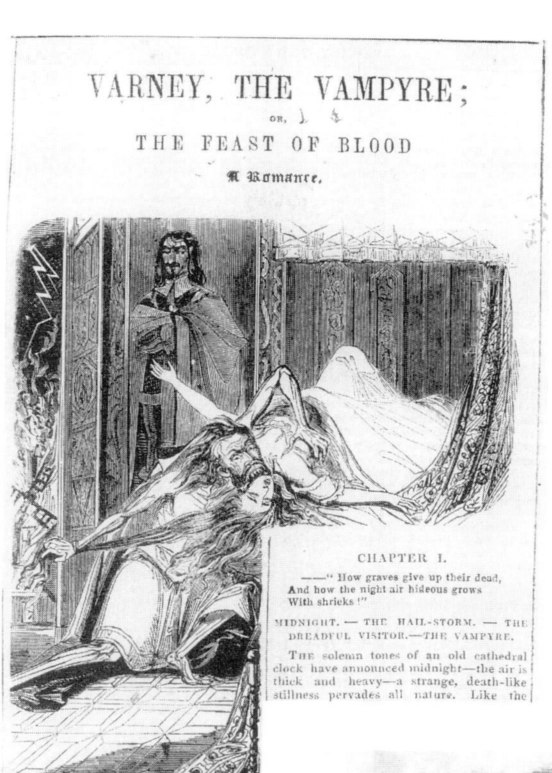

VARNEY, THE VAMPYRE;

OR,

THE FEAST OF BLOOD

A Romance.

CHAPTER I.

——"How graves give up their dead,
And how the night air hideous grows
With shrieks!"

MIDNIGHT.—THE HAIL-STORM.—THE DREADFUL VISITOR.—THE VAMPYRE.

THE solemn tones of an old cathedral clock have announced midnight—the air is thick and heavy—a strange, death-like stillness pervades all nature. Like the

40. Scene from Malcolm Errym's *Varney the Vampire*, 1847

41. The murderer Greenacre and his victim, *Newgate Calendar*, 1845

chief artist to put an extra dollop of saleable 'vigour' into illustrations destined for the dreadfuls. 'There must be more blood—', Lloyd ordered, 'much more blood!'[11]

Blood was not only a staple of tales of supernatural horror, but, as figure 41 shows, it was also a basic ingredient in fictional and fact-based tales of crime. The illustration reproduced here is from one of the many abridgements of that popular anthology of notorious felons and their crimes, the *Newgate Calendar*. Like so many examples of the depiction of crime and horror, this one presented the viewer with a gratifyingly lurid scene of gruesome violence, spiced with the sexual suggestiveness of the murderer's saw and the victim's naked body, which somehow manages to look both nubile and in a state of incipient rigor mortis.[12]

Of all the *Calendar*'s murderers and miscreants, there were no two more renowned than Dick Turpin, the legendary highwayman, and his contemporary, Jack Sheppard, the one-time carpenter's apprentice turned 'housebreaker', who was especially famous for his daring escapes from various places of incarceration—until Newgate and the gibbet finally claimed him. Apart from the *Calendar*'s accounts, an array of pamphlets, penny abridgements, and full-length novels, some cheaply, some handsomely produced—most of them illustrated—provided readers of the 1830s, 1840s, and 1850s with a seemingly endless number of versions of the daring exploits of Turpin and Sheppard. Figures 42 to 46 give some indication of just how pervasive were the mid-century tales and images of these two swash-buckling felons.[13]

With their high popular appeal, Jack Sheppard, Dick Turpin, Varney, and, indeed, all of the villains, heroes, heroines, incidents, events, and imagery associated with entertainment together predominated in the cultural life of the English worker at mid-century. But the transformed popular culture of this period also took in other categories of imagery and experience. As it had in the earlier period, religion and its cultural expressions figured large in many working

[11] 'An Old Printer' [J. Forbes Wilson], *A Few Personal Recollections* (London, 1896), 50.

[12] The *Calendar* was originally published in 1774 and ran to five volumes. The edition from which figure 41 comes was published in 1845 and is typical of the numerous 19th-cent. abridgements that many popular publishers produced. For additional commentary, see Neuburg, *Popular Literature*, 165–7.

[13] The Barry Ono Collection, British Library, contains many such examples.

42. Turpin's ride to York, *Life of Richard Turpin*, 1842

43. Bilking the toll, *Dick Turpin's Ride to York*, 1839

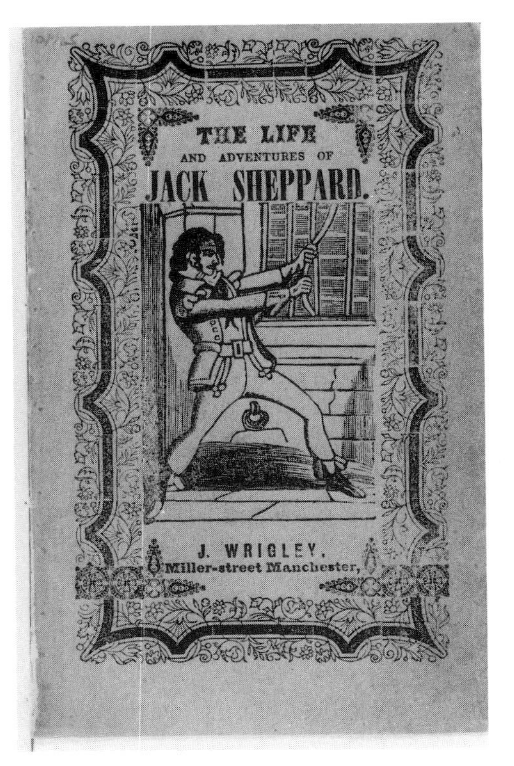

44. Title-page, *Life and Adventures of Jack Sheppard*, *c.*1840

45. Sheppard in Newgate, *History of Jack Sheppard*, 1840

46. Sheppard in Newgate, *Life of Jack Sheppard*, 1840

people's lives.[14] This was reflected in the success of publications such as Charles Knight's *Pictorial Bible* (1835–7, with numerous subsequent editions) and several illustrated religious magazines such as the *Sunday School Penny Magazine* and the *Leisure Hour*, both published in the 1850s. The *Leisure Hour* was a periodical of the Religious Tract Society, which was among those Evangelicals who recognized that religious literature must find a way to match the popular appeal of secular competition like the *London Journal*.[15] The *Leisure Hour* offered its readers fiction, but of a moralistic sort, mildly titillating accounts of idolatry and other heathenish practices in uncivilized corners of the world, pietistic aphorisms, and a generous amount of improving general information. The magazine's layout and style of engravings were reminiscent of the old *Saturday Magazine*, and as a whole the publication has a dated look when compared to the livelier form and content of the *Journal* and its like. However, it apparently pleased a great many readers for, according to John Cassell, the *Leisure Hour* and two other such contemporary religious periodicals enjoyed a combined monthly circulation of 600,000.[16]

For those workers whose creed was self-improvement—both intellectual and moral—a transformed popular culture included a greater number of affordable educational publications. As we have come to expect, many of these had pictures. Cassell was a leader in the field of illustrated educational publishing with his *Working Man's Friend* (1850–51) and the *Popular Educator* (begun in 1852).[17] Both of these penny weekly periodicals were serious-minded publications for the dedicated autodidact: the latter featured series of lessons in science, foreign languages, history, literature, and so forth; the former offered weighty discussions and occasional tiny illustrations of such general-knowledge subjects as the solar system, the wonders of vegetation,

[14] Burt, *Autobiography*, 113; 'An Irreconcileable' [W. B. Rands], 'The Penny Magazine', *St. Pauls Magazine*, 12 (1873), 544.

[15] See e.g. Revd. S. G. Green, *The Working Classes of Great Britain* (London, 1850), chap. 8, on the contemporary religious press. For more extensive discussion of religious periodicals than what is offered here, see Louis Billington, 'The Religious Periodical and Newspaper Press, 1770–1870', in A. J. Lee and Michael Harris (eds.), *The Press in English Society* (London, 1986), 126 ff.; and Margaret Dalziel, *Popular Fiction One Hundred Years Ago* (London, 1957), chap. 6.

[16] Cassell to Brougham, 30 Sept. 1858, Brougham correspondence, University College London Library.

[17] For commentary on these two publications, see S. Nowell-Smith, *The House of Cassell, 1848–1958* (London, 1958), 26–7, 40, 44–8, and *passim*.

Cromwell and his times, Wordsworth, gravity, and the properties of water. Neither publication included fiction, and the *Working Man's Friend* even went so far as to run an essay which, with some force, argued that novels and the reading of them contributed to shallow thinking, immoral tendencies, and the wasting of time and money.[18]

Cassell was by no means alone in his efforts to promote self-improvement and provide workers with inexpensive reading and pictorial matter. Until 1858 when it finally ceased publication, the *Mechanic's Magazine* pursued its aim of instructing and improving its readers; Charles Knight also brought out new editions of some of his earlier classics like the *Pictorial Shakespeare* (1837; 1851), while the *Penny Cyclopedia* and a few other of his educational publications continued to be sold into the 1850s; and many publishers of general fiction and non-fiction produced educational series of one sort or another, textbooks, and manuals of self-instruction in various subjects.[19] Mechanics' institutes also continued to promote the intellectual improvement of working men, and the increased availability of low-cost educational publications, especially after the 1850s, must have eased what had been until as late as the mid-1840s a constant battle to keep members adequately supplied with sufficient fresh material for their continuing intellectual stimulation.[20]

The new educational publications that found their way into working men's associations and into individual hands for private study were replete with articles and anecdotes extolling that set of civilized and civilizing virtues with which we are now well acquainted: self-improvement, thriftiness, hard work, emotional restraint, perseverance, and temperance.[21] The encouragement of the last virtue was of such widespread concern that by the 1850s temperance publi-

[18] *Working Man's Friend*, 2 (1850), 289–93.

[19] For a discussion of one such publisher of general and educational works, see Neuburg, *Popular Literature*, 177–9, on William Milner, who had offices in Halifax and London.

[20] The correspondence of the SDUK includes a number of requests from mechanics' institutes for donations of 'any works tending to forward the cause of knowledge': e.g. the Westminster Mechanics' Institution to SDUK secretary T. Coates, 2 July 1838; and the Finsbury Mutual Instruction Society to Coates, 17 Mar. 1845, SDUK papers, University College London Library.

[21] See e.g. the index to volume 1 of the *Working Man's Friend*, especially the items in the section labelled 'Scraps'; and see also the *Popular Educator* 1/3, with its illustration depicting the enhancing or adverse 'Influence of Morality or Immorality on the Countenance', cited, with the illustration reproduced, in Nowell-Smith, *House of Cassell*, 45–7.

cations constituted a major sub-genre of the literature of improvement. In addition to the myriad pamphlets and tracts in support of the cause, a number of magazines made their appearance in the 1840s and 1850s: among others were Cassell's *Teetotal Times*, the *Weekly Record*, *British Temperance Advocate*, and *Band of Hope Review*. Illustrative material in support of the cause also became fairly common at this time and was not confined solely to the pages of certain temperance publications; we will recall, for instance, that in 1847 the *London Journal* ran a set of illustrations showing the degradation resulting from drunkenness.[22] Cassell, who was throughout his adult life an active and unwavering advocate of temperance, was understandably more ambitious in his pictorial support of the cause. In 1858, as his biographer recounts it,

> He issued a pair of engravings, 16 inches by 24, entitled GIN and WATER, the artist being Kenny Meadows, and it was hoped that these would be hung on the walls of schools, workshops, and cottage houses. 'In the first—GIN—we have the interior of the drunkard's home with a glimpse of the horrors which belong peculiarly to such homes; in the second—WATER—we see how comfort, cleanliness, and peace attend the steps of the temperate man.'[23]

We have no evidence of who actually purchased these engravings, although they appear to have been aimed primarily at working people, and some presumably must have purchased them. Many more must have seen the new temperance magazines, for according to Cassell their 'joint issue' in 1858 was 200,000 to 300,000.[24] He did not specify the precise period of time to which this figure applied, but it is still suggestive that a substantial number of people, workers among them, must have practised, aspired to, or at the very least taken a mild interest in temperance.

As we saw in Chapter 1, for many workers of the late eighteenth and early nineteenth centuries, the cultivation of such civilized virtues as temperance and the quest for intellectual improvement often went with a commitment to some form of social or political protest. After 1832 the same was true of several of our autobiographers, and, presumably, many of their contemporaries also embraced the two sides of radicalism.[25] Certainly, the later period not

[22] See Chap. 4, n. 11, above.

[23] G. H. Pike, *John Cassell* (London, 1894), 115–16.

[24] Cassell to Brougham, 30 Sept. and 8 Oct. 1858, Brougham correspondence, University College London Library.

[25] For example, the radical shoemaker Thomas Cooper pursued intellectual

only saw an increase in the imagery of self-improvement, but also in the pictorial expressions of protest. We will note examples of the latter kind at a further point in the discussion. For the moment, we will continue our survey of working people's widening pictorial world.

By about 1840 that world abounded in a pictorial type which had been comparatively scarce before 1832: the printed imagery of advertising. Advertisers who used the medium of print (rather than painted signboards, for example, or moving displays on horse-drawn vehicles) now increasingly appreciated the value of imagery for enhancing their messages. At mid-century and thereabouts, the majority of printed advertisements were in the form of posted bills and handbills or insertions in magazines and newspapers. In either case, illustration figured often. The firm of Warren's, the Strand, for example, used handbills with a range of images from black cats to portraits of Shakespearian characters, all to advertise their superior brand of boot-blacking. Other advertisers similarly used pictorial bills to promote a variety of household goods, food, patent medicines, and cosmetics.[26] Illustrated theatrical playbills also became common by the late 1830s and, in addition to engravings of dramatic scenes, they often used two or three colours of print to advertise such entertainments as the Dramatic Spectacle of MAZEPPA! and THE WILD HORSE!, the BAZAAR OF WONDERS!!, and a host of other spectacles, romances, comedies, and melodramas—many of the latter taking as their subject the dashing, if not wholly civilized, deeds of Dick Turpin and Jack Sheppard.[27]

Advertising in the press became perhaps even more prevalent than bills from the 1840s. In its later years, even the *Penny Magazine* succumbed to the lure of advertising revenue, and while much of its

enlightenment with the same avidity with which he espoused political causes, and Adam Rushton, the farm and factory worker turned Unitarian minister, was both a Chartist sympathizer and an enthusiast for the *Penny* and *Saturday Magazines*.

[26] For general commentary on advertising at mid-century see J. D. Burn, *Commercial Enterprise and Social Progress* (London, 1858), 46–7; id., *The Language of the Walls* (London, 1855), 3–4 and *passim*; Fraser, *Coming of the Mass Market*, 134 ff.; and Terry Nevett, *Advertising in Britain: A History* (London, 1982), 40–61. For commentary on advertising bills and illustration of examples, see James Cleaver, *History of Graphic Art* (London, 1963), 176; and Michael Twyman, *Printing, 1770–1970* (London, 1970), 11; and for a reproduction of one of the Warren advertisements, see Leslie Shepard, *The History of Street Literature* (Newton Abbot, 1973), 155.

[27] The text's commentary is based upon Playbills 171 and 176A, British Library.

contents might still have dealt in high culture, its wrappers now presented a contrasting study in the mundane, with imagery used to advertise Parr's Life Pills and the like.[28] Similarly the *Journal*, *Miscellany*, and *Paper*, as well as their many imitative competitors, all carried numerous pictorial advertisements, usually grouped together on one or two pages of endpapers.[29] Figure 47 reproduces pictorial examples from an advertising page appended to an 1855 issue of the *Paper*. Regardless of the publications in which they appeared, such pages were markedly similar to one another, and each reflected the variety of imagery that now commonly transmitted the messages of advertising through the medium of the press.

The press was also the medium through which working people began to acquaint themselves with yet another comparatively new pictorial type: the illustration of the news. But even as late as the 1850s this was necessarily a nodding acquaintance, for periodicals such as the *Illustrated London News* and daily newspapers were all well beyond the budgets of working people and, indeed, those of many members of the middle class.[30] The 1840s and 1850s saw the beginnings of a change in this situation with the emergence of penny weekly papers; and such papers further proliferated after the repeal of the newspaper tax in 1855. Of the three most popular mid-century weeklies two—*Reynolds's News* and *News of the World*—were not illustrated. The third, however, *Lloyd's Weekly Newspaper*, offered readers of limited means relatively serious news reporting and illustrations of some of the most important events. The paper's publisher, the same Lloyd who led the penny dreadful market, clearly had a keen eye for what sold: in 1855, at a circulation of about 100,000, his *Weekly* matched the sales of *News of the World* and achieved double those of *Reynolds's News* in the same year.[31] Thus, by 1860, through the enterprise of Lloyd—and, as we will remember, through the occasional publication of war and other current-event illustrations in the *Journal* and *Cassell's Paper*—growing numbers of working people could begin to enlarge their knowledge of the contemporary world through the imagery of the news.

[28] Wrapper, *PM* monthly part 10, Oct. 1841, John Johnson Collection, under 'Charles Knight', box 1, Bodleian Library, Oxford.

[29] See e.g. *Home Magazine*, 1/2 (1856–7), 282–3; *LJ*, 29 (1859), between 384 and 385; and 31 (1860): endpaper.

[30] Richard Cobden to Cassell, 6 Sept. 1850, Add. MS, 43668, British Library.

[31] Altick, *Common Reader*, 394; H. R. Fox Bourne, *English Newspapers*, 2 vols. (London, 1887), ii. 121–2; and see also E. Lloyd, *Papermaking* (London, 1895), 1.

ILLUSTRATED FAMILY PAPER ADVERTISEMENTS.

TO INVALIDS.

COOPER'S DISPENSING ESTABLISHMENT,
26, Oxford Street, London.

THE Preparation of Prescriptions is carried on entirely distinct from the Retail Business. Competent assistants only are engaged; no apprentices are employed. Invalids in the country sending Prescriptions by post, can have Medicines forwarded the same day to any railway station, at prices considerably under the usual charges.—See Cooper's Illustrated Catalogue of Medicine Chests, Enemas, Drugs, etc., forwarded free by post.

MAHOGANY MEDICINE CHESTS for travelling, containing Six Cut-Glass Stoppered Bottles, 14s.; Oak Chests, containing Eleven Stoppered Bottles, 23s.; with every variety for Families, Clergy, and Travellers, at equally moderate prices.

COOPER'S EYE DOUCHE, for bathing the eye, is self-acting and so simple that it may be used by a child. To all who suffer from weak eyes produced by reading, writing, or close application to minute work, it is highly recommended. Price 20s, carriage paid.

IMPROVED LAVEMENT APPARATUS, for administering the whole of the injection at one stroke of the piston, thereby preventing admission of air into the bowels, price 35s. Every other variety at prices from 10s. upwards. Stoppered Bottles in Boxwood Cases, from 1s.

WILLIAM T. COOPER, Pharmaceutical Chemist, 26, Oxford Street, London.

CLEANLINESS

A STOVE most brilliantly Polished in two minutes for less than One Farthing.—W. G. NIXEY'S Registered BLACK LEAD, a new domestic discovery, cannot be wasted, and is a preservative of furniture from the injurious effects of the common article now in use, as it creates no dust, and requires comparatively no labour. Sold throughout the United Kingdom, 1d., 2d., 4d., and 1s boxes.

W. G. NIXEY'S EXTRACT OF FULLER'S EARTH in CRYSTALS, for Softening Water, Clearing and Beautifying Linen, Lawn, Woollen, &c. The want of an article as the above has been long felt by Families who know the trouble of mending, that more destruction to the Clothes is caused in the wash-tub than the wear and tear of actual use. "THE EXTRACT OF FULLER'S EARTH is the quickest and most effective article ever introduced, incapable of injury to the hands or the finest fabric, and requires only to be tried to be appreciated."—*Times, August 11th, 1854.*

Sold by Oilmen, Grocers, and Chemists, in Sample Packets, 6d., or 46s. per cwt. Manufactory, 22, Moor Street, Soho Square. Warehouse, 83, Upper Thames Street.

BEAUTIFUL CLEAN LINEN.

HEAL AND SONS,
ILLUSTRATED CATALOGUE OF BEDSTEADS
SENT FREE BY POST
196 TOTTENHAM COURT ROAD LONDON.

DOES YOUR HAIR FALL OFF? OR IS IT CHANGING GRAY?

IF so, consult MR. TAYLOR, who has made the Diseases of the Hair his Study for 18 Years; and he cautions those who may be suffering from loss of their Hair against using remedies that are advertised; for, as the Hair falls off and changes Gray from a variety of causes, each case requires peculiar treatment. Letters particularly attended to.
19, NEW BOND-STREET.

SLACK'S NICKEL SILVER

IS the hardest and most perfect White Metal ever invented, made into every article for the table, as Cruet Frames, Teapots, Candlesticks.

Per Doz.	Fiddle Pattern.	Strong Fiddle.	Thread Pattern.	King's Pattern.
Tablespoons or Forks	12s and 15s	19s	28s	30s
Dessert do.	10s and 13s	16s	21s	25s
Teaspoons	5s and 6s	8s	11s	12s

A sample Teaspoon sent on receipt of Ten Postage Stamps.

SLACK'S NICKEL ELECTRO-PLATED

Is a coating of Pure Silver over Nickel. A combination of two metals possessing such valuable properties renders it both for appearance and wear equal to sterling silver.

Per Doz.	Fiddle Pattern. £ s. d.	Strong Fiddle. £ s. d.	Thread Pattern. £ s. d.	King's Pattern. £ s. d.
Tablespoons and Forks	1 10 0	2 0 0	2 16 0	3 4 0
Dessert do.	1 0 0	1 10 0	2 0 0	2 6 0
Teaspoons	0 12 0	0 18 0	1 5 6	1 11 6

Slack's Nickel Electro-plated can be had only at 336 Strand.

SLACK'S TABLE CUTLERY

AND FURNISHING IRONMONGERY has been celebrated for nearly 50 years for quality and cheapness. Iron Fenders, 3s 6d; Bronzed Ditto, with standards, 8s 6d to 10s. Fire-irons 2s 6d to 5s 6d. Patent Dish Covers with handles to take off, 18s. the set of six. Table Knives and Forks, 8s per dozen. Roasting Jacks, complete, 7s 6d. Set of Three Trays, 6s 6d. Coal Scuttles, 2s 6d. Metal Teapots, with plated knobs, 5s 6d. Set of Cottage Kitchen Furniture, £3. As the limits of an advertisement will not allow of a detailed list, purchasers are requested to send for their Catalogue, with two hundred drawings, and prices of every requisite for furnishing, at the lowest prices, can be had gratis, or post free. Orders above £2 sent carriage free.

RICHARD and JOHN SLACK, 336, Strand, opposite Somerset House.
(Established nearly Fifty Years.)

CHINA AND GLASS.
J. W. SHARPUS,
49 & 50, Oxford-street, and Portland Bazaar, Langham-place.

These extensive establishments are now filled with thousands of the newest patterns, from the first manufacturers, at moderate prices, and offer advantages to be obtained at no other house in London.

MARION'S RESILIENT BODICE AND CORSALETTO DI MEDICI.

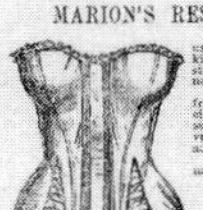

"We think few who have seen it will be disposed to disagree with us, when we assert that it is infinitely superior to anything of the kind yet introduced; it is admirably constructed, and in point of style and workmanship, it is alike unexceptionable."—(Editorial notice in "Le Follet," Journal of Fashion.)

They combine firmness with elasticity, fit closely, fasten easily in front, retain the original symmetry of their adjustment, are judiciously adapted to every varying condition of the female form, and suitable to every age, figure, and habitude. Ladies in health, convalescents, and invalids, wear them with equal satisfaction and advantage.

ENLARGED PROSPECTUS WITH ILLUSTRATIONS, papers for self-measurement, &c., sent post-free to any address.

All Country Orders sent, without extra charge, carriage paid or post free.

MESDAMES MARION AND MAITLAND,
PATENTEES, 11, CONNAUGHT TERRACE, HYDE-PARK.

A CLEAR COMPLEXION.

GODFREY'S EXTRACT OF ELDER FLOWERS

Is strongly recommended for Softening, Improving, Beautifying, and Preserving the Skin, and in giving it a Blooming and Charming Appearance, being at once a most fragrant Perfume and delightful Cosmetic. It will completely remove Tan, Sun-burn, Redness, &c., and by its balsamic and healing qualities, render the skin soft, pliable, and free from dryness, scurf, &c., clear it from every humour, pimple, or eruption; and, by continuing its use only a short time, the skin will become and continue soft and smooth, and the complexion perfectly clear and beautiful.—In the process of Shaving it is invaluable, as it annihilates every pimple, and all roughness, and will afford great comfort if applied to the face during the prevalence of cold easterly winds.

Sold in Bottles, price 2s. 9d., with Directions for using it, by all Medical Vendors and Perfumers.

PLUMBE'S GENUINE ARROW ROOT

SHOULD be used in preference to any other. It is patronised by the most eminent Medical Men in London, being the most nutritious imported. It is extensively used in the families of the Nobility and Gentry; it bears the signature of A. S. PLUMBE, 3, Alie Place, Great Alie Street.

Sold also by Snow, Paternoster Row; Williams, Moorgate Street; Ford, 11, Barnsbury Place, Islington; Morgan, Sloane Street; Medes, Camberwell; Pouit, Hackney; Bromfield, Conduit Street; Greenwell, Queen's Terrace, St. John's Wood; Jefferies, Stoke Newington; and others.

SIGHT and HEARING.—RECONNOITRING GLASSES.
Messrs. S. and B. Solomons, Opticians, 39, Albemarle-street, Piccadilly. Observe, opposite the York Hotel.

BY Her Majesty's Royal Letters Patent, for valuable and extraordinary improvements in the most powerful and brilliant Telescopes, Camp, Race-course, Opera, and Perspective Glasses, to know the distances of objects viewed through them; of great importance to the army, navy, and others. These telescopes possess such extraordinary powers that some three and a-half inches, with an extra eye-piece, will show distinctly Jupiter's moons, Saturn's ring, and the double stars. With the same telescope can be seen a person's countenance three and a-half miles distant, and an object from 16 to 20 miles. For the waistcoat pocket, and are of larger, and all sizes, with increasing powers accordingly. While others, varying from four to six inches, enable us to discover more than the above and the Georgium, with his six satellites, &c.

THE ROYAL EXHIBITION, 1851.—A valuable newly invented very small powerful Waistcoat Pocket Glass, the size of a walnut, by which a person can be seen and known a mile and a-half distant. They answer every purpose on the race-course and Opera houses; country scenery and ships are clearly seen at 12 to 14 miles. They are invaluable for shooting, deer stalking, yachting; to sportsmen, gentlemen, gamekeepers, and tourists. Opera, camp, perspective, and race-course glasses, with wonderful powers. Invaluable preserving spectacle lenses of the greatest transparent power. The great advantage derived from this invention is, that vision becoming impaired is preserved and strengthened, and very aged persons are enabled to employ their sight at the most minute occupation—can see with these lenses of a much less magnifying power, and they do not require the frequent changes to the dangerous effects of further powerful assistance.

DEAFNESS.—NEW DISCOVERY.—The Organic Vibrator, an extraordinarily powerful small newly invented instrument for deafness, entirely different from all others; surpasses anything of the kind that has been, or probably ever can be, produced. Being of the same colour as the skin it is not perceptible. It enables deaf persons to hear distinctly at church and at public assemblies; the unpleasant sensation of singing noises in the ears is entirely removed, and it affords all the assistance that possibly could be desired.—39, Albemarle-street, Piccadilly. Observe—opposite the York Hotel.

PATTERNS SENT FREE PER POST.

SPENCE AND BUCHANAN,
SILK MERCERS & DRAPERS,
77 and 78, ST. PAUL'S CHURCHYARD
LONDON.

RIMMEL'S TOILET VINEGAR

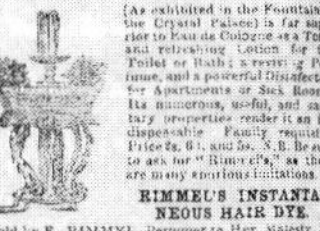

(As exhibited in the Fountain in the Crystal Palace) is far superior to Eau de Cologne as a Tonic and refreshing Lotion for the Toilet or Bath; a reviving Perfume, and a powerful Disinfectant for Apartments or Sick Rooms. Its numerous, useful, and sanitary properties render it an indispensable Family requisite. Price 2s. 6d. and 5s. N.B. Be sure to ask for "Rimmel's," as there are many spurious imitations.

RIMMEL'S INSTANTANEOUS HAIR DYE.

Sold by E. RIMMEL, Perfumer to Her Majesty, 39, Gerrard-street, Soho, London, and at the Crystal Palace, Sydenham; and by all Perfumers and Chemists.

Improvement in Wax Vestas, Patented by R. Letchford and Co.

THE inconvenience in the use of Wax Vestas is the bending of the wick when lighting the match, besides the risk of burning your fingers; this is now obviated by R. Letchford and Co., enclosing in every box of their Vestas (without charge) a Patent Ignitor, which will be found a simple little contrivance for lighting as well as for holding the match when lighted.

Ask for Letchford's Vestas, which are sold by all Chemists, Stationers, &c., in every sort of fancy boxes and japanned tins, from 1d. to 2s. each, including an enclosed Ignitor.

R. LETCHFORD and CO., Wax Vesta Manufacturers, Old Montague Street, Whitechapel, London.

THE TEETH AND BREATH.

ROWLAND'S ODONTO, OR PEARL DENTIFRICE, Compounded of the choicest and most recherché ingredients of the Oriental Herbal, and of inestimable value in PRESERVING and BEAUTIFYING the TEETH, strengthening the Gums, and in rendering the Breath Sweet and Pure. Price 2s. 9d. per box.

CAUTION.—The words ROWLAND'S ODONTO are on the label, and A. ROWLAND and SONS, 20, Hatton Garden, engraved on the Government Stamp affixed on each box. Sold by them and by Chemists and Perfumers.

GUTTA PERCHA TUBING,
FOR WATERING GARDENS, SPREADING LIQUID MANURE, &c. &c.

THE GUTTA PERCHA COMPANY HAVE BEEN FAVOURED WITH THE FOLLOWING

TESTIMONIALS:

From Mr. J. FARRAH, Gardener to BOSWELL MIDDLETON JALLAND, Esq., of Holderness House, near Hull.

I have had 400 feet of your Gutta Percha Tubing (in lengths of 100 feet each, with Union Joint) *in use for the last twelve months for watering these gardens, and I find it to answer better than anything I have yet tried.* The pressure of the water is very considerable, but this has not the slightest effect on the Tubing. I consider this Tubing to be a *most valuable invention for Gardeners,* inasmuch as it enables us to water our gardens in about one-half the time, and with one-half the labour formerly required.

From J. H. ECCLES, Esq., Surgeon, Plymouth.

The Tubing I have found most convenient in watering my garden, and doubt not that it may be substituted for lead pipe in most instances with great advantage, as well on account of its remaining unchanged by the action of acids, &c., as by its power of remaining uninjured by the action of intense cold.

From JAMES KENNEDY, Esq.

Myremill, by Maybole, Ayrshire, May 20th, 1850.

I have received your inquiry as to my experience in the use of Gutta Percha Tubing. I had 350 yards of it from your firm, and I have used it for the last few months in distributing liquid manure from my tanks over my fields, having often a pressure of 300 feet on it; and have been able to get the liquid from the end of the Tubing by the pressure from the steam-engine upwards of 400 yards. I have 350 Scotch acres laid with metal pipes under ground, for the conveyance of Liquid Manures over my farm, and your GUTTA PERCHA TUBING HAS GIVEN ME GREAT FACILITY IN SPREADING IT OVER THE SURFACE OF THE LAND.

I likewise think highly of the GUTTA PERCHA UNION JOINT.

Every variety of GUTTA PERCHA ARTICLES, such as Mill Bands, Tubing, Soles, Goloshes, Sheet, Pump Buckets, Fire Buckets, Bosses, Union Joints, Flask Bottles, Bowls, Chamber Vessels, Toilet Trays, Sponge Bags, Curtain Rings, Galvanic Batteries, Talbotype Trays, &c. &c., Manufactured by the GUTTA PERCHA COMPANY, and Sold by their Wholesale Dealers in Town and Country.

THE GUTTA PERCHA COMPANY, PATENTEES, 18, WHARF ROAD, CITY ROAD, LONDON.

47. Illustrated advertisements, *Cassell's Paper*, 1855

When they were not taking in the news through pictures, or wistfully studying some expensive product in an illustrated advertisement, or losing themselves in the flamboyant world of Jack Sheppard, some working people might well have paused for a few seconds' glance at a picture on the wall of their own small room or cottage. After 1832 this would have been more and more likely a possibility, as inexpensive printed imagery of all kinds and from several sources became widely affordable and available. For example, a working person who wished to relieve a little of the cheerlessness of his or her surroundings might paste a pictorial broadside on the wall, or do the same with an engraving cut from the *Penny Magazine* or any of its illustrated successors. Alternatively, there were also cheap prints of popular actors, society beauties, children, and cats to be had from street sellers. In addition, for only a penny apiece, Cassell offered the *Paper's* readership 'splendid engravings' of subjects of 'national and historic interest'—all executed 'in the first style of art, with the view of contributing to the adornment of the dwellings of the people'.[32]

From what evidence we have, it appears that an interest in adorning the walls of their dwellings was widely shared amongst working people. As we might gather from figure 48, it was not just relatively prosperous artisans in moderately comfortable accommodation, but also people in much humbler circumstances, who made an effort to brighten their walls and turn their surroundings into a home. The room pictured was in one of London's rookeries; the dimensions of this single room, which housed a young couple and their child, were 6 feet wide by 7 long, with a claustrophobic ceiling height of 6½ feet at the highest point; the roof had gaping holes and the walls were 'green and mildewed with damp'.[33] Yet, as the contemporary observer recognized, the room evinced 'a perception of the beautiful', 'a dash of taste', and perhaps, judging by the subject matter of the first two prints, an optimistic hope for brighter and more prosperous times to come:

Above the fireplace are several little prints; one representing two lovers walking on a terrace, overlooking trees and gardens bright in the light of the

[32] CIFP NS 3 (1859), 224. On the sale of prints in the street, see H. Mayhew, *London Labour and the London Poor*, 4 vols. (1851; enlarged edn., 1861–2, reprinted London, 1967), i. 215 and 302–3.

[33] George Godwin, *London Shadows: A Glance at the 'Homes' of the Thousands* (London, 1854), 5.

Fig. 2.—Interior of House in Court.

48. Interior of a working-class home, London, *c.*1854

clear sky: another shows a richly furnished chamber, with a couple of more mature years: there are also some unframed prints of the young royal family, and a row of small beads are festooned in the centre.

The commentator concluded by remarking that 'poor as this place is, it is *still a home*; and there are several thousand of these struggling homes in London'.[34] And indeed there must have been. Evidence from various sources leaves little doubt that life in a comfortless cottage or even the meanest tenement room did not necessarily damp people's enthusiasm for imagery or quash their efforts to make their individual dwellings part of the mid-nineteenth century's expanding pictorial world.[35]

In structuring our understanding of that world as a whole, there are two crucial points to bear in mind. First of all, rapid though it was, the expansion of popular culture and pictorial experience between 1832 and 1860 was not only a matter of change—of the new emerging and the old disappearing. Rather, side by side with all the artefacts of a transformed popular culture—weekly newspapers, pictorial advertisements, mass-circulation magazines, and penny dreadfuls—there remained pictorial survivals with their origins in an earlier popular cultural experience: for example, chapbook-style reissues of such traditional favourites as *Robinson Crusoe*, *Foxe's Martyrs*, and *Pilgrim's Progress*, murder and execution sheets, religious broadsides, and ballad sheets with old stock woodcuts.[36] In other words, the transformation of popular culture did not come about through the repression or wholesale replacement of older cultural forms and experiences. The dynamic was more complex than that, involving continuity as well as change.

It is even more important to remember the second major point about the expanded pictorial world and the culture that it reflected.

[34] Godwin, *London Shadows*, 6.

[35] Ibid. 17; Arthur Armitage, *Heads of the People*, vol. ii, *c.*1846, excerpted in Bernard Denvir, *The Early Nineteenth Century: Art, Design and Society, 1789–1852* (New York, 1984), 247; *Fortnightly Review*, Oct. 1868, commenting on the dwellings of Lancashire factory operatives in the 1840s, ibid. 67–8; P. E. Razell and R. W. Wainwright, (eds.), *The Victorian Working Class: Selections from Letters to the* Morning Chronicle (London, 1973), 167–8 and 198; Robert Roberts, *Life and Opinions* (Cardiff, 1885), excerpted in John Burnett (ed.), *Destiny Obscure* (Harmondsworth, 1984), 183.

[36] For commentary and representative illustrations, see Thomas Gretton, *Murders and Moralities* (London, 1980), figs. 90, 91, 93, pp. 125 and 127; Louis James, *Print and the People* (London, 1976), 155; anon., 'Literature of Labour', *Meliora*, 2 (1860), 4; and Mayhew, *London Labour*, i. 280.

That is, despite the evidence of survivalism, it would be a mistake to regard the transformed popular culture of mid-century as merely an enlarged version of the older culture described in Chapter 1. As our examination of certain of its important pictorial forms has shown, the new culture was not simply the non-élitist lived experience of working people, although it was partly that. More significantly, through the primary agency of wide-circulation magazines like the *Penny Magazine* and its three main successors, a transformed popular culture was increasingly a mass experience. Several magazines and newspapers now regularly reached hundreds of thousands of people; and some successful books, *Uncle Tom's Cabin*, for instance, had initially traded in the tens of thousands, and might in exceptional cases top 1 million in total sales over the course of a year and several editions.[37]

A mass experience entailed more, however, than just high sales and circulation figures, and more even than the great number of people that these figures represented. It is most crucial to remember that the most widely sold artefacts of the new culture reached a social cross-section of people, not just a single definitive group or class of them. We have seen this in our consideration of the readership of the *Penny Magazine* and its three successors, and might reasonably assume that imitative magazines like *Lloyd's Miscellany* drew a similarly diverse market. Additionally, the *Saturday Magazine* reached both the middle and working classes, and this was perhaps true of later religious magazines—although a good deal more research would have to be done before we could pronounce conclusively on this point. Still other kinds of cultural expression also drew a large, mixed—or mass—audience: *Uncle Tom's Cabin* and presumably at least a few other such successful books attracted both middle- and working-class readers. Advertisements in the *London Journal* and other such examples would necessarily have reached the same cross-section as the magazines themselves—although, judging by the cost and kind of most of the wares advertised, it seems likely that the actual purchasers of these goods were mainly middle-class. Finally, we might compare the differences of style, quality, and technique between the illustrations in figures 42 and 43, and among figures 44 to 46. These and other examples not reproduced here indicate a range from simple woodcuts and engravings to detailed, good-quality

[37] Altick, *Common Reader*, 384 and 394–5.

lithographs. From such comparisons we can gather that the publications which these images illustrated varied in cost and hence in readership. Indeed, contemporary sources confirm that at mid-century it was not just working people, but also 'the educated classes [who] were revelling' in the 'picturesque daring' of Jack Sheppard and Dick Turpin.[38]

Of course not all cultural expressions of the time engaged a social cross-section. It is, for example, difficult to believe that a publication like Cassell's *Working Man's Friend* could attract anyone other than a fairly select segment of the working class in search of intellectual improvement. Even so, from 1832 popular experience was dominated by the magazines, books, advertisements, and imagery that spoke to, pictured, and reflected the interests of a range of people of different, ages, sexes, occupations, and classes—that cultural formation which is best characterized by the term 'mass'.

II

In choosing to participate in the new mass experience, working people consented to the civilizing values embedded in many cultural artefacts; in giving such consent they served both their personal need for information and entertainment and their collective interest in acquiring a repertoire of social and cultural values to enhance a developing class identity.[39] We are hardly surprised to find a panoply of social virtues—industriousness, thrift, continence, and so on—promoted in religious, temperance, and other forms of respectable literature. However, as we have seen with the *Journal*, *Miscellany*, and *Paper*, such values also permeated the literature and imagery of entertainment. We find further evidence of this in other similar contemporary magazines. To pick one out of many, *Lloyd's Miscellany* followed the lead of its three competitors and offered 'domestic entertainment and useful knowledge'—both conceived to 'maintain the high majesty of virtue over the turbulence of vice'.[40] Accordingly, in a way that will now be familiar, *Lloyd's Miscellany* clothed civilizing values in the trappings of entertainment, and

[38] Frost, *Forty Years'* 323; and 'Popular Literature', 242, 245–6.

[39] For a useful study of the ways in which one stratum of workers adapted the values of respectability to serve their particular interests, see Geoffrey Crossick, 'The Labour Aristocracy and Its Values', *Victorian Studies*, 19 (Mar. 1976), 301–28.

[40] *Lloyd's Weekly Miscellany*, 1 (1843), Preface.

presented its readership with short, light, often humorous items illustrating the folly of vice; it featured stories of hard drinkers and notorious spendthrifts who come to grief, and paraded an array of heroes and heroines who conversely prosper through hard work, honesty, perseverance, and—in the case of the heroines—beauty and chastity.[41]

At the same time that this and other pictorial magazines were pursuing their useful course of simultaneously entertaining and civilizing the reader, a good deal of penny fiction, some it rather lurid, was following the same path. Once again to choose from many, take Malcolm Errym's *Ada, the Betrayed, or, The Murder at the Old Smithy*: this was a colourful tale replete with accounts and engravings of exciting chases, plentiful corpses, and narrow escapes from fire and sundry attacks by axe, sword, and pistol. In the tradition of the old murder broadsides, we find that villains and murderers are not only bloodthirsty, but also idle, extravagant, and intemperate. As its preface said, *Ada, the Betrayed* sought to ennoble 'good actions' and demonstrate 'the degradation and misery to which vice subjects its possessor'.[42] The *Newgate Calendar* similarly moralized as it sensationalized violence and crime, purporting to serve as a dire warning to all would-be offenders.[43] Finally, it would do to remember that even such a dashing character as Jack Sheppard started his career as an idle apprentice; and, despite all of his glamorized escapades and legendary escapes, he ultimately paid at the gallows for his crimes—and for his want of industry and other civilized virtues.

As we know from earlier discussion, the civilizing values contained in penny fiction, magazines, and other cultural forms could only have been effective through the consent of those at whom such content was often aimed. The most conspicuous way that workers signalled their consent to these values was through their widespread purchase of entertaining miscellanies and the stories of Sheppard, Turpin, and Ada. But, as we will also remember, such consent had to be negotiated. For working people, the return on partaking of socially restrictive values was the benefit of a new, varied, and enlarged cultural experience. This, though, is not to imply that workers had engaged in a straightforward trade-off and chose to tolerate unpalatable values

[41] *Lloyd's Weekly Miscellany*, 5 (1846), and NS 1 (1850–2): The text's commentary is based on a sampling of several representative issues.

[42] Preface to Errym, *Ada, the Betrayed* (London, 1847).

[43] Neuburg, *Popular Literature*, 167.

in exchange for an enriched cultural life. Rather, a brief examination of what we can learn about working people's taste suggests that consent to certain forms of civilizing content was not a matter of toleration or even active acceptance. Often such consent was simply the exercise of long-standing, widespread preference.

By the mid-nineteenth century there had grown up a mythology about the taste of the English worker. It was, or so the myth ran, debased—impure, corrupt, vulgar, prurient, low, ignorant; it took its sustenance from murder, horror, superstition, and 'guilty indulgence'; it was at best desultory, at worst diseased.[44] Now it was certainly true that flamboyant and slightly salacious fiction attracted a large number of working people: in fact we have already seen how largely such fiction was central to the commercial success of the *Journal*, *Miscellany*, and *Paper*. It is probably also true that many workers never read anything but romantic thrillers: Mayhew's costermongers, for example, displayed a fairly consistent taste for stories about girls with names like Venetia, whose distinguishing features were 'glowing cheeks, flashing eyes, and palpitating bosoms', and who invariably landed themselves in situations of torture, imminent rape, or general adversity, any of which eventualities invariably led to distress and *déshabille*.[45]

These qualifications aside, the weight of the evidence is that the myth that all working people shared a uniformly degraded taste was just that—a myth. In actual fact, far from being debased, the taste of some working men was notably rarefied. For example, the weaver Joseph Gutteridge recorded that his favourite books were Gibbon's *Decline and Fall of the Roman Empire*, Volney's *Laws of Nature*, Rollin's *Ancient History*, and Mosheim's *Ecclesiastical History*; and the Northumberland pitman Thomas Burt recalled that among the preferred reading of his circle of Primitive Methodist friends were Paley's *Natural Theology*, Alison's *History of Europe*, and Humboldt's *Cosmos*.[46] As we have previously recognized, working-class autobiographers were an exceptional group, and their taste was

[44] 'Cheap Literature', 330, 337, 339; H. Dixon, 'Literature of the Lower Orders', *Daily News*, 9 Nov. 1847; 'New and Cheap Forms of Popular Literature', *Eclectic Review*, 4th ser., 18 (1845): 76; 'Popular Literature', 242 ff.: this last writer also considered middle-class taste to be equally degraded.

[45] Mayhew, *London Labour*, i. 25.

[46] Burt, *Autobiography*, 105 and 120; Joseph Gutteridge, *Lights and Shadows in the Life of an Artisan*, in V. E. Chancellor (ed.), *Master and Artisan in Victorian England* (London, 1969), 130.

clearly not representative of the whole of their class. But we have other evidence that if many workers' taste was less elevated than that of Gutteridge and Burt, it was still far above the level of debased. For instance, working people crowded into minor theatres and fairground booths to see performances of Shakespeare; according to the 'journeyman engineer' Thomas Wright, they also had a widespread liking for the works of Scott, Byron, and Tennyson; others, like the brick-burner who read the *Penny Magazine*, favoured the sentimental, mildly religious couplets of sundry minor poets; and we have already seen the effort that even the poorest made to beautify their mean surroundings.[47]

What all this implies is that working people's taste cannot properly be understood as uniformly one way or another: it was neither degraded nor lofty—it was both, and more than that. Broadly viewed, working people's taste embraced every conceivable level of cultural expression: literary, lurid, radical, religious, respectable, morbid, moralistic, serious, sensational, salacious, educational, escapist. And this is not merely to suggest that we will find these levels represented only if we look at taste as a cumulative whole, within which any given individual would be all or mostly respectable, or all or mostly raffish, and so on, in his or her preferences. Rather, it is common to find more than one cultural level, often several, embodied in the taste of individual working-class people. We have, for example, the Chartist readers of the politically innocuous *Penny Magazine*; the autodidact who confessed to a taste for almanacs and penny story books; the chimney-sweep who read history books, Shakespeare, *Uncle Tom's Cabin*, the *News of the World*, and 'shoals of tracts and pamphlets upon doctrinal subjects'; the tenant farmer who adorned his walls with the images of a sailing ship (illustrating a ballad about a calamitous storm), the Chartist riots at Newport, and 'two or three small engravings of wonderfully ill-favoured Nonconformist divines'; and, finally, there was the shoemaker Thomas Cooper, whose taste ran the gamut of cultural levels: among other works, he fondly recalled the essays of Lamb and Hazlitt; Goldsmith's histories of England, Greece, and Rome; Byron's *Childe Harold*, Milton's *Paradise Lost*, and Shakespeare's plays; the *London Magazine*, *Quarterly Review*, *Edinburgh Review*, and *Black-*

[47] T. B. Clark to Coates, 15 Nov. 1842, SDUK papers, University College London Library; James, *Print*, 83; Wright, *Some Habits and Customs of the Working Classes By a Journeyman Engineer* (London, 1867), 177.

wood's; *Pilgrim's Progress* and *Robinson Crusoe*; Hone's publications and the Chartist *Northern Star*; and stories about beautiful serving girls, gypsies, and Dick Turpin.[48]

In view of the multifarious nature of working people's individual and collective taste, we begin to see one of the crucial factors that determined the appeal of certain kinds of reading-material at mid-century. It seems that the popularity and hence commercial success of a book or magazine lay in its ability to address and accommodate all or most of the different cultural levels that people's taste might embody at a particular time. In the 1830s the *Penny Magazine* achieved sales of 200,000 because it reflected, responded to, and cultivated people's then overriding taste for serious education leavened with some uplifting moralizing, a little poetry, and here and there some mild humour.[49] As taste changed and people wanted their educational fare spiced with a little fiction, the magazine did not react to this change and by 1845 its circulation had declined to 40,000. Even so, it still far outpaced the circulation figures of publications with a highly particularized focus—the Chartist *Northern Star*, for example, had an 1842 circulation of 12,500.[50]

Meanwhile publications that ran the range of cultural levels, and included entertaining fiction as well as educational and moralistic content, had begun to make their appearance in the field of inexpensive publishing. In sales and circulation figures, these miscellanies eclipsed the *Penny Magazine*. As we know, the *Journal*, *Miscellany*, and *Paper* were foremost among such magazines and had by 1855 achieved respective regular sales of 450,000, 200,000, and 250,000. At the same time, one other equally successful publication also flourished and now warrants mention: the *Family Herald*, like the

[48] T. Cooper, *Life of Thomas Cooper* (London, 1872), 22, 33–6, 52, 65, 179, 228; Elson, *Last of the Climbing Boys*, 208–9; John Plummer, *Songs of Labour, with Autobiographical Preface* (London, 1860), p. xvii; Roberts, *Life*, in Burnett, *Destiny Obscure*, 183; Adam Rushton, *My Life* (Manchester, 1909), 64–9, 70–1; and see also Angus B. Reach, 'The Coffee Houses of London', *New Parley Library*, 2 (1845), 293–4. The notion of multiple cultural levels within the taste of one individual is consistent with the view that the behaviour of any individual worker was not necessarily consistently rowdy or consistently respectable: see Peter Bailey, 'Will the Real Bill Bailey Please Stand Up?: Towards a Role Analysis of Mid-Victorian Working-Class Respectability', *Journal of Social History*, 12 (1978/9), 336–53.

[49] On people's interest in educational reading-material in the early 1830s, see 'Present Taste for Cheap Literature', *Bee* (1833), 9.

[50] All circulation figures cited in this and the following paragraph are from Altick, *Common Reader*, 393–4.

second generation of pictorial miscellanies, offered the familiar winning mix of amusement and instruction, and regularly provided short stories, instalments of serial fiction, poetry, essays on general-knowledge subjects, chess problems, housekeeping hints, cooking advice, and, as one observer described them, 'mild moralizings and pleasant platitudes'.[51] In 1849 the *Herald*'s circulation was 125,000, and by 1855 it had climbed to about 250,000.

There were two significant differences between the *Herald* and its three main rivals. Of these the more obvious one was the fact that the *Herald*, with the exception of its logo, contained no pictorial material. This indicates that, although it was a great selling-point, illustration was not the ultimate determinant of a magazine's success. More fundamental, it seems, was a publication's ability to encompass the variety of cultural levels that both individual and collective taste embodied. This is not to say, though, that illustration could not, or did not, greatly enhance this ability.

We must also take into consideration the other difference between the *Herald* and the *Journal*, *Miscellany*, and *Paper*. Of these four magazines the first was more serious in tone, more overtly respectable and moralistic than its pictorial competitors—a fact that did not escape the notice of contemporary commentators.[52] This suggests that the *Herald*'s readership—presumably a mixed one, somewhat like that which we identified in the previous chapter—might have had a high proportion drawn from the lower middle class, labour aristocracy, and other social strata who energetically pursued respectability; conversely it may not have attracted readers from the lowest social levels. This is speculation only, but it is offered in order to make another, more important point. That is, the *Herald*'s popularity, despite its lack of illustration, should not lead us to underestimate the centrality of imagery in capturing and holding a large audience of the humblest members of society—those, we might add, who were the most likely to be illiterate or only able to read with

[51] Francis Hitchman, 'The Penny Press', *Eclectic Magazine*, June 1881, 841; the text's description of the *Family Herald*'s content is based on the following sampling: 25 Feb. 1843, 4 May 1850, and 13 Jan. 1855; for other information and commentary on the *Family Herald*, see J. G. Bertram, *Some Memories of Books, Authors and Events* (London, 1893), 140; 'An Old Printer', *Recollections*, 16 ff.; and W. A. Smith, *Shepherd Smith, the Universalist* (London, 1892), 222–3, 226 ff., and *passim* (Shepherd Smith was the *Herald*'s first editor).

[52] 'Cheap Literature', 340–1; Charles Knight, *The Old Printer and the Modern Press* (London, 1854), 284.

difficulty. In support of this caution, we need only recall the enthusiasm that Mayhew's costermongers, particularly the illiterate among them, showed for pictures. Would the dense, unillustrated, earnest columns of the *Herald* have done as much as the *Miscellany*'s lively pictures to distract an arthritic sweep from his pain and poverty?[53]

III

In satisfying their collectively and, often, individually eclectic taste with pictorial magazines, or even with the *Herald*'s heavier sustenance, working people had not abandoned either their class interests or the pictorial expressions of such interests. The period between 1832 and 1860 yielded a number of printed images of social and political protest. These images were either produced or likely to have been seen by working people. A few were reiterations or survivals of a social critique that had its origins in the radicalism of the late eighteenth century. We can point, for instance, to the old Tree of Taxation image which recurred in various similar depictions until at least the late 1830s; and occasionally we can find late broadsides protesting over old corruption: in one such example, published in about 1850, the image of a shoemaker hard at work illustrates a ballad protesting at the abuses of the robber lords and 'coroneted vagabonds' who prosper while working people 'are daily starving' (figure 49).[54]

Still other pictorial expressions of the radical tradition can be found occasionally in Owen's *Crisis*, here and there in the Chartist *Northern Star*, and among the 378 illustrations in the *Struggle*, a paper which the weaver-turned-printer Joseph Livesey published in the 1840s to protest against the Corn Laws.[55] An issue of the first-named publication, for example, depicted the image of a lunatic asylum as a symbol of the old, corrupt, unjust ('irrational') society where poverty and madness abound; in contrast, the same page included a visionary image of a model ('rational') community where industry, people, and

[53] See Chap. 5, end of sect. II, above.

[54] For a reproduction of the Tree of Taxation which appeared in the *Northern Liberator*, 1838, see Max Beer, *History of British Socialism* (1919; reprint edn., Nottingham, 1984), 129.

[55] In aligning Owenism and Chartism with an old-style radical social critique, I am following Gareth Stedman Jones, 'Rethinking Chartism', in *Languages of Class* (Cambridge, 1983), 117–27 and 168 ff.

England's going down the Hill.

ENGLAND'S GOING DOWN THE HILL

Tune—" Never push a man going down the Hill."

We talk of England's greatness,
And England's riches rare,
We talk of England's brightness,
And freedom that is there.
But I've been thinking lately,
That she has some faults and ills,
That with all her grandeur stately,
England's going down the hill.

Then never be down-hearted, boys, the rich may have the run,
Your voices raise together, and let's see what's to be done;
We are in a land of plenty, tho' there's plenty starving still,
And that's the reason England, boys, is going down the hill.

The titled lord may rob and steal,
And not be brought to book,
But the poor hard working labourer,
Is not allowed to look;
For stealing of an egg he's sent
Three weeks to tread the mill,
And that's the reason England, boys,
Is going down the hill.

They talk of emigration,
To help the working man,
While coroneted vagabonds,
Have robbed them of their land;
They will not part their riches,
But they want more riches still,
And that's the reason England, boys,
Is going down the hill.

Ye lordlings of Belgravia,
Who on fashions grandeur feast,
Go see the half-starved woman,
Make your shirts a penny a piece;
You are wearing out her life's blood,
And abusing of her skill,
And that's the reason England, boys,
Is going down the hill.

You'll often find in London Streets,
Where poverty abounds,
A man that served his country,
Begging through the town.
They've worn him out, and when he's
He may go where'er he will,
And that's the reason England, bo
Is going down the hill.

They store ill-gotten thousands,
These lords of wealth and rank,
While some are daily starving,
On the doorsteps of the bank.
The weapon of starvation,
Does dozens daily kill,
And that's the reason England, boys,
Is going down the hill.

They talk of revolution,
But that they need not fear,
A man to fight must be well fed,
And we can't get it here.
If they drive us off we'll tell the world,
How we knew no peace until,
We left the starving country,
And England going down the hill.

Some say you've sung of England's faults,
For remedy we call,
Then I say England's large enough,
To find work for us all.
For every Englishman that leaves,
There's two to fill his place,
Of course the end of that will be,
There'll be no English race.

We do not want the workhouse,
But our hard honest crown,
Then don't let foreign countries,
Run our English workmen down,
Set the wheel of trade in motion,
'Twill the workman's pockets fill,
And perhaps some day again we'll say,
She's at the summit of the hill.

W. S. FORTEY, Printer and Publisher, Monmouth Court.

49. 'England's going down the Hill', broadside, *c.*1860

plant life flourish. The *Northern Star* ran images of a similar sort —for instance, the 1846 engraving of the editor Feargus O'Connor's model farm, O'Connorville, 'the people's first estate'.[56] The *Struggle*, as Livesey recalled in his autobiography, relied heavily on the imagery of political satire 'after the fashion of Punch'; but sometimes its pictures were more sombre social critiques, stressing the deprivation of many and articulating the radical notion that the fruits of labour ought to go to labourers. For example, in one illustration a poor family sits down to a meal of potatoes, and in the text underneath, the father says: 'it is a hard case that we who *work most* should be *worst fed*; that a poor man like myself must toil early and late and yet never taste a bit of *beef*, nor *butter*, nor scarcely *bread*'.[57]

Other imagery of the period addressed itself to more specifically contemporary issues: illustrated broadsides, for example, might protest against low wages, unemployment, or the New Poor Law. The last perhaps aroused the greatest bitterness of all. The text of a mid-century broadside captured the cruelty of this 1834 Act which sentenced many to what was effectively imprisonment in the workhouse. In this vignette an official has just relegated a family to a dung cart bound for 'the New Workhouse' and arranged for their disposition on arrival: 'Put the man in 11th cell, and the woman in 394 ward, and take the children to the barn twelve miles from there, and tell them not to let them see each other for once in two years, for we must enforce the rule of the New Poor Law Bill.'[58] The illustration accompanying this grim description of an even bleaker reality appears to have been a stock image and shows only a contextless group of ragged paupers apparently engaged in begging. More graphically to the point were the radical caricatures that appeared in various satirical magazines and representatives of the unstamped press in the 1830s and 1840s. Such imagery spared no one's sensibilities, portraying, for example, soldiers using swords to force the Poor Law down the throat of a working man tied to a chair, or depicting the walled-in claustrophobia of the dejected inmates of a women's

[56] *Crisis*, 3 (1833), 1; *Northern Star*, 22 Aug. 1846, 1; for another example of this paper's illustration, see 10 Jan. 1846, 1.

[57] *Struggle*, no. 61, [1842 or 1843] (issues are not dated); for a reproduction of the *Struggle*'s imagery of political satire, see Joanne Shattock and Michael Wolff (eds.), *Victorian Periodical Press* (Toronto, 1982), plate 9; and see Joseph Livesey, *The Life and Teachings of Joseph Livesey* (London, 1886), 21–2.

[58] This and other such contemporary examples of protest are in the John Johnson Collection of street ballads, Bodleian Library, Oxford.

workhouse. Radical caricatures also addressed themselves to a variety of other issues and injustices: the Reform Bill, truck system, and so on. These have been well documented and copiously reproduced elsewhere and must certainly have played a key role in the development of class identity.[59]

With the rise of mass-circulated imagery such as that in pictorial magazines, caricature and similar kinds of radical imagery declined.[60] It would not be long, though, before another group of images signalled that a specifically working-class consciousness was beginning to take shape. By the 1850s the English worker's expanding pictorial world took in the engraved emblems printed on trade union certificates. Figure 50 reproduces a representative example.[61] As in many other similar cases, the iconography of this emblem communicated workers' craft pride and emphasized the value and dignity of labour, while mottoes like 'united to protect' and 'union is strength' conveyed a belief in the efficacy of unity in protecting workers' common interests. Other mottoes, such as 'not combined to injure', indicate that the organized working class had no revolutionary intent, but envisioned itself united within a stable society. This view is further suggested in this and several other emblems' images of the solid, roughly triangular, classically styled architectural edifice and the classicizing figures disposed in orderly fashion from base to apex. As one historian has aptly put it, such iconography signified that the unions chose to draw an analogy between their 'own civilization of labour' and 'a civilization of legendary stability'.[62]

IV

The classicizing figures and architecture that typified the iconography of trade unionism were collectively one example of an increasing

[59] Celina Fox, *Graphic Journalism in England during the 1830s and 40s* (Ph.D. diss. (Oxford, 1974) published, London and New York, 1988); for the examples mentioned, see ibid. 77 and figs. 114, 147, and 167.

[60] Ibid. 201.

[61] This emblem was actually engraved in 1866, but it is typical of the engraving style and iconography of emblems of the 1850s.

[62] I owe this idea on the iconography of stability to Bernard Waites, 'Popular Culture in Late Nineteenth- and Early Twentieth-Century Lancashire', in the Open University, *Popular Culture* (Milton Keynes, 1981; reprint edn., 1985), 86. For other commentary on trade union emblems, see John Gorman, *Images of Labour* (London, 1985), 16–17; R. A. Leeson, *United We Stand* (Bath, 1971); for illustrations, see F. D. Klingender, *Art and the Industrial Revolution* (1947; reprint edn., 1975), 110; and Waites, 'Popular Culture', 84–5.

50. Membership certificate, Amalgamated Society of Carpenters and Joiners, 1866

rarity in working people's pictorial world: the imagery of fine art. Here and there, we can point to other instances in which art, or the discussion of it, were in some way part of common cultural experience at mid-century: there were, for example, the artists' lectures offered by some mechanics' institutes and the reproductions of paintings that from time to time illustrated playbills.[63] On the whole, though, after 1845 and the demise of the *Penny Magazine*, the visual forms of high culture retreated from the cultural and pictorial experience of working people, back to their traditional place among the privileged and powerful: back, that is, to the walls, specimen cabinets, and bookcases of the wealthy; back into expensive periodicals; and back to the galleries, museums, and exhibition halls that were closed on Sunday, the only day of leisure for most working people.[64]

We have seen already how this retreat was signalled in the second generation of pictorial miscellanies, in their limited use and trivialization of art. We find similar signals elsewhere in the transformed popular culture at mid-century. For example, the new abundance of cheap illustrated magazines drove a number of the old umbrella print-sellers out of a business which occasionally offered fine-quality engravings.[65] Now people had increasingly less need of the printed wares of a street vendor: they could cut their choice of any sort of image out of the pages of a used *Journal* or *Miscellany*. There is no more ironic indicator of how far art had withdrawn from common experience than Cassell's *Magazine of Art* (1853–6), which, at twopence an issue, was the only art periodical of the time that at least a few working people could afford. Despite its title, this publication devoted much of its content to general-knowledge subjects, and offered comparatively little of the discourse and imagery of art.

At this point we might be forgiven for wondering if possibly all of this came about in response to people's taste. Perhaps workers wanted only visually and intellectually undemanding material. Certainly there would be partial truth in such a surmise—it seems unlikely that

[63] C. P. Darcy, *The Encouragement of the Fine Arts in Lancashire, 1760–1860* (Manchester, 1976), 106; Playbills 171, fo. 233, British Library.

[64] The most important art periodical of the time was the *Art Union*, which, at the price of a shilling per issue, was well beyond working-class means; on the prevalence of Sunday closings of art galleries and so on, see Burn, *Language of the Walls*, 29; Elson, *Last of the Climbing Boys*, 207; and J. A. Roebuck, 'The British Museum', in *Pamphlets for the People*, 1 (1835), 13.

[65] Peter Jackson, *George Scharfe's London* (London, 1987), 48.

the costermongers who enthused over the *Miscellany*'s pictures, the factory-girls who revelled in illustrated serial fiction, and a host of others like them would have bypassed such diverting pictorial entertainment in favour of a magazine of fine art (assuming, of course, that there was an affordable version of such a magazine).

But acknowledging the existence of a widespread taste for escapist entertainment does not negate the fact that the withdrawal of art from working people's lives was a manifestation of the uneven social, economic, and power relations of the time. Furthermore, there is no evidence that, given the choice, many working people would not have wanted to incorporate the imagery of art into their lives, in preference to, or at least along with, other kinds of pictures. There is in fact considerable evidence from various sources that a large part of the working class was not satisfied with a steady diet of the pictorial fare of penny dreadfuls and illustrated magazines, but would also have liked more purely aesthetic nourishment. Among the many workers who professed a taste for the visual forms of high culture were the factory operative who admired pictures of Greek sculpture and architecture; the east London labourer who was 'possessed' by the works of 'pictorial art' which he saw displayed in shop-windows; the many working men who petitioned for Sunday opening at the British Museum; and, perhaps most notably, there was the Northampton shoemaker who, after a night of drunken brawling and domestic violence, did not neglect to restore his now headless casts of Milton and Shakespeare to their proper place on the mantelpiece.[66]

At the same time that fine art was retreating from the lives of most workers—even those who actively sought aesthetic experience—the idea became current that there were really two kinds of art: for the privileged, paintings, sculpture, and high-quality prints; for the people, the imagery to be found in the textbooks and manuals of practical design. We have already seen how contributors to the new pictorial miscellanies communicated this idea, and we might now

[66] Plummer, *Songs*, pp. xviii–xix; Razell, *Letters*, 80–1; Rushton, *Life*, 102; David Vincent, *Bread, Knowledge and Freedom* (London, 1981), 155–6; and see also Samuel Bamford, *Walks in South Lancashire* (1844; reprint edn., Brighton, 1972), 253; Burn, *Commercial Enterprise*, 27; Charles Eastlake on 'The Love of Pictures of the Lower Orders' (1843; excerpted in Denvir, *Nineteenth Century*), 68–9; J. C. Robertson, evidence given before the Select Committee on Arts and Manufactures, 2 Sept. 1835, *Report*, vol.5, item 1628; C. Thomas, *Love and Work Enough* (Toronto, 1967), 165–6; Wakefield Mechanics' Institution to T. Coates, 21 Aug. 1842, SDUK correspondence, University College London Library.

take note of the many others who shared the same view: there were, for example, witnesses before government select committees, the committee members themselves, teachers of art, magazine editors, and several writers for various periodicals.[67] Among these individuals, there was a single instrumental rationale for advocating practical, as opposed to fine, art education: improved working-class design skills would also improve British manufactures. As schools of design multiplied, and as many other educational establishments introduced rudimentary design education for working-class students, class-differentiated aesthetic experience became institutionalized—even though class did not necessarily dictate taste.

With the formal and informal withdrawal of fine art from common experience, working people had by 1860 sustained an aesthetic loss. But at the same time they had also made considerable gains over the prior three decades. For many, there remained the lingering memory and lasting intellectual benefit of the ground-breaking *Penny Magazine* and its art reproductions. For many, many others there were the present pleasures to be taken from the pages and pictures of the *London Journal*, *Reynolds's Miscellany*, and *Cassell's Illustrated Family Paper*. If all of this were not enough, there were also the myriad other informative, humorous, horrific, romantic, and thrilling stories and illustrations in all the inexpensive pictorial magazines and penny story-books that now flourished.

In other words, by 1860 the printed imagery of entertainment proliferated in the English worker's expanded and expanding pictorial world. That imagery, and the wide-circulation publications which transmitted it, were together the nucleus of a transformed popular culture. This nucleus, moreover, was the source of a cultural experience so different from any that people had known in the late eighteenth and early nineteenth centuries that we should now stop describing it merely as popular. For the large and growing centre of a transformed popular culture had from its outset been an experience of many different kinds of people—people of both sexes and varied age, from the country as well as the towns and cities; their number included the illiterate, the comparatively well educated, and those in between; they came from both the middle and the working classes. They were, of course, that large social cross-section typified by the readership of mass-circulation pictorial magazines. And the lived

[67] See Chap. 4, n. 15, above; and see also G. Sutton, *Artisan or Artist* (London, 1967).

experience that they now shared through choice, and through the medium of print and its imagery, was in effect a formative mass culture.

But as extensive as this culture was by 1860, it was not, and never became, all-encompassing. As their class feeling developed, working people managed to keep certain cultural expressions of that feeling —trade union emblems, for example—distinct from the domain of the mass. In other words, class and mass had begun to emerge at about the same time. Meanwhile another kind of cultural experience remained largely untouched by the momentous changes of the past thirty years. Apart from the *Penny Magazine*'s short-lived assault on its exclusivism, art had managed to remain aloof from all but the most privileged and powerful members of society. In 1860 those who bought pictorial miscellanies and those who patronized the Academy exhibition room lived in different worlds.

Conclusion
The Making of a Mass Culture: A Perspective from 1860

A SOURCE from the mid-nineteenth century with whom we are now well acquainted expressed the opinion that during the past few decades the newspaper and popular periodical press had grown in a way that was no less than revolutionary. This was yet another observation from our perceptive and unfortunately anonymous authority on 'cheap literature'.[1] We will recall that he—or perhaps she—was writing in 1859, a vantage-point not far removed from the 1860 perspective that we will now adopt. But unlike our commentator, who could contemplate only the present and the immediate past, we have the benefit of being able to look back from and beyond our mid-century viewpoint. We will presently survey the direction of the future, but now let us turn our gaze the other way and briefly reconsider the developments of the last thirty years.

Most immediately apparent is the fact that from the early 1830s the printed word and its associated image had proliferated to an extent unimagined only a decade or so earlier. Here, as our commentator might well have remarked, was a kind of revolution. As we noted earlier, it was in part a revolution in printing technology complemented by a trend towards the reduction and repeal of the 'taxes on knowledge'. But, as we have also come to recognize, new technology, increasingly lenient fiscal policies, and the attendant growth of the publishing industry were really at the bottom of a larger, cultural transformation: as a result of increased access to inexpensive printed material, the everyday experience of working people dramatically expanded to take in an unprecedented quantity and range of information, entertainment, and illustration. We have also looked closely at the most significant and widely circulated artefacts of this trans-

[1] 'Cheap Literature', *British Quarterly Review*, 29 (1859), 319–29 and *passim*.

formed and expanded popular culture: the *Penny Magazine* and its three main successors. Now, as we glance one last time at these publications and the widening array of similarly entertaining magazines and inexpensive books that appeared from 1840 on, we can see more clearly than before that these publications were more than just part of a bigger, latter-day version of the popular culture of the late eighteenth and early nineteenth centuries. They were in fact the centre of this expanded popular culture, and from that centre there began to emerge another, very different, culture.

Crucial though they were, such artefacts did not create this emergent culture. Rather, it was the creation of people. There were first of all the cultural producers: the men of vision in the field of publishing—reformers like Knight and entrepreneurs like Stiff—and all those men and women, the writers and artists, who contributed essays, stories, and pictures to penny miscellanies, and who conceived the escapist fiction and dashing images that were the stock-in-trade of low-cost story-books. Apart from those who created culture through its production there were all those who purchased the new magazines and penny fiction. These people, as we have already recognized, were a large and socially diverse group of men and women of varying ages: working people, and members of the middle class—all of whom together came from farms, villages, towns, and cities throughout Great Britain. This cross-section of the population—the mass—not only bought magazines and books, but also read these publications, looked at their images, discussed their stories and articles in booksellers' shops, at home, and in coffee-houses and pubs; this mass market of readers pored over serial fiction, fashion news, chess problems, and recipes; they wrote countless comments and queries to editor after editor; cut illustrations out of penny magazines and pasted them on their walls; and in dozens of other ways of which we now have no record this mass of people incorporated the printed word and image into their lived experience. Through their joint interaction, both the consumers and producers of new artefacts like the *Penny Magazine* and its successors made their own cultural experience. And this experience—at the heart of an expanded and transformed popular culture—was an emergent mass culture.

As we continue to look back on this newly made mass culture we can begin to identify characteristics about it that we had not previously observed. First of all, we have yet to take notice that the

Penny Magazine not only circulated throughout Britain, but also found a market in the eastern United States; Knight additionally sold casts of its engravings to publishers all over western Europe for use in various foreign-language versions of the magazine. We also find that Reynolds's most popular stories circulated widely in the United States; and, of course, that 'best-seller' in England, *Uncle Tom's Cabin*, was the work of an American author, and the book had enjoyed as much popularity in its own country as it had abroad. As we survey these and a few other such examples of international participation in the new mass culture, it appears that here we may have the first foundations of what would eventually become a 'global village'.[2] If this is an exaggerated view, it is none the less apparent that because of the new and widespread geographic diffusion of words and images, the world by the end of the 1830s had become smaller and more closely knit than it had been before.

As we proceed with our overview, still looking back from 1860, we can now see the first growth to maturity of what a later age would call the 'cult figure'. Dick Turpin was probably one such figure. More certainly, this was true of his 'housebreaking' contemporary—that master of escape from lawful detention—Jack Sheppard. As we have previously observed, in the 1840s and 1850s his image proliferated in countless books and penny serials covering a range of quality and prices. In addition, print-sellers did their best to meet the popular demand for inexpensive single-sheet engravings of Sheppard to paste on the walls of domestic interiors; and working people crowded into the cheap seats of theatres to see dramatizations of the intrepid escape artist's reprehensible but compelling adventures.[3] Indeed, this particular cult figure, or anti-hero, so pervaded the new mass culture that by the mid-1850s any daring escape or bold criminal exploit had come to be called 'Jack Sheppardism'.[4] Finally, what is especially interesting about this figure is the fact that we can trace his evolution from an earlier existence. As the previous chapter noted in passing, he had begun his career as a lazy and insolent apprentice who was soon dismissed by the carpenter who employed him. The great Jack Sheppard was thus none other than a later, swashbuckling

[2] For discussion of the present-day phenomenon, see Marshall McLuhan and Bruce R. Powers, *The Global Village* (New York, 1989).

[3] Henry Mayhew, *London Labour and the London Poor*, 4 vols. (London, 1851; enlarged edn., 1861–2; reprinted, London, 1967), i. 304; 'Popular Literature of the Day', *British and Foreign Review* 10 (1840), 242.

[4] *News of the World*, 9 Sept. 1855, 7.

incarnation of those old negative exemplars, the shiftless apprentices of the Cheap Repository's *Two Shoemakers*, and the *Penny Magazine*'s reproductions of Hogarth's *Industry and Idleness*.

As we take one last backward glance at Sheppard pursuing his dashing but doomed course to the gallows, we notice a different kind of contemporary persona on the new cultural horizon. This was no swaggering anti-hero, but an increasingly common and disturbing image: the female victim of vampires like Varney and murderers like Greenacre. What is most disturbing about this image is not just the passivity of the victim, but the suggestion that she may have enjoyed her victimization. Let us, for example, take a second look at the *Newgate Calendar*'s depiction of the corpse of Greenacre's victim, Hannah Brown (figure 41). Is there not a certain ambivalence in this image? Can we be sure of the meaning of Mrs Brown's stiff-looking legs and feet? Was she in the early stages of rigor mortis or still rigid with the sexual excitement of her last living moments? And what of Varney's victims? Did their backs arch in pain or the pleasure of masochistic eroticism? Here was the dark side of the female image we looked at earlier.

Here was also one of the least savoury aspects of an emergent culture that had brought with it many other more positive kinds of imagery, fantasy, and information. We have already looked at length at the most important examples of this brighter side of mass culture: the general information, art reproductions, and other engravings in the *Penny Magazine*; and the stories, essays, fashion news, items of humour, poetry, and pictures in the *Journal*, *Miscellany*, and *Paper*. For the moment there is nothing more to see or say about these magazines and their content than what we have noted before. So now we will turn our gaze to that other view that our current perspective offers: the years following 1860.

Eventually, as we can just manage to see, the printed medium would share the mass domain with other popular modes of communication and entertainment: film, radio, and television. But for the most part these cultural forms occupy the far distance which we can only see too indistinctly for meaningful observation. We will thus direct our gaze towards the near and middle distance where we can see clearly the persistent popularity and ever-widening diffusion of the printed word and its associated image.

Our three successors to the *Penny Magazine* would continue to flourish, two of them—the *Journal* and the *Paper*—surviving into the twentieth century. Of course, as we have already gathered, they would not have the market all to themselves. The 1861 repeal of the paper duty would enhance the profits of publishers and contribute to the growth of the industry. In the next thirty or so years an increasing number and variety of magazines and weekly papers would enter the field of popular publishing, and the most successful of them attain circulations comparable to, and eventually surpassing, those of the *Journal*, *Miscellany*, and *Paper*. In 1896 *Lloyd's Penny Weekly Paper* would become the first weekly serial publication to achieve a regular circulation of 1 million—and a possible actual readership of five times that figure. Similarly, during the two or three decades following 1860 advertising would enjoy further expansion, both in its use of technology and in the breadth of the audience that would more and more feel its influence. For example, by the 1880s, pictorial advertising would not only use the black and white engraved image to sell its wares, but also the photoreproduction and the coloured lithograph.[5] And, from about 1870, working people would become ever more able to purchase the products that such imagery publicized.

But increasing consumer choice with the improved and improving standard of living that went with it represented only a small incursion on the unequal power relations which still flourished, and which continued to be enacted in cultural and other arenas.[6] Working-class consciousness thus developed further, and we see this reflected in an expanding stock of working-class images designed to express class solidarity or protest over social and economic injustices. The continuing formation of new trade unions would lead to an increase in pictorial membership certificates of the sort reproduced in figure 50; and, increasingly, posters, pamphlets, and socialist and trade union papers and magazines would use the printed image to help articulate working-class interests and discontents in the latter years of the nineteenth century.[7]

[5] Bryan Holme, *Advertising: Reflections of a Century* (London, 1982), 13.

[6] Government fiscal policy continued to be one such arena. Although the House of Lords' 1860 rejection of the repeal of the paper duty did not long hold, other government policies such as the security system continued to curb the free expression of social and political protest: see Alan J. Lee, *The Origins of the Popular Press in England* (London, 1976), 95 ff.

[7] For examples see John Gorman, *Images of Labour* (London, 1985), 8, 16, 67, 78–82, 138, and *passim*; by the end of the century the printed imagery of protest would encompass photoreproduction and lithography as well as engraving: examples can be found in the John Johnson Collection, under 'Leaders of Reform', boxes 1–8, Bodleian Library, Oxford.

The interests and discontents of another group—women—would have to wait a decade or so more before finding at least partial expression in the imagery of suffragism. In the meantime, and long after, that self-contradicting, restrictive image of women that we found at mid-century would continue to proliferate and exert its effect on those who allowed themselves to 'succumb' to such 'despotism'—as one source would describe the dictates of fashion and the ideals of feminine attractiveness.[8]

As we pursue our survey of the printed imagery of magazines, weekly papers, advertising, and so on, we cannot fail to notice the scarcity of one kind of image: art, we can see as we look ahead, would continue its retreat from the domain of mass culture. As it had done before 1860, and would continue to do in the latter part of the century and beyond, art would withdraw further and further from common experience, returning to expensively appointed homes, costly books and magazines, and galleries and museums that would long remain firmly closed on Sundays.[9]

Of course, art would never manage entirely to effect its retreat from everyday life. Here and there it would remain accessible to the people. The vanishing street vendors of inexpensive prints might still on occasion be able to offer a penny art reproduction or other fine print that they would in turn have purchased cheaply from a waste-paper dealer; and, for more than two decades after it had ceased publication, the *Penny Magazine* would find its way into booksellers' shops in working-class neighbourhoods, where it would sell for ninepence to a shilling for a bound volume.[10] And art would soon establish itself as a presence in the realm of advertising. In the next few decades after 1860, and into the following century, art would help to sell all manner of products from Pears soap to ballpoint pens and chocolate bars.[11]

[8] Lucy Crane, *Art and the Formation of Taste* (1882), excerpted in Bernard Denvir, *The Late Victorians: Art, Design and Society, 1852–1910* (London, 1986), 209.

[9] The *Art Journal*, for example, cost 1*s*. an issue; the majority of galleries and museums were still closed on Sunday as late as 1890: see *Quarterly Journal of the Sunday Society*, 1876–90, *passim*; this society worked to have museums, art galleries, libraries, and gardens open on Sundays.

[10] Thomas Wright, *The Great Unwashed* (London, 1868), 224.

[11] For illustrations and further commentary, see P. Anderson, 'Pictures for the People', *Studies in Art Education*, 28 (1987), 138 and 140; John Berger, *Ways of Seeing* (Harmondsworth, 1972; reprint edn., 1976), 135; Frank Presbrey, *The*

In observing this incongruent alliance of art, soap, ink, and confectionery, we reach the far limit of our view beyond 1860. But we will try to retain the after-image for a short while as we turn the other way for a final look at the years between 1830 and 1860. We see again the early phase of a new mass culture as it emerged from the centre of a transformed, greatly expanded, popular culture. As we recognized at the outset, this was not the fully commercialized mass culture that would develop in the latter part of the nineteenth century.[12] Nevertheless, still bearing in mind our after-image of the future, it becomes apparent that what we are now surveying for the last time here is the emergence and growth of a fundamentally modern mass culture. For this was a culture whose central artefacts—the *Penny Magazine* and its three main successors—depended upon and fostered new technology, increasingly commercialized their operation, continually augmented the amount and range of their written and pictorial content, and persistently reached and communicated with an ever-widening, socially and geographically diverse, or mass, body of readers and viewers. In this way the new culture accommodated all the necessary preconditions for the development of the twentieth-century mass media.

But in 1860 there was no such phenomenon as a mass media. There was, though, the mass medium of print, with all its increasing quantity and variety of imagery. Even so, some people's visual experience remained little altered from what it had been a half-century or so ago. As they long had done, devotees of Academy art congregated at the annual exhibition. Meanwhile, those who interested themselves in the welfare of the very poorest members of society took note of, and attempted to alleviate, the visual deprivation of the inmates of charitable institutions.[13] But at mid-century there was little to show for such effort. In both urban and rural parishes all over England, in the midst of a burgeoning, ever more pictorial mass culture, the workhouse walls remained bare.

History and Development of Advertising (New York, 1929; reprint edn., New York, 1968), between 110 and 111.

[12] See Introduction, sec. III.

[13] *Journal of the Workhouse Visiting Society*, 32 (1865), 278.

Select Bibliography

PRIMARY SOURCES:

Manuscript Collections

Brougham, Henry, Correspondence, 1850–63, University College London Library.

Cobden, Richard, Correspondence with J. C. Cassell, 1849–65, Add. MSS 43668–9, British Library.

Knight, Charles, Correspondence with Richard Bentley, Rowland Hill, and William Hone, Add. MSS 46632B, 31978, 40120, British Library.

Longman Archive, Ledgers, vols. 51–2, Box II, 26A/1–24 and 27, University Library, Reading.

Place, Francis, Papers, Add. MSS 27827–8, British Library.

Society for Promoting Christian Knowledge (SPCK), General Literature Committee Minutes, 1832–47, 4 vols., SPCK Archive, Holy Trinity Church, London.

Society for the Diffusion of Useful Knowledge (SDUK), Minutes and Correspondence, 1826–48, University College London Library.

Broadside, Ephemera, and Memorabilia Collections

Ballads and Other Broadside Sheets Published by J. Pitts *et al.* [1665–*c.*1870], unnamed collection, British Library.

Baring-Gould, Sabine, Collection of Ballads, 10 vols., London, 1800–70, British Library.

—— Collection of Ballads, 2 vols., Newcastle, [1730?–1830?]. British Library.

Broadsheets Relating to . . . Various Traitors, Murderers and Malefactors, East Anglia, [1707–1832], unnamed collection, British Library.

Collection of Curious Advertisements and Handbills, 1682–1836, unnamed collection, British Library.

Crampton, Thomas, Collection of Ballads, 7 vols., London, [1860?], British Library.

Creed, G., Collection of Drawings of Inn Signs . . . 14 vols. [1855?], British Library.

Goldsmiths' Library Broadside Collection, 3 vols., University of London.

John Johnson Collection, Bodleian Library, Oxford.

Memorabilia, National Museum of Labour History, London (now in Manchester).

Miscellaneous Broadsides . . . of Almanacks and Accounts of Criminal Trials and Executions [1801–58], unnamed collection, British Library.

Ono, Barry, Collection of Nineteenth Century Bloods and Penny Dreadfuls, British Library.

Playbills, vols. 10, 20, 171, 176–7, 300, 358, and 361, British Library.

Tracts, Broadsides, and Newspaper Cuttings . . . London and Newcastle, [1807–23], unnamed collection, British Library.

British Government Documents

Select Committee on Arts and Manufactures, *Report* vols. 5 and 9.1, 1835 and 1836.

Select Committee on National Monuments, *Report* vol. 6, 1841.

Select Committee on Industrial Design, *Report* vol. 43, 1851.

Select Committee on Newspaper Stamps, *Report* vol. 17, 1851.

Newspapers and Magazines

Bentley's Miscellany, 1837–8.

Bookseller, various obituaries.

Cassell's Illustrated Family Paper, 1853–60.

Chambers' Edinburgh Journal, 1832–3.

Cobbett's Two-Penny Trash, 1832.

The Crisis, 1832–4.

Family Herald, 1842–60.

Home Magazine, 1856–7.

Lloyd's Weekly Miscellany and Penny Sunday Times, 1850–2.

London Journal, 1845–60.

Mechanic's Magazine, 1823–48.

Methodist Magazine, 1798–1821.

Mirror of Literature, Amusement and Instruction, 1823–32.

Northern Star, 1838–52.

Penny Magazine, 1832–45.

Poor Man's Guardian, 1832.

Reynolds's Miscellany, 1846–60.

Reynolds's Political Instructor, 1849–50.

Saturday Magazine, 1832–44.

The Struggle, 1842–6.

The Welcome Guest, 1858–61.

Working Man's Friend and Family Instructor, 1850–1.

(With the exception of *Chambers' Journal*, all of the above were published in London.)

Books, Articles, and Published Memoirs

ACKERMANN, R., *The Microcosm of London*, 3 vols. (London, 1808).

ARCH, JOSEPH, *Joseph Arch: The Story of His Life* (London, 1898; reprint edn., London, 1966).

BAMFORD, SAMUEL, *Early Days* (London, 1848–9; reprint, ed. W. H. Chaloner, New York, 1967).

—— *Passages in the Life of a Radical* (London, 1848–9; reprint, ed. W. H. Chaloner, New York, 1967).

—— *Walks in South Lancashire* (Blackley, 1844; reprint edn., intro. J. D. Marshall, Brighton, 1972).

BASSET, JOSIAH, *The Life of a Vagrant* (London, 1850).

BATHGATE, JANET, *Aunt Janet's Legacy to Her Nieces: Recollections of Humble Life in Yarrow* . . . (Selkirk, 1894).

BERTRAM, JAMES G., *Some Memories of Books, Authors and Events* (London, 1893).

BRIERLEY, BENJAMIN, *Home Memories and Recollections of a Life* (London, 1886).

BROUGHAM, HENRY, *Practical Observations on the Education of the People* (1825; reprint edn., Boston, 1826).

—— 'Society for the Diffusion of Useful Knowledge', *Edinburgh Review*, 46 (1827); 235–44.

BURCH, WILLIAM, *Life, Sermons and Letters*, ed. T. Russell (n.p., 1866).

BURN, JAMES DAWSON, *The Autobiography of a Beggar Boy* (London, 1855).

—— *Commercial Enterprise and Social Progress* (London, 1858).

—— *A Glimpse at the Social Condition of the Working Classes During the Early Part of the Present Century* (London, 1865).

—— *The Language of the Walls and the Voice from the Shop Window* . . . (Manchester and London, 1855).

BURT, THOMAS, *An Autobiography* (London, 1924).

BUSBY, T. L., *Costume of the Lower Orders of London* (London, 1820).

CARTER, THOMAS, *Memoirs of a Working Man* (London, 1845).

CHATTO, W. A., 'The History and Practice of Wood-Engraving', *Illustrated London News*, 11 May 1844, 309–10, and 22 June 1844, 405–6.

'Cheap Literature', *British Quarterly Review*, 29 (1859), 313–45.

[Cole, Henry], 'Modern Wood-Engraving', *London and Westminster Review* 31 (1838), 265–78.

Cooper, Thomas, *Life of Thomas Cooper* (London, 1872).

Curwen, Henry, *A History of Booksellers: the Old and the New* (London, 1873).

Dixon, Hepworth, 'Literature of the Lower Orders', *Daily News*, 9 Nov. 1847.

Elmes, James, and Shepherd, Thomas, *London and Its Environs in the Nineteenth Century* (London, 1829).

Elson, George, *The Last of the Climbing Boys: An Autobiography* (London, 1900).

Frost, Thomas, *Forty Years' Recollections* (London, 1880).

Godwin, George, *London Shadows: A Glance at the 'Homes' of the Thousands* (London, 1854).

—— *Town Swamps and Social Bridges: The Sequel of 'A Glance at the "Homes" of the Thousands'* (London, 1859).

Green, S. G., *The Working Classes of Great Britain* (London, 1850).

Gutteridge, Joseph, *Lights and Shadows in the Life of an Artisan: The Autobiography of J. Gutteridge* (1893). In Valerie E. Chancellor (ed.), *Master and Artisan in Victorian England* (London, 1969).

Harris, John Howard, *John Harris, the Cornish Poet: The Story of His Life* (London, 1884).

Herbert, Henry, *Autobiography of H. Herbert, a Gloucestershire Shoemaker . . .* (Gloucester, 1866; reprint edn., 1876).

Hindley, Charles, *Curiosities of Street Literature* (London, 1871; reprint edn., with foreword by Michael Hughes, New York, 1970).

Hitchman, Francis, 'The Penny Press', *Eclectic Magazine*, June 1881, 836–849.

Holyoake, George, *Sixty Years of an Agitator's Life* (London, 1892; reprint edn., London, 1906).

Hutton, William, *The Life of William Hutton* (London and Birmingham, 1817).

'An Irreconcileable' [W. B. Rands], 'The Penny Magazine', *St. Pauls Magazine*, 12 (May 1873), 542–9.

Knight, Charles, 'Diffusion of Useful Knowledge', *Plain Englishman*, 3 (1823), n.p.

—— 'Education of the People', *London Magazine*, 3rd ser., 1 (1828), 1–13.

—— *The Old Printer and the Modern Press* (London, 1854).

—— (ed.), *Pictorial Gallery of the Arts* (1845–7), 2 vols. (1845–7; 2nd edn., London and New York, [1858]).

—— *Passages of a Working Life*, 3 vols. (London, 1864).

LANGDON, ROGER, *The Life of Roger Langdon* (London, 1909).

LENO, J. B., *The Aftermath, with Autobiography of the Author* (London, 1892).

LIVESEY, JOSEPH, *The Life and Teachings of Joseph Livesey* (London, 1886).

LOVE, DAVID, *The Life, Adventures and Experience of D. Love* (Nottingham, 1823).

MAYHEW, HENRY, *London Labour and the London Poor*, 4 vols. (London, 1851; enlarged edn., 1861–2, reprinted London, 1967).

'New and Cheap Forms of Popular Literature', *Eclectic Review*, 4th ser., 18 (1845), 74–84.

'An Old Printer' [J. Forbes Wilson], *A Few Personal Recollections* (London, 1896).

PIKE, G. HOLDEN, *John Cassell* (London, 1894).

PLUMMER, JOHN, *Songs of Labour, with Autobiographical Preface* (London, 1860).

'Popular Literature of the Day', *British and Foreign Review*, 10 (1840), 223–46.

PYNE, W. H., *Costume of Great Britain* (London, 1808).

REACH, ANGUS B., 'The Coffee Houses of London', *New Parley Library*, 2 (1845), 293–4.

ROGERS, FREDERICK, *Labour, Life and Literature* (London, 1913).

ROWLANDSON, THOMAS, *Sketches of the Lower Orders* (London, 1820).

RUSHTON, ADAM, *My Life as a Farmer's Boy, Factory Lad, Teacher and Preacher* (Manchester, 1909).

TAYLOR, W. C., 'On the Cultivation of Taste in the Operative Classes', *Art Journal*, 11 (1849), 3–5.

THOMSON, CHRISTOPHER, *Autobiography of an Artisan* (London, 1847).

THORNBURY, WALTER, and WALFORD, EDWARD, *Old and New London*, 6 vols. (London, 1887).

VIZETELLY, HENRY, *Glances Back through Seventy Years*, 2 vols. (London, 1893).

'A Working Man', *Scenes from My Life*, ed. R. Maguire (London, 1858).

WRIGHT, THOMAS, *Some Habits and Customs of the Working Classes, By a Journeyman Engineer* (London, 1867).

—— ('The Journeyman Engineer'), *The Great Unwashed* (London, 1868).

—— *Johnny Robinson: The Story of an 'Intelligent Artisan', By 'The Journeyman Engineer'*, 2 vols. (London, 1868).

Secondary Sources:

ALLEN, W. O. B., and MCCLURE, EDMUND, *Two Hundred Years: The History of the Society for Promoting Christian Knowledge, 1698–1898.* (London, 1898).

ALTICK, R. D., *The English Common Reader* (Chicago and London, 1957).

ASHTON, J. (ed.), *Chap Books of the Eighteenth Century* (London, 1882; reprint edn., New York, 1966).

ASHWIN, CLIVE., *Art Education: Documents and Policies: 1768–1975* (London, 1975).

BAILEY, PETER, *Leisure and Class in Victorian England*, (London, 1978).

—— Introduction to the paperback edn. of *Leisure and Class in Victorian England* (London, 1987), 8–20.

BARTHES, ROLAND, 'The Photographic Message,' and 'The Rhetoric of the Image', in *Image-Music-Text*, trans. Stephen Heath (New York, 1977), 15–31 and 32–51.

BENJAMIN, WALTER, 'The Work of Art in the Age of Mechanical Reproduction', in *Illuminations* (Frankfurt, 1955: *Illuminationen*. trans. Harry Zohn, New York, 1969; reprint edn., New York, 1978, 217–51).

BENNETT, SCOTT, 'Revolutions in Thought: Serial Publication and the Mass Market for Reading', in J. Shattock and M. Wolff (eds.), *The Victorian Periodical Press* (Leicester and Toronto, 1982), 225–57.

—— 'The [Editorial Character] and Readership [of the *Penny Magazine*]', *Victorian Periodicals Review*, 17 (1984), 126–41.

BENNETT, TONY, 'Theories of the Media, Theories of Society', in M. Gurevitch, T. Bennett, J. Curran, and J. Woollacott (eds.), *Culture, Society and the Media* (London, 1982).

—— 'Popular Culture and the Turn to Gramsci', in T. Bennett, C. Mercer, and J. Wollacott (eds.), *Popular Culture and Social Relations* (Milton Keynes, 1986), pp. xi–xix.

BERGER, JOHN, *Ways of Seeing* (Harmondsworth, 1972; reprint edn., 1976).

BRIGGS, ASA, *Mass Entertainment: The Origins of a Modern Industry* (Adelaide, 1960).

BURNETT, JOHN (ed.), *Destiny Obscure: Autobiographies of Childhood, Education and Family* (1982; reprint edn., Harmondsworth, 1984).

—— *Useful Toil: Autobiographies of Working People from the 1820s to the 1920s* (Harmondsworth, 1984).

CIRKER, BLANCHE (ed.), *1800 Woodcuts by Thomas Bewick and his School* (New York, 1962).

CLARKE, W. K. L., *The History of the SPCK* (London, 1959).

CLEAVER, JAMES, *A History of Graphic Art* (London, 1963).

COLLINSON, ROBERT, *The Story of Street Literature* (London, 1973).

CUNNINGHAM, HUGH, *Leisure in the Industrial Revolution* (London, 1980).

DALZIEL, MARGARET, *Popular Fiction One Hundred Years Ago* (London, 1957).

DARCY, C. P., *The Encouragement of the Fine Arts in Lancashire, 1760–1860* (Manchester, 1976).

DE MARE, ERIC, *The Victorian Woodblock Illustrators* (London, 1980).

DENVIR, BERNARD, *The Early Nineteenth Century: Art, Design and Society, 1789–1852* (London and New York, 1984).

—— *The Late Victorians: Art, Design and Society, 1852–1910* (London, 1986).

DOBSON, AUSTIN, *Thomas Bewick and His Pupils* (London, 1884).

ELKINS, CHARLES, 'The Voice of the Poor: The Broadside as a Medium of Popular Culture and Dissent in Victorian England', *Journal of Popular Culture*, 14 (1980), 262–74.

ENGEN, RODNEY K., *Dictionary of Victorian Engravers, Print Publishers and Their Works* (Cambridge, 1979).

FOX, CELINA, *Graphic Journalism in England during the 1830s and 40s*. Ph.D. diss. (Oxford, 1974); published, London and New York, 1988.

—— 'The Development of Social Reportage in English Periodical Illustration during the 1840s and Early 1850s', *Past and Present*, 74 (1977), 90–111.

—— 'Political Caricature and the Freedom of the Press in Early Nineteenth-Century England', in G. Boyce, J. Curran, and P. Wingate (eds.), *Newspaper History* (London, 1978), 227–46.

—— and WOLFF, MICHAEL, 'Pictures from Magazines', in H. J. Dyos and M. Wolff (eds.), *The Victorian City* (London, 1973), ii. 559–82.

GAMMAGE, R. G., *History of the Chartist Movement* (London, 1894).

GARRETT, ALBERT, *A History of British Wood Engraving* (Atlantic Highlands, NJ, 1978).

GEORGE, M. D., *Hogarth to Cruikshank: Social Change in Graphic Satire* (London, 1967).

GORMAN, JOHN, *Images of Labour* (London, 1985).

GRAMSCI, ANTONIO, *Selections from the Prison Notebooks*, ed. and trans. Quintin Hoare and Geoffrey Nowell Smith (London, 1971; reprint edn., 1986).

GRAY, ROBERT, 'Bourgeois Hegemony in Victorian Britain', in T. Bennett, G. Martin, C. Mercer, and J. Woollacott (eds.), *Culture, Ideology and Social Process* (London, 1981), 219–34.

GRETTON, THOMAS, *Murders and Moralities: English Catchpenny Prints, 1800–1860* (London, 1980).

GROBEL, MONICA, 'The Society for the Diffusion of Useful Knowledge, 1826–1848', 4 vols. Ph.D. diss., University of London, 1932.

HAINING, PETER, *The Penny Dreadful* (London, 1975).

HALL, STUART, 'Cultural Studies', in S. Hall (ed.), *Culture, Media, Language* (London, 1980), 15–47.

—— 'Notes on Deconstructing the "Popular"', in R. Samuel (ed.), *People's History and Socialist Theory* (London, 1981), 227–40.

HARRISON, J. F. C., *Learning and Living, 1790–1960* (Toronto, 1961).

HINDLEY, CHARLES, *The History of the Catnach Press* (London, 1887; reprint edn., Detroit, 1969).

HOLLIS, PATRICIA, *The Pauper Press* (London, 1970).

HUMPHERYS, ANNE, 'The Geometry of the Modern City: G. W. M. Reynolds and *The Mysteries of London*', *Browning Institute Studies*, 2 (1983), 69–80.

—— 'G. W. M. Reynolds: Popular Literature and Popular Politics', in Joel Wiener (ed.), *Innovators and Preachers: The Role of the Editor in Victorian England* (New York, 1985), 3–21.

IVINS, WILLIAM M., *Prints and Visual Communications* (London, 1953; reprint edn., New York, 1969).

JACKSON, MASON, *The Pictorial Press* (London, 1885).

JAMES, LOUIS, *Fiction for the Working Man, 1830–1850* (Oxford, 1963; Harmondsworth, 1974).

—— *Print and the People* (London, 1976).

—— 'The Trouble with Betsy: Periodicals and the Common Reader in Mid-Nineteenth-Century England', in J. Shattock and M. Wolff (eds.), *The Victorian Periodical Press* (Leicester and Toronto, 1982), 349–66.

JONES, GARETH S., 'Working-Class Culture and Working-Class Politics in London, 1870–1900; Notes on the Remaking of a Working Class', *Journal of Social History*, 7 (1974), 460–507.

—— 'Rethinking Chartism', in *Languages of Class* (Cambridge, 1983), 90–178.

KLANCHER, JON P., *The Making of English Reading Audiences, 1790–1832* (London and Madison, Wis., 1987).

KLINGENDER, FRANCIS D., *Art and the Industrial Revolution* (1947; reprint edn., St Albans, 1975).

LACLAU, ERNESTO, and MOUFFE, CHANTAL, *Hegemony and Socialist Strategy* (London, 1985).

LAQUEUR, T. W., *Religion and Respectability: Sunday Schools and Working-Class Culture, 1780–1850* (New Haven, Conn., 1976).

LEAVIS, Q. D., *Fiction and the Reading Public* (London, 1932).

LEESON, R. A., *United We Stand: An Illustrated Account of Trade Union Emblems* (Bath, 1971).

LINDLEY, KENNETH, *The Woodblock Engravers* (Newton Abbot, 1970).

MCKECHNIE, SAMUEL, *Popular Entertainments through the Ages* (New York and London, 1931; reprint edn., London, 1969).

MCKENDRICK, NEIL, BREWER, JOHN, and PLUMB, J. H., *The Birth of a Consumer Society: The Commercialization of Eighteenth-Century England* (London, 1982).

MATHEWS, H. F., *Methodism and the Education of the People, 1791–1851* (London, 1949).

MEGGS, PHILIP B., *A History of Graphic Design* (New York, 1983).

MITCHELL, SALLY, 'The Forgotten Woman of the Period: Penny Weekly Family Magazines of the 1840s and 1850s', in M. Vicinus (ed.), *A Widening Sphere* (Bloomington, Ind., 1977), 29–51.

MOUFFE, CHANTAL, 'Introduction: Gramsci Today' and 'Hegemony and Ideology in Gramsci', in *Gramsci and Marxist Theory* (London, 1979), 1–18 and 168–204.

—— 'Hegemony and Ideology in Gramsci', in T. Bennet, G. Martin, C. Mercer, and J. Woolacott (eds.), *Culture, Ideology and Social Process* (London, 1981), 219–34.

NEUBERG, VICTOR E., *The Penny Histories* (London, 1968).

—— 'The Literature of the Street', in H. J. Dyos and M. Wolff (eds.), *The Victorian City* (London, 1973), i. 191–209.

—— *Popular Literature* (Harmondsworth, 1977).

NOWELL-SMITH, SIMON, *The House of Cassell, 1848–1958* (London, 1958).

PEARSON, EDWIN, *Banbury Chap Books . . .* (London, 1890; reprint edn., New York, 1972).

PRESBREY, FRANK, *The History and Development of Advertising* (New York, 1929; reprint edn., New York, 1968).

RAZELL, P. E., and WAINWRIGHT, R. W. (eds.), *The Victorian Working Class: Selections from Letters to the* Morning Chronicle (London, 1973).

RICKWORD, E. (ed.), *Radical Squibs and Loyal Ripostes* (Bath, 1971).

SHEPARD, LESLIE, *The History of Street Literature* (Newton Abbot, 1973).

SMITH, HAROLD, *The Society for the Diffusion of Useful Knowledge, 1826–1846: A Social and Bibliographic Evaluation*, Dalhousie Library Occasional Paper, 8 (Halifax, Nova Scotia 1974).

SUMMERS, MONTAGUE, *A Gothic Bibliography* (London, 1940).

SWINGEWOOD, ALAN, *The Myth of Mass Culture* (London, 1977; reprint edn., 1979).

THOMPSON, E. P., *The Making of the English Working Class* (1963; reprint edn., Harmondsworth, 1978).

TWYMAN, MICHAEL, *Printing, 1770–1970: An Illustrated History of its Development and Uses in England* (London, 1970).

VICINUS, MARTHA, *The Industrial Muse: A Study of British Working-Class Literature* (London, 1974).

VINCENT, DAVID, *Bread, Knowledge and Freedom: A Study of Nineteenth-Century Working Class Autobiography* (London, 1981; reprint edn., 1982).

WAKEMAN, GEOFFREY, *Victorian Book Illustration: the Technical Revolution* (Newton Abbot, 1973).

WEARMOUTH, R. F., *Methodism and the Working-Class Movements of England, 1800–1850* (London, 1937).

WEBB, R. K., *The British Working Class Reader, 1790–1848* (London, 1955).

WILLIAMS, RAYMOND, *The Long Revolution* (London, 1961).

—— 'Radical and/or Respectable', in R. Boston (ed.), *The Press We Deserve* (London, 1970).

—— 'Minority and Popular Culture', in M. A. Smith, S. Parker, and C. S. Smith (eds.), *Leisure and Society in Britain* (London, 1973), 22–7.

—— *Keywords: A Vocabulary of Culture and Society* (New York, 1976).

YEO, EILEEN, 'Culture and Constraint in Working-Class Movements, 1830–55', in E. and S. Yeo (eds.), *Popular Culture and Class Conflict, 1590–1914* (Atlantic Highlands, NJ, and Brighton, 1981).

Index